Bournemouth's Airports
A HISTORY

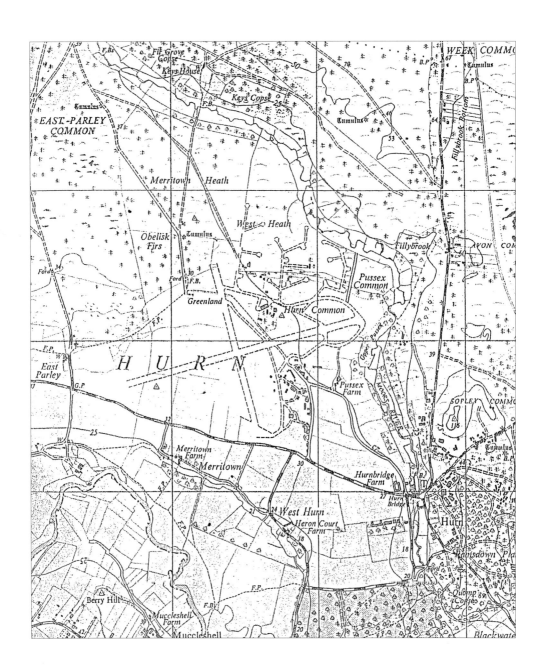

Bournemouth's Airports
A HISTORY

MIKE PHIPP

TEMPUS

Frontispiece: A 1950 Ordnance Survey map which omits the western end of Bournemouth Airport.

First published 2006

Tempus Publishing Limited
The Mill, Brimscombe Port,
Stroud, Gloucestershire, GL5 2QG
www.tempus-publishing.com

British Library Cataloguing in Publication Data.
A catalogue record for this book is available from the British Library.

ISBN 0 7524 3923 5

Typesetting and origination by Tempus Publishing Limited
Printed in Great Britain

CONTENTS

ACKNOWLEDGEMENTS

Material for this book has been gathered from information collected over many years. As airport historian, I have been able to build up a number of contacts over the years. A main source of information has been the collection of photographs, press cuttings, timetables and so on which have accumulated in the Archive Room at the airport. This leads to the problem of knowing where some of the information has come from, so I would like to say that there has been no intention of overlooking any source when I acknowledge the following for their assistance: Henry Beck, Colin Cruddas, Tony Dean, Ken Dyer, Lawrence Hayward, Tony Needham, Allen Rustell, Stephen Skinner, Hazel Thorby and the various individuals whose reminiscences appear throughout the book.

I also acknowledge: Air-Britain (variety of publications), BAE Systems, Bath Travel, Bournemouth Airport, Bournemouth Aviation Museum, *Bournemouth Daily Echo*, Bournemouth Red Arrows Association, European Aviation, FR Aviation, Hampshire CC Museum Service (Red House Museum), VT Aerospace, various operators around the airport, 397 Bomb Group Association.

Books I used for reference include:

BAC One-Eleven, Stephen Skinner
Bransgore and the Valiant, John Peatey
Christchurch Airfield, Allen White
Ensbury Park Airfield, John Barker
In Dorset's Skies, Colin Cruddas
Test Pilot, Brian Trubshaw
Wings over Dorset, Leslie Dawson

Finally, without the understanding of my wife this book would have stalled well before the end of the runway. By Chapter 20 her proof-reading was becoming tested but, thankfully, she has joined me in seeing the project through to the end, even asking what the next one would be! So, once again my grateful thanks to her for all her patience.

INTRODUCTION

Four years ago Tempus published my previous book on Bournemouth Airport. Encouraged by the comments received, I decided to go ahead with a history of all the airports in the Bournemouth area over the years. Consequently, this volume contains fewer photographs than before, thereby saving them up for a possible Mk.2 pictorial version in a couple of years time.

Having lived in the Bournemouth area all my life, my early enthusiasm for aviation has developed into something more substantial in recent years. Interest in the activity at the local airfields has led to greater research on the subject, building up into much fuller histories. Covering a similar subject, the introductory comments of *Bournemouth International Airport* apply equally to this book. The pioneering efforts of Messrs Drexel and McArdle preceded Bournemouth's International Aviation Meeting by a few months. Regrettably, the meeting brought fame to the area for the wrong reason – the death of Charles Rolls. First World War pilot training took place at Talbot Village Aerodrome, the site of the present-day Bournemouth University at Wallisdown. Later the Royal Flying Corps used a site at Ensbury Park which local businessmen tried to develop as The Aerodrome, Moordown. Alan Cobham's efforts to encourage Bournemouth to establish a municipal aerodrome in the 1930s came to nothing and he turned his attention to a new airfield at Christchurch. This traded under the name of Bournemouth Airport, which then jolted Bournemouth to join forces with Poole for another attempt to establish a municipal aerodrome. The plans floundered and Christchurch was left to continue as Bournemouth's airport.

The needs of the Second World War saw the hasty move of BOAC flying-boat services to Poole Harbour as it was considered more secure that Southampton. These services continued after the war until Southampton was ready to take them back. RAF Hurn had a hectic three-year period of wartime activity before being selected as the country's main civil airport. Christchurch lost its services on the outbreak of war and these were not re-established on the return to peace, so it was left to Hurn to continue as the local airport during the 1950s and 1960s.

One problem has been deciding what name to use when describing the airport. Originally RAF Hurn, it became Bournemouth (Hurn) during the 1950s before becoming Bournemouth International. So it seemed logical to use the name Bournemouth from the 1950s. However, both Vickers-Armstrongs and BAC continued to use the Hurn name for their factory site until closure in 1984. For the section relating to the aircraft industry, the name Hurn has been used.

There have been many ups and downs in its history, mainly tied in with its rival airport at Southampton. Bournemouth is most definitely on the up at the moment with an increase in low-cost operations. It has the advantage of a longer runway and less flight restrictions. Hopefully this will continue, so putting Bournemouth Airport back in the major airport role that it was sixty years ago.

1

THE EARLY YEARS

The Bournemouth area had an early association with aircraft, bearing in mind that the first officially recognised flight in Great Britain was by Samuel Cody at Farnborough on 16 October 1908. Other flights followed, with The English Channel being crossed by Louis Bleriot on 25 July 1909.

BOURNEMOUTH PIONEERS

These well-publicised events came to the attention of William McArdle – a well-known Bournemouth garage owner – who took a keen interest in this new sport of aviation. His 'Motor Mac's' Garage near the Lansdowne in Holdenhurst Road (later to become George Hartwell's) claimed to be the 'Finest Garage in England', supplying the latest automobiles to the gentry of the town. McArdle decided to follow his new interest and in August built a Bleriot-style monoplane, along with Mr Gould of Boscombe. However, the frail craft did not take to the sky as neither of them knew how to fly it. The fact they could not find a suitable test site did not help the situation. In order to receive flying lessons McArdle had to visit France, and was taught at the Bleriot Aviation School at Issy, near Paris. He successfully completed his flying tests at Pau early in the spring of 1910, where his instructor commented, 'flying during these tests was to a far higher standard than that reached by any previous pupil here'. While there, McArdle struck up a friendship with a wealthy American, J. Armstrong Drexel, who had also qualified as a pilot and wanted to build an aircraft. Both returned to Bournemouth in the spring of 1910 in order to build another Bleriot, where early test flights gave them encouragement to proceed with further aircraft. News of their enthusiasm reached Lord Montague at Beaulieu, who wanted to promote this new sport of flying. He offered the two new aviators a field on his estate where they established the New Forest Aviation School in May 1910, and in due course the school boasted seven Bleriots for training. At the same time, McArdle and Drexel arranged a flying display for the people of Bournemouth during the Whitsun Bank Holiday (16–18 May), held at Vines Farm, Talbot Village (now the site of Bournemouth University). A souvenir brochure, *Flying in Bournemouth*, gave details of McArdle's flying exploits, but surprisingly made no mention of Drexel. For the evening events, four Bleriots were available, but strong winds on the first day prevented the flyers demonstrating their new 'toys' as much as they would have liked. Nevertheless, a large number of townspeople made their way to Talbot Village each day to witness the events. It was the evening of the third day before the flyers achieved success, with McArdle undertaking a number of flights. Drexel was not so lucky, his Bleriot failing to climb after take-off, resulting in two forced landings. However, Drexel was later to gain the British height record at 1,100ft, although he bettered this to 6,600ft when he returned home to New Jersey in August.

CENTENARY MEETING

McArdle and Drexel's display was regarded as a prelude to a much grander event. To mark the 100th anniversary of the town, the spectacular Bournemouth Centenary Fêtes were held in various locations between 6 and 16 July 1910. As part of the fête the Bournemouth International Aviation Meeting was held on 11–16 July. Flying was undertaken from a specially cleared site to the east of Belle Vue Road known as Southbourne Aerodrome (now occupied by The Broadway), stretching from Tuckton Bridge in the north to the cliff tops in the south. The event had the patronage of HRH Prince Arthur of Connaught, as well as a large number of earls, countesses, lords and ladies. Bleriot attended the meeting but did not take part in the events. He had already given up flying after suffering a number of crashes. Prize money totalling £8,500 attracted over twenty British and Continental pilots to the meeting, these numbers showing how popular flying had quickly become. Already, pilots such as Cody, Grahame-White and Rolls had become internationally famous, and gained entry for 2s, although a carriage would be an extra 2s 6d. The best seats at £1 were in the Grandstand (with the benefit of the Music Lawn), with those arriving by motorcar paying an extra 10s to park (including uniformed drivers). However, the majority of people travelled from the town centre to Southbourne or Tuckton by tramcar. The variety of events required the pilots to fly round a 3,140-yard course which was marked out by four pylons. The Speed Prize of £1,000 needed the frail aircraft to cover five circuits of the course, with a bonus of £100 for the fastest lap. The Greatest Altitude Prize was also £1,000, with an additional £200 for the greatest height attained by a Britain. To qualify for the Weight-Carrying Prize, a minimum of 25 stone had to be carried aloft for one circuit, with the competitor responsible for any mishap to his passenger. The Sea-Flight needed one circuit of the course, then out and back over the Bay to the Needles. The competing aircraft arrived by road, except for McArdle who flew in from Beaulieu in Drexel's Bleriot. As ever, the meeting was plagued by wind and rain (no change from today's shows).

Regrettably, the meeting was marred when The Hon. Charles Rolls was killed around midday on 12 July when part of the tail-plane of his Wright biplane broke off under stress during the alighting competition. The aircraft stalled at a low height and crashed to the ground, with Rolls dying almost instantaneously. This was the first fatal accident to an aviator in England.

The Bournemouth International Aviation Meeting was held at Southbourne in July 1910. This view of the 'control tower' was taken from a competing Farman biplane; photographs taken from aircraft were rare at the time.

The Hon. Charles Rolls flying his Wright biplane at the Aviation Meeting, with Christchurch Priory in the background. It is thought that adjustments made to the tailplane resulted in his aircraft breaking up during the second day of the competition with fatal consequences.

Charles Rolls and Henry Royce had formed Rolls-Royce in 1906 – destined to become Great Britain's most famous car manufacturer. In June 1910 Charles Rolls received great publicity when he became the first person to make a non-stop return crossing of the English Channel. Following the Bournemouth crash, Royce (himself not in good health) decided to continue with the Rolls-Royce name, although as a mark of respect the Rolls-Royce badge was now in black, not red. It was not until 1914 that the company branched out to make its first aero engine.

The 12 July meeting continued, with further accidents, but none as serious. The Speed Prize was won by Claude Grahame-White, the Longest Flight by William McArdle (all the way from Beaulieu!). Robert Loraine encountered heavy rain near the Needles and was forced to land at Afton Down near Freshwater, so becoming the first aircraft to land on the Isle of Wight. The overall winner of the meeting was Frenchman Leon Morane in a Bleriot, who collected prize money totalling £3,425. To give an indication of the value of the prizes, a Bleriot XI would cost £480, and a Farman (without engine) £450. Grahame-White supplemented his prize money by giving people flights in his Farman biplane; the term 'pleasure flights' would probably not be correct for these early passengers.

VISITING PIONEERS

The Aviation Meeting enabled people to see the new breed of flyers in action. Later events enabled them to obtain a first-hand taste for flying. McArdle and Drexel concentrated their efforts on the New Forest Aviation School until they sold up at the end of 1911, moving on to new ventures. At the time, Lord Northcliffe, owner of the *Daily Mail*, supported flying with various prizes, also promoting a 'Grand Aviation Tour of England' during 1912. In July Mr Fischler gave flights in his 70hp Farman waterplane from alongside Bournemouth Pier, and in the summer a Bleriot XI also visited the town, flown by the Frenchman Henri Salmet, who was a flying instructor at Hendon. Salmet was already well known for his displays and he returned to Pokesdown the following year. He suffered a crash at Tuckton when his Bleriot ran into a tree on landing, and although Salmet and his passenger were alright, the aircraft required substantial repairs. For Christmas 1913 he flew Father Christmas in his Bleriot along the seafront into Meyrick Park, close to the town centre, en route to his annual visit to Beale's store. The park was used the following April for demonstration flying by Gustav Hamel which included twenty-one loops. Entry into the park enclosure was from 1s to 2s 6d, although many people had excellent views from outside. Already a famous name, Hamel had crossed the Channel more times than any other pilot. An Englishman, he also toured the country sponsored by the *Daily Mail*, and for his local manager he employed businessman Frederick Etches, of whom more later. Hamel was lost at sea the following month while returning across the Channel once again.

These events provided the townspeople of Bournemouth with their first tastes of a new mode of transport.

During the summer of 1912 the *Daily Mail* sponsored a 'Grand Aviation Tour of England' by a number of pilots. Mr Fischler visited Bournemouth and the south coast during July with this Farman 'waterplane'.

FIRST WORLD WAR

The outbreak of war between Great Britain and Germany on 4 August 1914 did not have an immediate effect on the Bournemouth area. Although the coastal region of the county was declared a prohibited zone on 14 August, life continued much as before. However, the reality of war was brought home to the townsfolk in October 1914 when they saw large numbers of wounded soldiers arriving for attention at local hospitals. Regulations were brought into force in January 1915, forbidding the showing of lights at night for fear of Zeppelin attacks. None ever came near the area, although further Air Raid instructions were issued in March 1916.

Above left and right: Two pilots of the era. Gustav Hamel (*left*) was already a famous name when he gave a display at Meyrick Park in April 1914. Herbert Smith (*right*) was one of the early pilots with the Bournemouth Aviation Co. at Talbot Village in 1916.

Bournemouth Aviation gave instruction to Royal Flying Corps pilots on Caudron biplanes at Talbot Village during the First World War. The public were able to view the flying, and flights were also available to the Isle of Wight and back for 5s.

TALBOT VILLAGE

Having acted as local manager for Hamel, Frederick Etches expanded his aviation interests (he was already a pilot) by forming the Bournemouth Aviation Co. Ltd in 1915 to operate a flying training school at Talbot Village Aerodrome, the site used by McArdle and Drexel in 1910. (In fact, the Aerodrome was in Poole as it was situated on the south side of Wallisdown Road, the dividing line between the two towns.) Promoted as 'Learn to Fly at Bournemouth', operations commenced in November 1915, with Etches as general manager and S. Summerfield as chief instructor. Although it was wartime, flights were available to civilians as well as prospective Royal Flying Corps (RFC) pilots; training was also being undertaken by Belgians and Canadians. Initially, Caudron biplanes were operated, flights being offered at £3 (more if you wanted to view the Isle of Wight), with spectators being charged 1s or 6d to gain entry to the Aerodrome, which was advertised as open for Private and Commercial Aircraft.

A fatality occurred on the morning of 24 April 1916 when a biplane piloted by Lt Edward Rebbeck, son of a former Mayor of Bournemouth, crashed on take-off just outside the Aerodrome. In August 1916 Etches responded to a request for one of his aircraft to be demonstrated over Poole for the benefit of its two hospitals. Summerfield landed in a field adjacent to Poole Park before giving a demonstration over the park – so being the first aircraft seen close-up at Poole. Etches insisted that there was no way he would accept payment for the fundraising event. Edgar Brynildsen, another instructor, had a scare one day when his aircraft's engine cut out while he was performing loops over Bournemouth Square; luckily it restarted before he hit the ground. While at Talbot Village, Etches first used the title of Bournemouth Aerodrome.

ENSBURY PARK

There had been a number of complaints over the noise of the aircraft flying at Talbot Village, including one from the owner of the adjacent Vines Farm, who reportedly fired his shotgun at aircraft that were disturbing his cows. In August 1916 the nearby 88-acre Ensbury Farm Estate was sold for £8,600, with 'road frontage ripe for building development', so it was anticipated that it would be developed for housing. Etches had other ideas, purchasing the land jointly with his new co-director, Bernard Mortimer, in December, in order to transfer operations of the Aviation Co. (At the time the estate was in Kinson Parish which was part of Poole, not Bournemouth.) The new aerodrome was known as Ensbury Park; after levelling the ground and erecting a large number of hangars on its south side, flying training commenced early in 1917. Avro 504s, Caudron G.IIIs and Curtiss JN-3s were operated, the company claiming it was the only civilian-operated flying school during the war providing pilots for the RFC and, later, the RAF. By the end of the war it claimed to be the finest equipped flying school outside of London.

Ensbury Park was also used by the military, who referred to the aerodrome as RFC Winton. On 1 April 1918 it passed to the newly formed Royal Air Force, with its Wireless Telephony School arriving post-war in November, operating diverse types such as BE.2Cs. FH.8s and RE.8s before moving on to Beaulieu by May 1919. There was a fatal accident involving a Bristol Fighter from Ensbury Park: it hit trees low-flying close to the Lansdowne on the afternoon of 22 July 1918, the crash in Christchurch Road attracting many sightseers. The return of peace in November 1918 brought to an end the need for pilot training. However, a further crash on 2 April 1919 saw two killed when their Avro 504 crashed on take-off from Ensbury Park. On 19 April a Handley Page 0/400 arrived from Plymouth while on a round-the-country War Savings campaign. Emblazoned with the words 'Joy Bonds – Last Days', it was piloted by Major Keith Park, who went on to attain the rank of Air Vice Marshal at the time of the Battle of Britain.

With the departure of the RAF in May, a number of surplus Avro 504s and Caudron G.IIIs were left behind in the hangars as being surplus to military requirements. These were to be made use of by Bournemouth Aviation Co.

RNAS UPTON

The only operational flying in the region during the war was by airships from the Royal Naval Air Station at Upton. Situated within a wooded area of the grounds of Upton House, the station became operational by the summer of 1917, housing three 'blimps' for submarine patrols over the English Channel. However, by this stage of the war, there was little threat from U-boats in the Channel. The airships comings and goings over Holes Bay and Poole finished with the end of the war.

2

THE BOURNEMOUTH AERODROME

FIRST AIR SERVICES

With the return to peace it was anticipated that civilian flying would be permitted again, following the signing of the Armistice in November 1918. This was not to be, as the British Government did not consider the war officially ended until the signing of the Peace Treaty in July 1919. Commercial interests raised their objections, and so a Bill was passed to allow civil operations from 1 May 1919. A number of prospective operators were geared up for this date, one being Air Transport & Travel Ltd of Hendon, to which fell the honour of operating the first official peacetime flight. One of their DH.9s prepared to depart Hendon at 12.01 a.m. on 1 May, bound for Bournemouth with newspapers, but poor weather delayed take-off until 4.30 a.m. The biplane headed south over Hampshire, with the intention of reaching the coast before flying westwards to Bournemouth. Thick fog was encountered north of Portsmouth, resulting in the DH.9 crashing into Portsdown Hills with injuries sustained by both its crew members. This was an inauspicious start to the day, with Bournemouth missing out on the anticipated publicity. Another firm which was ready for operations was the Handley Page Co. of Cricklewood, North London, which had converted a fleet of surplus Handley Page 0/400 bombers for passenger-carrying purposes. Following the lifting of flying restrictions, one flew a proving flight from Cricklewood to Ensbury Park on 4 May. Another arrived on a South Coast newspaper flight five days later, the papers being packed into its bomb bay.

Handley Page Transport was formed in June 1919 to operate the fleet of 0/400s on various passenger services, including 'The Bournemouth Aerodrome'. For the inaugural flight at the beginning of the month, the Deputy Mayor and civic leaders travelled to Cricklewood by train in the morning, returning home in 0/400 *Vulture*, which then gave pleasure flights to local residents. Handley Page's chief pilot was Lt-Col. William Sholto Douglas, who was to become Marshal of the RAF at the end of the Second World War, followed by Managing Director of BEA in the 1950s. Press reports of the event announced, 'Bournemouth has a town aerodrome'. However, the new service did not prove as popular as anticipated, ending on 18 August with a planned extension to Weymouth having never been operated. The service did not prove competitive with the train service from Waterloo.

A number of surplus HP 0/400 bombers were modified by Handley Page during 1919 for more peaceful duties. This one operated newspaper flights from North London to the south coast and Bournemouth in May 1919.

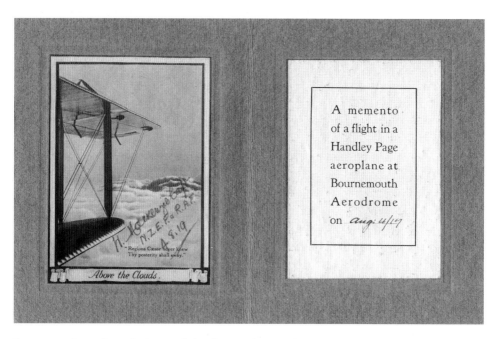

Passengers who undertook pleasure flights from Ensbury Park in an HP 0/400 received a souvenir from Handley Page Transport to mark the event. This one was issued in August 1919 after a flight with Capt. Mackenzie NZEF RAF.

On 26 June an Avro 504M stopped off to refuel whilst flying a couple on honeymoon from Chorley Wood to Fowey – the first peacetime charter flight.

BOURNEMOUTH AVIATION

The Bournemouth Aviation Co. was well placed to undertake a peacetime role at Ensbury Park, anticipating that pilots would still be needed, and having a supply of training aircraft left behind by the RAF. In 1919, Frederick Etches and Bernard Mortimer advertised instructional and pleasure flights from 10s (50p) to £1 1s (£1.05) in a fleet of Avro 504Ks, plus a DH.6 and FE.2B from what was initially referred to as The Aerodrome, Moordown.

Bournemouth Aviation organised a flying display with races on Easter Monday, 5 April 1920, mostly with Avro 504Ks which still retained their wartime RAF markings. Instructor Reg Tollerfield won the main race of the day, Christchurch Priory and back. Tollerfield became well-known in these events, although later in the year he was fined £50 for undertaking aerobatics and low-lying over the town. A similar event on 1 May saw another Avro 504 win the 12-mile race, with the pilot receiving a prize of 25gns (£26.25). Large numbers of visitors took pleasure flights in the Avro 504s, with a Handley Page 0/400 giving flights along the seafront. The day finished with a parachute descent by Professor W. Newell, from a tethered balloon. During the summer there were a number of flights to Bath and Weymouth, but civilian flying in the country did not develop as anticipated. The former military aircraft proved unsuitable; there were limited facilities at the new airfields and flying could only take place in good weather. With the activities at Ensbury Park virtually coming to a halt, the chief instructor, Mr Summerfield, left to form his own flying school on the east coast, taking some of the Avro 504s with him.

SEASIDE AND SCHNEIDER

There was another 'Aerodrome' at Bournemouth in 1919, situated on the seafront! Supermarine Aviation of Woolston, Southampton, converted a number of surplus Channel reconnaissance flying boats for passenger services, and from the end of July 1919 some of them operated pleasure flights around Poole Bay from the pier. These cost 3gns, with the three passengers seated in the open in front of the pilot, proving popular in giving views of warships anchored in the bay. One flight was for an intrepid seventy-five-year-old man and his seventy-two year-old wife. Services were flown to the Isle of Wight between July and September, but these were frequently interrupted by bad weather. During a storm in August, one of the Channel's overturned, resulting in rather damp passengers! At the end of September, copies of the *Southern Daily Echo* newspaper were flown from Woolston to Bournemouth during a national rail strike, the flight taking forty-five minutes to arrive off the pier where the papers were taken ashore by boat.

September 1919 also saw the Royal Aero Club organise the Schneider Trophy Race for seaplanes over the bay on 10 September, with entries from France, Italy and Great Britain.

The Schneider Trophy Race held in Bournemouth in September 1919 was not a success, as fog over the bay interrupted flying. Here crowds surround the Sopwith Schneider entry, causing problems for the mechanics trying to work on the racer.

The event was attended by two Royal Navy battleships moored in Poole Bay. Most of the aircraft arrived from Cowes in the morning to be parked on the beach alongside the pier, with their mechanics complaining of limited facilities and crowds of onlookers getting in their way. The British entered a team of three aircraft – a Fairey III, a Sopwith Schneider and a Supermarine Sea Lion. The French did not fare well as their Spad was damaged on arrival and their Nieuport failed to start. The Italians did better with both their Savoias starting the race. The course was ten laps out to Swanage, back to Hengistbury Head, and returning to the Pierhead, but the race afternoon was fog-bound which prevented racing until tea-time. Regrettably, the race turned into a fiasco because of confusion between the organisers and the Italian and British teams. Two of the British entries retired at the end of the first lap due to the fog. The Sea Lion was damaged whilst taking-off near Studland when the pilot tried to establish where he was. He then flew on but, when landing again off Boscombe Pier, the damaged aircraft promptly nosed over with its tail sticking into the air! This should have left the race open to the Italians, with the Savoia pilot, Janello, claiming the trophy for completing the course. But the officials declared the win void as his aircraft had missed the correct marker buoy off Swanage, turning over a reserve buoy near Studland. Naturally, this did not please the Italian team and, after an official objection, they were declared winners twelve days after the event, although the race was still declared void.

RACE MEETINGS

Etches and Mortimer decided on a new form of racing at Ensbury Park, and formed the Bournemouth Racecourse Syndicate in 1921. Delays with their plans meant that the first horse race at the excellently laid out course did not take place until April 1925. Six race days were held during the year but the lavish events did not prosper as hoped and the following year saw the introduction of air racing as well. The landing area was situated within the race course, with 12,000 people flocking to the site for the 'Bournemouth Summer Aviation Race Meeting' on 21/22 August 1926. There were a number of races using a 5-mile triangular course northwards to East Parley and Kinson Manor Farm. One competitor in an Avro was Wing-Cdr Sholto Douglas, now with his RAF title. There were parachute jumps by Doris Marshall and Miss June, aerobatics by the well-known aviator of the day, Bert Hinkler, in an Avro Gosport, and sky writing by an S.E.5A. Hinkler flew straight down the horse-race course, lifting his Avro over each of the jumps! Objections to the horse racing had been raised by townspeople, and these objections continued, mainly because air racing was held on Sundays. This led to the Killjoy Trophy at the Easter 1927 Flying Meeting, named after the killjoys in the town who wanted Sunday racing banned. An irate local farmer took his shotgun to the low-flying aircraft, managing to hit a participating Blackburn Bluebird. The fastest race aircraft were wartime SE.5A fighters, although three races were won by Hinkler in an Avro Avian. The public were offered joy flights in an Avro 504K for 5s 6d (27p), or the luxury of a Hampstead airliner of Imperial Airways for £1 1s (£1.05).

The Whitsun Meeting at the beginning of June 1927 was marred by two crashes. During a test flight on 4 June, DH.37 *Lois* collided with a racecourse number board on take-off, the passenger being killed when the plane hit the ground. There were then a number of races on the Monday, involving the triangular course to the north. During one race, a Blackburn Bluebird and a Westland Widgeon collided over the Parley turning point, the aircraft bursting into flames in the ensuing crash which killed both pilots. One was Laurence Openshaw who had only married in April, having flown his bride to Bournemouth for their honeymoon and also to publicise the Easter Meeting. The smoke from the crash could be seen across the fields by the crowd at Ensbury Park, which included the families of the pilots. An enquiry into the crashes concluded that layout of the horse-race course placed too many restriction on aircraft operations, resulting in plans by the Royal Aero Club to hold the prestigious Kings Cup Air Race at Bournemouth in 1927, being scrapped. Complaints were also received by the Parish Council, concerning, 'damage to property with the flying machines on Flying Race Days'. All this sealed the fate of Ensbury Park as 'The Bournemouth Aerodrome', although further horse races were held during 1927 and 1928.

END OF ENSBURY PARK

Etches had not yet finished with his plans for the Ensbury Park site. In another new venture in September 1927, he became one of the directors of the Ensbury Park Greyhound Co. Snow delayed the first meeting until January 1928, and others were held over the following weeks. These activities came to a sudden end on 19 February when the National Hunt Club said they would not permit any further horse racing unless greyhound racing ceased.

During April and May the site was also used by the Bournemouth Gypsy Motor Club for grass-track racing. The last horse-race meeting was held at Ensbury Park on 11 April, the Racecourse Co. having been in financial difficulties for some months. It went into liquidation in June 1928, and the agents acting for the sale of the land enquired whether Poole Council were interested in retaining it as an airfield or sports ground. However, the Council had decided that the land should be developed for housing, the site being offered for sale at auction in December 1928. It failed to reach its reserve price, and remained unsold until November 1930. Its use as Bournemouth's Aerodrome was reconsidered, but by now the site had become so enclosed by housing that there was no way the Air Ministry would grant an aerodrome license. The final traces of the old airfield disappeared in spring 1934, when the grandstand at the western end was demolished as it had been surrounded by new housing developments.

Racing at Ensbury Park during the 1927 Easter Holiday. Turning over the shed is Bert Hinkler who won three races during the weekend. As well as the races, Imperial Airways offered pleasure flights for 10s 6d or cross country flights for £1 1s.

Additional excitement to the air racing at Ensbury Park was provided by the aircraft finishing along the home straight of the horse-race course. Leading the field during the 1927 Easter Meeting to cross the winning line is Bert Hinkler in his Avro Avian.

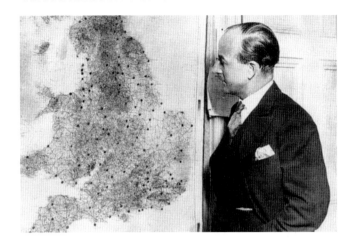

In 1929 Sir Alan Cobham undertook his Municipal Aerodrome Campaign to encourage air mindedness amongst the people of the country. Here he studies his planned route with one of the drawing pins marking Bournemouth.

MUNICIPAL AERODROME NO.1

In October 1928 the Air Ministry issued a recommendation that all cities and towns with populations of over 20,000 should be connected by air services through their own municipal aerodrome, 'with as little delay as possible'. In conjunction with the Ministry, Bournemouth viewed three sites in May 1929 – Ensbury Park, Holdenhurst and Wick – with the Ministry considering the one at Wick (adjacent to the 1910 Southbourne site) most suitable. At the time, the well-known pioneer aviator Sir Alan Cobham, was surveying a number of towns around the country during his municipal aerodrome campaign in DH.61 *Youth of Britain*. He arrived from Yeovil in August to meet town officials, before flying on to Weymouth and Dorchester. In September, Sir Alan advised Bournemouth that he had a number of local sites in mind, and so was tasked by the corporation's newly formed Aerodrome Committee to find a suitable one. His view was that such an aerodrome should be for commercial use, not private use, and that it should not necessarily be profit making, as it was regarded as part of the infrastructure of the town. His report of April 1930 covered twelve possible locations, including Kinson, Littledown, Southbourne and Talbot Village. However, Sir Alan favoured the sites at East Parley, Throop, Muscliff and, his main recommendation, West Parley, which he considered, 'would make a very fine aerodrome, and could accommodate the largest types of air-liner. I would say West Parley should be developed'. It was accessible from the road into Northbourne (New Road), although it was a considerable distance (3½ miles) from the town centre. It would also be the cheapest to develop, with two planned runways of 1,200 yards east to west, and 1,400 yards north-east to south-west. He considered the Air Ministry's choice of Wick too far from the town, but Throop and Muscliff were much nearer, being south of the River Stour, and both were considered suitable. East Parley suffered from being some way from the town centre, although it was excellent from a flying point of view, situated between the hamlet of East Parley and Pussex Farm, the site of the present-day airport. Sir Alan considered the land, 'capable of being made into a magnificent aerodrome. I could recommend it for development as Bournemouth Aerodrome'. Sir Alan's fee for the report was just under £100.

Despite the recommendation of Sir Alan and the Air Ministry, Bournemouth's council members argued for some years as to where and when to proceed with a municipal aerodrome. One of the councillors wrote to the papers in September 1932, saying that Bournemouth, 'had left matters too late and was going to be left behind'. Sir Alan was not too concerned as he had plenty of other activities to keep him busy, including overseeing the aerodromes that were built by the likes of Blackpool, Bristol and Plymouth. Bournemouth had missed out on another opportunity to acquire an airport.

MISCELLANY

Amy Johnson made an official visit to Bournemouth on 23 August 1930, having recently returned from her record-making solo flight to Australia. She landed in the morning at the site of the former Talbot Village Aerodrome in her de Havilland Gipsy Moth *Jason*. Then off with her flying helmet, on with the make-up, and she was ready to meet her public at the Hospital Fête. After the visit she flew on to Shoreham for a week's visit to the Brighton area.

Bournemouth residents saw a new form of air travel when the airship *Graf Zeppelin* flew over on 2 July 1932 while on a round-the-country flight from Hanworth. Then, on the evening of 6 July 1936, the *Hindenburg* flew over eastbound, having recently made the news with its first transatlantic crossing in May.

The Royal Air Force frequently undertook goodwill tours of the country. Here Supermarine Southampton flying boats of 480 Flight from Calshot are moored off Bournemouth beach during summer 1926.

3

THE FIRST
'BOURNEMOUTH AIRPORT'

During the 1920s and 1930s the term aerodrome was used in Great Britain to apply to airfields used for airline services; the term airport did not come into general use until after the Second World War. However, the Bournemouth area was well to the fore as it used the title 'Airport' in 1934.

MUNICIPAL AERODROME NO.2

In January 1933, the Boroughs of Bournemouth and Poole announced that they were planning a jointly run municipal aerodrome, and were examining various sites in the area. Bournemouth did not refer back to Sir Alan Cobham's recommendations of 1930, saying they were no longer available, and Poole had no obvious sites. However, during 1933 Poole had expanded northwards to take in Canford and Merley. The advice of the Air Minister, Lord Semphill, was sought, and his views were received in September 1934. He considered that the new aerodrome should be used for both commercial and private flying, with thought being given to accommodating sea-planes. The short list of sites considered by the councils were White Cliff (adjacent to Poole Harbour), Haymoor Bottom (Canford Heath), Canford Magna (part of Canford Estate) and Studland (adjacent to Poole Bay).

CHRISTCHURCH AIRPORT...

Christchurch had seen pleasure flying undertaken from fields adjacent to Mudeford Lane, in June 1926, by Avro 504s of Surrey Flying Services, offering passenger flights from 5s (25p). Also advertised were 'Great Death-Defying Spectacles [wing-walking at 1,000ft] and Thrilling Parachute Descents'. Then, in 1930, Fisher Aviation Co. arrived from Shoreham with 'generous circular flights from 5/-' in the usual mount of an Avro 504. The company was owned by Flying Officer Francis Fisher, described as a flashy and flamboyant stunt-flyer, who spent the first few months living in a tent alongside his Avro at Somerford Bridge. A couple of fields to the west was another site used for a while by the Hampshire Aero Club, known as Burry's Field (after the farmer who owned the land), and being listed by the Automobile Association as a suitable light aircraft landing ground with a 650-yard landing run. By 1930 the AA was diverging into aviation interests as well as motoring ones, issuing its first Register of Aircraft Landing Grounds in 1932. The AA issued visiting pilots to these Landing Grounds with a 'Permit to Use'. The register advised them to visit the local Somerford Garage for fuel, but warned them to look out for cattle and haystacks when arriving at Burry's Field! The highlight of 1933 was the visit of Cobham's Flying Circus on Sunday 30 April, which attracted 8,000 spectators, and disquiet from churchgoers.

At the Priory Church that morning the Vicar protested from the pulpit against the air display being held on a Sunday, also protesting to the Air Ministry that the Sunday Observance Act of 1677 should not be disregarded. Among the congregation were the Deputy Mayor, Aldermen and Councillors – most of who later flew in the afternoon with Cobham in the Astra airliner!

On the instigation of Fisher Aviation, expansion of the site took place from January 1934, following permission to combine the various adjoining fields. Advertised as Christchurch Airport (not Aerodrome), the site attracted a scheduled air service from Bristol, commencing in the middle of May and operated by DH Dragons of Western Airways at a fare 37s 6d return. The airport was also included in Provincial Airways' Croydon to Plymouth service, also being served from Portsmouth by the impressively named Portsmouth, Southsea & Isle of Wight Aviation Co. (PS&IoW). Bournemouth passengers for the 'Shamrock and Rambler Air Station' were provided with a taxi from Beale's Store and the Lansdowne.

A postcard issued by Fisher Aviation in 1930 to promote the pleasure flights operated from a field adjacent to Somerford Bridge at Christchurch. 'Enchanting Panorama of Coast-Line and Country to be seen in comfort from our Avro 504, a veritable Magic-Carpet.'

Bournemouth Airport's terminal at Christchurch airfield in the mid-1930s. Although plans had been drawn up for an impressive art deco terminal building, the lack of finance meant that these wooden sheds continued to be used until the outbreak of war.

... INTO BOURNEMOUTH AIRPORT

After only a few months, the grass landing strip at Christchurch developed soft spots and dangerous ruts, resulting in the airlines having to suspend their services. In order to undertake improvements, Fisher Aviation needed to raise further cash, and decided to do this by forming Bournemouth Airport Ltd in February 1935. This title was used as it was felt that Bournemouth was more well known than Christchurch, a fact that did not go down well in the town. The new company purchased the 94-acre site for £17,000 in March, with plans for an impressive modern terminal building, but in fact only wooden sheds on the north side were available. Three grass runways were provided, each of 1,000 yards. Fisher achieved a major coup in obtaining the services of Sir Alan Cobham as technical adviser and one of the new directors. For this he received £250 p.a., with Fisher receiving £400 p.a. as general manager and director. (Other directors were Lord Dorchester of Basingstoke and Viscount Fitzharris of Winchfield.)

Cobham had recently formed his own small airline company, Cobham Air Routes, so the airport could now feature in its route plans. A brochure issued by the airport showed the grand design of the terminal, plus the intention to operate services with their own aircraft via Birmingham to Manchester, in addition to the existing services, which included the 'Express London service from Bournemouth' operated by Airspeed Envoys. The other airlines returned, the summer of 1935 seeing services by Cobham Air

Routes from Croydon to Guernsey, Great Western & Southern Airlines to Plymouth, PS&IoW to Portsmouth, Ryde and Sandown, plus Western Airways to Bristol and Cardiff. Example fares were Croydon 57s return, Cardiff 55s return and Guernsey 67s return. Although sounding impressive, it must be remembered that airliners at the time were the likes of single-engined, four-seater DH Fox Moths or twin-engined, eight-seater DH Dragons. On the evening of 3 July, Cobham's Westland Wessex airliner suffered an engine failure whilst returning from Guernsey, and came down in the sea south of the Needles. The sole passenger was eventually rescued by a passing ship, but the pilot drowned and, as a result of the accident, Sir Alan sold his airline. Cobham's Flying Circus visited again on 10 August with its usual variety of aircraft for pleasure flights, aerobatics and displays, plus flights in the 'giant' airliner *Astra*. To expand their activities, the Airport Co. formed the Bournemouth Flying Club in December 1935, operating from early in the following year from a wooden clubhouse adjacent to the terminal. Flying instruction was given on the popular DH Moth trainer at £1 per half hour, with solo flying at 18s per half hour. During the first year of operation the airport handled 3,573 aircraft and 6,170 passengers.

COBHAM'S FLYING CIRCUS

Following his efforts to get aerodromes established at every major town, Sir Alan Cobham turned his attention to getting the public air-minded. For this, he established his National Aviation Day campaign early in 1932, which toured the country giving spectacular displays and offering many people their first chance of a flight. Normal admission prices were 1s 3d, children 6d, and flights started at 4s. The crowds were entertained by championship aerobatics, parachute descents from the wing of an airliner, crazy flying, autogiros and much more. The displays soon became referred to by the public as Cobham's Flying Circus, but Sir Alan was horrified at this title which implied a different slant on his intention of bringing aviation to the public. However, he achieved his aim as a large number of the public recall having their first flight for 5s in one of his Avro 504s or Airspeed Ferries. Over the years, the displays would draw crowds like the Red Arrows do currently.

   On its first visit to Bournemouth, the National Aviation Day was based at fields between Holdenhurst Road and Iford Bridge (the present-day Tesco site), and displayed on 12/13 August 1932. The fields were also used by Prince George in October when he arrived to open the extension to Boscombe Hospital. Cobham visited again on 22 August 1933, when he was based at East Parley (the site he recommended to the council), although it proved more difficult for people to get to. For the visits on 7 July 1934 and 6 July 1935, the event was based at Wick Lane, Southbourne (Bournemouth Centenary site), but at the end of the 1935 season Cobham gave up the flying circus to concentrate on other aeronautical matters. The circus also visited Wimborne during these years, where it was based at fields alongside Magna Road, Canford, in August 1933, July 1934 and August 1935.

For passenger flights with Cobham's Flying Circus, two Airspeed Ferries were utilised during 1932/33, each carrying six passengers. Both had been built by Airspeed at York at the specific request of Sir Alan Cobham for his National Aviation Days.

MOORTOWN AERODROME

Bournemouth and Poole Councils were heartened to be advised by the Air Minister in September 1934 that he did not consider the existing aerodrome at Christchurch could adequately serve all of Bournemouth. The councils were seriously considering the site at Moortown on Lord Wimborne's land, but at a meeting in December, Francis Fisher suggested that the councils, instead of the newly formed Bournemouth Airport Ltd, should purchase the newly developed Christchurch site. The councils did not go along with this line of thinking, saying that Christchurch was too far out for intending passengers. The town councils again considered the Parley sites recommended by Sir Alan Cobham (and used by his Flying Circus in 1933), making an approach in May 1935 to the landowner, the Earl of Malmesbury, who replied that he, 'could not see his way to sell the property for the purpose of an aerodrome'. The councils agreed to settle on Moortown (named after an adjacent farm), where in June the borough engineers took an option on the 130-acre site, which comprised undulating land, to the west of Bear Cross, south of Magna Road. Situated within the new boundary of Poole, approval to proceed was received from the Air Ministry in November 1935, although they recommended that additional land should be purchased to give an extended area of 180 acres. Anticipated costs were: site, £13,000; adjacent woods, £2,000; prepare land and erect buildings, £10,000. There would be an east–west grass runway, with terminal building and hangars adjacent to Magna Road. Fisher, on behalf of Bournemouth Airport Ltd, opposed the plans of the two boroughs, requesting that they should invest their money in Christchurch. The boroughs replied again that intending passengers would prefer Moortown Aerodrome. They also announced that the Straight Corporation had shown interest in operating the aerodrome and that Spartan Air Services were considering suitable routes. In January 1936 agreement was reached by the councils to borrow £18,530 for the outright purchase of the site.

In a letter to *The Aeroplane* magazine in April 1936, Sir Alan Cobham expressed his fury that having recommended sites in 1930, Bournemouth took no action, and most of the sites were now used for other purposes. He considered Poole Council had belatedly joined in the action, 'surveying wild pieces of heathland to convert to an aerodrome for the benefit of one or two belated yachtsmen in the town'.

MOORTOWN ABANDONED

At a public enquiry in March 1936, the Air Ministry said that they were against the idea of two aerodromes close together, where, by now, Christchurch had established regular services. In July Bournemouth Airport Ltd again wrote to Bournemouth and Poole Councils, saying that their Christchurch site should be developed as the airport. After months of further consideration, Bournemouth Borough confirmed in June 1937 that it had allocated £88,000 towards the development of Moortown, the borough aiming to double the size of the site to handle international services, rather than develop the original plan which had only been intended to operate local services. The Air Ministry advised that they considered a 1,300-yard runway would be needed, which would entail the levelling of a larger area of land, plus the removal of adjacent woodland. Matters dragged on until May 1938 when Poole pulled out of the scheme due to the increasing costs of the enlarged site, with Bournemouth stating that it would be unable to finance the project by itself. Although the boroughs had purchased the land, no construction work had been undertaken and in due course the land reverted to agricultural use. So for yet another occasion, Bournemouth had missed out on its own airport (as opposed to one at Christchurch).

Sixty years later the site was still referred to as Moortown Aerodrome, even though there had never been any flying there. The site was eventually developed by the councils in 2000 as the Canford Park Arena leisure and sporting complex. However, there was now aerial activity – the occasional visits by helicopters or hot air balloons for special events.

SLOW EXPANSION AT CHRISTCHURCH...

Bournemouth Airport Ltd did not prosper as had been hoped, and the intentions of Bournemouth and Poole Councils relating to Moortown had not helped. Despite the prospect of a rival airport, new partners were sought during 1936 to introduce further capital for expansion and improvements. Fisher sought advice from the Air Ministry on how to expand their activities to more fully serve Bournemouth, and in September he even approached the Southern Railway in the hopes they might consider a new station on the main London line to serve the airport, thereby increasing passenger numbers. New airlines seen during the year were Air Dispatch, Channel Air Ferries, Crilly Airways and Olley Air Service (who had bought out Cobham Air Routes). Something new for the local residents was Empire Air Day, held on 23 May 1936 to enable the public to see the RAF in action. Displays were given by Hawker Audax fighters from Old Sarum and Hawker Nimrod naval fighters from Eastleigh. On 22 March 1937 five RAF Ansons of 51 Sqdn diverted into the airfield low on fuel whilst on exercises over the Channel and lost in a heavy snowstorm. The local press described them as, 'double engined Army fighting planes of a crack RAF fighting squadron operating from Boscombe Down'.

... AND FURTHER DIFFICULTIES

The RAF had been undergoing expansion during the mid-1930s, and in February 1937 the Bournemouth Flying Club approached the Air Ministry to set up a reserve Training School to assist in the increasing requirement for RAF pilots. Their request was turned down, mainly due to the small size of the airfield. Land adjoining the eastern end of the airport, forming part of the Somerford Grange Estate, came up for sale in June 1937. The Airport Co. realised it was just what they needed for expansion, but was unable to raise any funds towards its purchase. Problems were mounting at Christchurch due to its restricted size, with the directors approaching the Under Secretary of State in August 1937 to see if he could help. But he confirmed that the physical restrictions on expansion would prevent them developing the grand municipal airport envisaged. So the directors decided to find a replacement site in the local area for future use. Another Empire Air Day was held on 28 May 1938, the RAF now having a number of monoplanes in front-line service to replace the biplanes seen in previous years. Avro Anson reconnaissance aircraft and Fairey Battle light bombers were displayed, along with older Gladiators, Hinds and Sharks. The display was to show the RAF's preparedness for any forthcoming conflict, the local population having already been issued with gas masks. In the meantime, the Flying Club joined the Government's Civil Air Guard Scheme in September to speed up the training of prospective RAF pilots – sixty being under instruction on DH Moths by the end of the month.

The year 1939 arrived with the prospect of war with Germany increasing. Flying activity continued as before at Christchurch, and the directors at last thought they had found a suitable site for a replacement airfield. This was the land at East Parley owned by the Earl of Malmesbury, who had been approached by Bournemouth and Poole Councils in 1935. He was still totally opposed to the idea, because, amongst other things, it was too close to his home at Hurn Court. The Earl would not even see Francis Fisher to hear of the plans, and so Fisher contacted the Air Ministry early in 1939 to see if they could bring any pressure on the Earl. They replied to say that earlier in the year they had undertaken their own survey which revealed two suitable airfield sites in the area, but they were unable to do anything to make the Earl change his mind. So no further progress could be made as

The initial fleet of the Bournemouth Flying Club in 1936 was made up of Fisher's Avro 504 plus de Havilland Moths. They are depicted in this painting which shows them to the north of the airfield. One of the Moths continues to fly from the south coast at the present time.

the Air Ministry were now involved in the more serious matter of preparing for war. The summer timetable included services by Great Western & Southern Air Lines thrice daily from Shoreham, via Ryde, with DH Dragon Rapides, and PS&IoW six times a day from Ryde with Airspeed Couriers. Fares were, Ryde 17s 6d return (87p) and Shoreham 41s 6d return (£2.07). The Flying Club added further DH Moths to its fleet to cope with the Civil Air Guard training, with the aircraft averaging five hours of flying a day.

Part of the land at Somerford Grange Estate was used by the Government for building premises adjacent to Lymington Road for the Air Defence Experimental Establishment (ADEE), which took up residence in 1939. The establishment was involved in the early development of radar, making use of scanners on the clifftop at nearby Steamer Point. There was little publicity concerning the ADEE, although in August 1939 the local paper said that trials included the development of a death ray for defence against the enemy – shades of H.G. Wells!

BAN ON CIVIL FLYING

On the outbreak of war in September 1939, all civilian flying in the area was prohibited and Civil Air Guard training ceased. The Airport Co. was informed by the Air Ministry that they had no use for the airfield, nor was there any military work for the Flying Club whose Moths remained out of use for some months before being collected by the RAF for other duties. So Bournemouth had lost another of its airports. (In fact, Bournemouth Airport Co. remained in existence until after the war, but only in a dormant capacity.)

4

THE SECOND WORLD WAR

The declaration of war on Germany on 3 September 1939 meant an end to existing air services within Britain, although emergency airline services were soon set up by the Government. However, Christchurch was not included among the routes.

PHONEY WAR

During the 1930s the Government and the RAF were concerned with the defence of the country, and there had been a great expansion of the RAF, both in the form of modern aircraft and new airfields. The majority of these airfields had been constructed in East Anglia, Lincolnshire and Yorkshire, as these were the areas closest to the threat from Germany. Initial offensive operations were conducted across the North Sea, with the winter months being known as the 'Phoney War' as there was little action on either side. This was to change in the spring when Germany concentrated its efforts on capturing further territories, resulting in the invasion of Holland and Belgium at the beginning of May 1940, followed by the north-eastern part of France later in the month. The invading troops encountered little resistance and were apparently poised on the northern coast of France prior to crossing the English Channel to complete their task by capturing Great Britain. Troops carried by gliders had been used for the earlier operations, and were expected again, followed up by barges, large numbers of which were appearing in French-occupied ports.

The threat of the Germans across the Channel threw the Air Ministry plans into disarray as the majority of the defences were along the east coast and around London. Hasty plans had to be drawn up for new airfields in the south to counter Luftwaffe attacks and the anticipated invasion, codenamed Operation Sealion.

EFFECT ON BOURNEMOUTH

The nearest RAF airfield to Bournemouth in spring 1940 was at Warmwell, south-east of Dorchester, which housed a Bombing and Gunnery School. July 1940 brought changes with the school moving out of the line of fire to Dumfries and the airfield transferred to Fighter Command as a forward base for Supermarine Spitfires normally housed at Middle Wallop. The fighters were tasked with defending the coast roughly within the Bridport to Southampton area, and much action was seen during the ensuing Battle of Britain, with the fighters up against attacking Luftwaffe forces often in excess of 200 aircraft.

Having suffered their first bombing raid on 2 July, the residents of Bournemouth soon became used to the sight of Hurricanes and Spitfires from Middle Wallop and Warmwell chasing the Luftwaffe in the skies high above the town. Poole was to suffer its first raid on 21 August. The Luftwaffe had based its fighters on the Cherbourg peninsular, with their bombers further inland, so the shortest crossing of the English Channel brought them between the Purbecks and the Isle of Wight. Many residents witnessed a Spitfire being brought down in the bay on 18 July. The pilot initially tried to swim to the beach, but then had to be rescued by the Navy. Not so fortunate was the pilot of a Spitfire from Middle Wallop who was attacked over the Purbecks on 15 August, crashing at Talbot Woods. Pilot Officer Cecil Hight was killed as a result of his parachute failing to open and, post-war, he was commemorated by the naming of 'Pilot Hight Road' in Kinson. (The event was commemorated again in September 2005 by the flypast of a RAF Spitfire.) From August 1940 residents had to contend with nightly flights by Luftwaffe bombers from France bound for raids further inland, and were kept awake by the local ack-ack guns opening up on them. Nationwide, the 'Buy a Spitfire Fund' was introduced, with towns being asked to raise £5,000 which they were told would purchase a Spitfire for the RAF. The first fundraising event in Bournemouth was during the summer of 1940, when sufficient funds were raised to buy a Spitfire, which was named *Bournemouth*; further funds later saw the purchase of *Bournemouth II*. The town hall was supplied with a photograph of the aircraft, which was also published in the *Bournemouth Echo* for the entire town to see. As part of the fundraising, a crashed Dornier Do.17 bomber was displayed in Dean Park during September, with four Spitfires giving an aerobatic display. Over in Poole, funds were raised to purchase Spitfire *Villae de Poole*, with a crashed Messerschmitt 109 on display in Poole Park. Bournemouth participated in War Weapon Week in February 1941, during which three Hurricanes from Ibsley gave an aerobatic display. Unfortunately, during this, one failed to recover from a roll, crashing on to a house at St Clements Road, Boscombe.

RAF HURN

Further airfields in the area were required by the RAF, but the existing one at Christchurch was considered unsuitable due to its limited size. The Air Ministry came up with two new sites. The first, at Ibsley, north of Ringwood, had originally been considered by the Fleet Air Arm just before the war. It was eventually constructed during the winter of 1940/41, opening as a Fighter Command station on 15 February 1941 as a satellite to Middle Wallop. The second site was one that the Air Ministry was well aware of – farm and heath land at East Parley on the Earl of Malmesbury's Estate. The land had been earmarked during 1939, but it was not until the following year that it was requisitioned from the Earl, with John Mowlem & Co. being contracted in August to build the airfield for £115,000. Three hard runways were provided, connected by a perimeter track, with hard standings for aircraft parking off of it. As well as buildings on the airfield, many administration buildings were situated in the woods at Hurn Village. Again, the airfield was intended as a Fighter Command satellite to Middle Wallop. However, these plans were changed during construction, with Mowlems being requested to extend the main runway to 1,600 yards so as to be capable of handling bombers in the future.

Arthur Porter was a fresh RAF recruit:

> I was one of a number of airmen posted from Catfoss (Yorks) in June, and as is often the case there was a mix up in our postings as the airfield was not ready. An officer drove up from Bournemouth and arranged for us new arrivals to sleep in the workmen's huts. Building work was going on all around, and the Earl of Malmesbury used to visit to see what was going on. At the end of July we were able to move into newly completed quarters.

The new airfield was officially opened on 1 August 1941, being handed over by Mowlems to Wing Commander G.K. Horner. By the time of the airfield's opening, the Battle of Britain was long over and the threat of an anticipated second attempt of Operation Sealion by the Germans during the summer of 1941 had receded. So the RAF had a new airfield which it initially did not know what to do with. The need for local fighter defence had been shown at the end of March when a lone Luftwaffe aircraft dropped two bombs on Branksome Gas Works. Thirty-four were killed in the lunch-time attack, which was Poole's worst during the war.

There were a couple of crash landings in Hurn's first weeks. The first was on the evening of 6 August when a Westland Whirlwind fighter, returning from combat over Cherbourg, force-landed with a damaged engine. Unfortunately, there was still builder's equipment and obstructions on the runway, which the Whirlwind hit, ending up on its nose. The pilot was able to climb safely down to the ground. The second crash-landing was made by a Short Stirling bomber on 20 September a long way from its home base at Oakington.

TELECOMMUNICATIONS FLYING UNIT

Plans had already been made in spring 1941 for Hurn to house the experimental aircraft of the RAF Special Duty Flight which was involved in the early development of airborne radar (or RDF as it was known as at the time). A research station had been built at Worth Matravers in the Purbecks (prior to the invasion of northern France) and a nearby airfield was required for their aircraft. Hurn had not been completed as early as anticipated, and so for a time the aircraft were based at Christchurch, moving to Hurn between August and November to make use of its longer tarmac runways. At

Operational Spitfires were never based at RAF Hurn. Occasionally, squadrons would arrive to undertake specific operations or else to refuel. This is one of a number used by the Telecommunications Flying Unit during 1941/42 for trials purposes.

the same time, the Special Duty Flight was renamed the Telecommunications Flying Unit (Research Section), with Christchurch airfield then becoming a satellite of Hurn. Airborne Interception (AI) radar was already in use with the RAF, initially used by night fighters to track down Luftwaffe aircraft. Using Bristol Blenheim IV's and Beaufighters, this was further developed along with a form of radar to track the aircraft's position over the ground. After early trials in a Blenheim IV, the radar was fitted into a Handley Page Halifax in March 1942, later being developed into the H2S radar used successfully by Bomber Command. Other aircraft in use by the unit ranged from ancient Fairey Swordfish biplanes to the latest Avro Lancaster, plus a Vickers Wellington with an early form of AWACS rotating radar mounted above its fuselage. (One of the Blenheim pilots was Flying Officer Jock Bryce, who returned to the airfield in 1951 as Valiant test pilot and again in 1963 as One-Eleven test pilot.) Any TFU trial flight undertaken usually meant flying over the English Channel with the danger of running into Luftwaffe fighters based on the Cherbourg peninsular. On a number of occasions the aircraft were attacked, luckily without loss. However, there was an early loss for the unit when a Blenheim IV force-landed on Chesil Beach at the end of November, after becoming lost over the Channel, with its pilot being killed when the aircraft overturned.

Joe Sieger was posted to Telecommunications Research Establishment at Worth Matravers in the spring of 1941:

I soon became Divisional Leader of Engineering which involved working on the aircraft at Christchurch and Hurn. There were about one hundred civilian draughtsmen and fitters working in various Nissen huts on trial radar installations, mainly for Blenheims and Wellingtons. The construction work on these early sets was moved to a new factory at Northbourne, with flight trials (sometimes on operational missions) continuing from Hurn.

Joe later retired to the area, forming the Hurn Airport Development Association in 1967 to drum up support for the airport's future.

The work being undertaken at Worth Matravers and by the TFU was considered secret enough for the Government to decide that future work should be carried out much further inland, and so a move to Defford was made almost overnight on 22 May 1942.

Despite the airfield having been in use for almost a year, much work was still to be done on accommodation. A report in April 1942 criticised the fact that water and drainage was still not connected to many buildings, necessitating Elsan toilets having to be installed, with the resultant offensive smells. There was also insufficient permanent accommodation, with 350 airmen having to be housed in tents. However, despite many of the buildings being described on the plans as 'Temporary Brick Construction', they were still in use sixty years later. When the airfield was built, it took in two farms (Greenland and Pussex) and associated buildings, most being put to new use. Pussex Farm, on the south-east, became home of the wartime commanding officer. In following years it was used by the airport commandant, Group Capt. Cox, and later still the airport director, Harry Longhurst, until his retirement.

BOAC AT POOLE

Prior to the war, long-range airline services were operated by Imperial Airways, mainly with their fleet of Short C Class flying boats, which were based on Southampton Water. These were used on the Empire Air Mail routes to places like Australia, Hong Kong and South Africa, and in summer 1939 there were joint operations with Pan American Airways across the North Atlantic to New York and Montreal. With war looming, Southampton was considered a prime target, and so a new base was sought. Following the Munich Crises of 1938, both Christchurch and Poole Harbours had been considered, but Poole's larger size made it the preferred choice. Runways, or trots in nautical terms, were planned, and terminal facilities sought. Imperial's move to Poole was officially made on 1 September 1939 with the airline's headquarters being 'Airways House' in the High Street. The 'Marine Terminal' was situated in the Poole Harbour Yacht Club at Lilliput, close to the end of one of the trots, with the crews housed at the Harbour Heights Hotel. Services continued during the early months of the war, with passengers arriving by special Pullman train from London and staying overnight in a local hotel before an early-morning departure. After checking in at the Yacht Club, passengers boarded a launch at Salterns Pier to be ferried out to the waiting flying boat. There were weekly services to Durban, Kisumu, Singapore and Sydney.

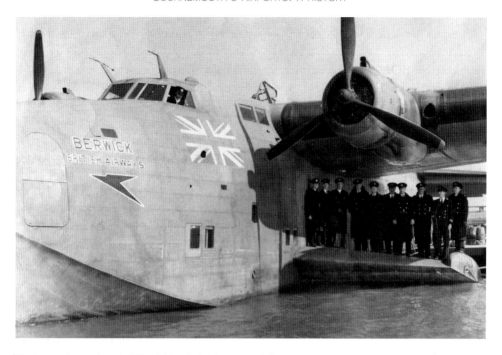

For non-stop services to West Africa, BOAC acquired three Boeing 314s in spring 1941. Like a number of their wartime aircraft, they carried British Airways titles, which were also used on the ground-crews' uniforms and the Poole Harbour launches.

As well as the move to Poole, Imperial Airways had to deal with its merger with British Airways to form British Overseas Airways Corporation (BOAC) which officially came into existence on 1 April 1940. No sooner had this happened, than the Germans invaded France in May, which cut off BOAC's route to Marseilles and the Mediterranean – the first stage of the majority of its flights. Then Italy entered the war in June, causing even more problems for the airline. For a while the C Class flying boats operated via Lisbon and Gibraltar to reach Cairo, but the route had to be abandoned as it soon fell prey to Luftwaffe fighters. In order to reach the Far East, BOAC were forced to set up the very much extended 'Horseshoe Route', flying from Durban, via Cairo, India and Singapore to Sydney. This resulted in the majority of their flying boats being based in Durban, with only three remaining at Poole. The route flown by C Class from Poole to East Africa was also in danger from Luftwaffe attacks, and BOAC needed a longer-range aircraft that could fly a route further to the west over the Atlantic to avoid the danger. Consolidated Catalinas had the range and the first, *Guba*, arrived in March 1941 to fly services to Lagos, soon being joined by others. However, the Catalinas had nowhere near the capacity of the C Class, resulting in three large Boeing 314's being purchased from America in May. These successfully operated from Foynes, flying non-stop to Takoradi – an important staging point in the Gold Coast. The new flying boats operated with British Airways titles, being seen on occasions at Poole.

America remained neutral on the outbreak of war, and so Pan American's limited New York services terminated at Foynes, Eire, with onward connections to Poole being provided by BOAC. A limited number of Air Mail services were flown by BOAC to Montreal and New York between August and November 1940, but the C Class flying boats did not have the range for regular services, having to refuel in Foynes and Newfoundland. These operations were under the control of Capt. J.C. Kelly Jones, who had the honour of piloting the first transatlantic flight of Winston Churchill. This was in January 1942 when the Prime Minister was flown home by Boeing 314 from Bermuda, but landed at Plymouth instead of Poole.

AIRSPEED SHADOW AIRCRAFT FACTORY

Although Christchurch had been rejected by the RAF, it still had a role to play in the war. With the guidance of Sir Alan Cobham, plans had already been drawn up for the construction of an aircraft production factory on the north-east side of the airfield, adjacent to the main road (site of Fisher Aviation's activities) – the land having already been purchased in June 1937. Construction work proceeded during 1940 under the auspices of the Ministry of Aircraft Production (MAP), who arranged for the new factory to be run by Airspeed Ltd whose existing factory was at Portsmouth. Airspeed were new to aircraft construction, having commenced business at Portsmouth in 1934, and produced a large number of Oxford trainers from 1937. Oxfords were also built at Christchurch and, by the time the factory was officially opened in March 1941, the first was almost complete. A total of 550 Oxfords were built at Christchurch compared with 4,400 at Portsmouth. Many of the Christchurch ones were shipped overseas for training in Australia, Canada, New Zealand and South Africa. The Christchurch factory was involved with the Horsa assault glider from the summer of 1942, and test flights involved being towed into the air by an old Whitley bomber. Many were then delivered to Brize Norton and Netheravon. On one occasion, one of the Whitley's engines failed on take-off. The Horsa was rapidly released to end up on the mud flats of Christchurch Harbour, with the Whitley struggling along the coast to end up on the mud flats of Poole Harbour.

Prior to the outbreak of war, PS&IoW had commenced sub-contract work for the Airspeed factory at Portsmouth. This included the major overhauls of Oxfords, and in 1941 a similar arrangement was brought into being at Christchurch. Overhauls were undertaken in a building provided by the MAP at Purewell, with aircraft being towed by tractor to the airfield for re-assembly and flight testing.

Christchurch was also used for a period by the Special Duty Flight which was involved in the early development of radar. A varied collection of aircraft arrived from St Athan at the end of April 1940, the original intention being that they should use Hurn. Trials were flown from Christchurch in connection with the TRE at Worth Matravers, one of the reasons being to establish whether the experimental radar scanners could pick up a wooden glider or a slow flying autogiro. On a test flight during September, a Blenheim IV crash

Initial production from the Airspeed 'Shadow' Christchurch factory was of Oxford trainers for the RAF and Commonwealth air forces. However, the majority were produced at Airspeed's main factory at Portsmouth, plus others from de Havilland and Percival Aircraft.

Following the Oxford, large numbers of wooden Horsa gliders were produced by Airspeed for Airborne Forces duties. They played vital roles during D-Day, Arnhem and the Rhine crossing. However, seen here is one of those overhauled at Christchurch during 1948/49.

landed after being attacked by a Junkers Ju.88. The crew were uninjured but the crews of a Blenheim and Defiant were not so happy when they were set upon by a RAF Whirlwind a few days later! The SDF aircraft moved out to Hurn in autumn 1941, having received a visit from the Minister for Aircraft Production in October 1941, and Air Commodore the Duke of Kent in November.

An earlier visitor in 1941 had been a Luftwaffe Jungmann trainer. Two Frenchmen had taken the biplane from the German-occupied airfield of Carpiquet in Normandy on 30 April, and had flown low crossed the Channel. They made landfall by the Needles before coming across the airfield at Christchurch. Luck was on their side as they landed safely and surrendered to the commanding officer. After interrogation in London, they were allowed to join the RAF. Questions were asked as to why the Jungmann had not been intercepted before landing. The local Army gunners said they were leaving it to the RAF, who said they were leaving it to the Army!

AIR SERVICES FROM HURN

The outbreak of war had thrown BOAC's landplane operations into confusion, with many of its aircraft taken over by the RAF. By the end of 1941, the Air Ministry had drawn up plans for resumption of limited BOAC services, with Hurn chosen as a suitable base. Amongst the reasons were that the airfield was under-utilised by the RAF at the time, and that BOAC already operated its flying-boat services from nearby Poole. So January 1942 saw the first airline services from Hurn. Initial flights were the re-establishment of services to Cairo, operated via Gibraltar, with a fleet of two Consolidated Liberator transports and a Curtiss CW-20 *St Louis*, all three carrying British Airways titles. The Liberator was chosen due to its long range, as flights to Cairo took twelve hours. Here they would connect with the Horseshoe Route services to South Africa and Australia. The first service to Cairo departed on 18 January, but disaster struck the Liberator on its return. Having flown out the long way round, it cut across France for its return on 15 February, only to be shot down in error by an RAF Spitfire south of Plymouth. All those on board were killed. Services continued with the remaining Liberator, frequently from Lyneham, with *St Louis* also being used for essential relief flights into Malta. There were also RAF Liberator transports of No.1425 Flight, which used Hurn as a servicing base, from January 1942. The Flight was concerned with the ferry flights of aircraft to the Middle East. The aircraft routed west of Portugal, refuelled at Gibraltar, then continued to Cairo and their final destination.

RAF IN BOURNEMOUTH

The town of Bournemouth was also seeing increased RAF activity. During 1941 a large number of the town's hotels were taken over by the RAF for administration and training purposes as No.3 Personnel Reception and Training Centre. The Royal Canadian Air

Force (RCAF) also arrived in July 1941, remaining until September 1945, and there were so many aircrews passing through, that the Canadians used forty-three hotels in the town. Still more were required when the Americans arrived later in 1943. The Royal Bath was the headquarters for the RAF and RCAF, the Ambassador and Palace Court for the US Army, with the Marsham Court used by the American Red Cross. The Pier Approach Baths – part of the town's emergency water supply – doubled as a training facility for Mae West and dinghy drill for aircrews.

5

RAF HURN OPERATIONAL

ARMY CO-OPERATION COMMAND

At last the RAF found a use for Hurn, transferring it to Army Co-Operation Command early in June 1942, with the arrival of 296 and 297 Squadrons and their Armstrong Whitworth Whitley Vs for paratroop training and, later, glider towing. There was also a new commanding officer – Group Capt. H.J.G.E. Proud. The RAF realised that it needed to develop its use of paratroops and glider-borne troops in connection with the Army's Airborne Division. Whitleys had served the RAF as bombers until spring 1942, but the Mk.V version seen at Hurn was equipped to carry ten paratroops that jumped from the aircraft by means of a hatch in the underside of the aircraft. From the summer they began to be equipped with towing gear which enabled them to tow Horsa gliders which could carry twenty-five troops. (Many of these gliders were built locally at the Airspeed factory at Christchurch.) The Horsas were piloted by members of the Glider Pilot Regiment, who received their basic flying training on Tiger Moths before moving on to the gliders. Advance training flights were carried out over Salisbury Plain, where Netheravon was a major training base. Also attached to Army Co-Operation Command were North American Mustang Is of 170 Squadron, which appeared briefly during the summer on tactical reconnaissance flights. There was a visit by the Duke of Kent in August to see the work of Army Co-Operation Command, but a mass parachute drop from their Whitleys had to be cancelled due to strong winds. Changes saw Army Co-Operation Command move out for a while at the end of September to make way for new occupants at Hurn.

The only reported 'visit' by the Luftwaffe to Hurn was on 14 August, when a Heinkel He.111 dropped bombs in the area, although there was little damage. The airfield AA gunners opened up at the bomber, claiming some hits.

FIRST USAAF ARRIVAL

The Americans had begun arriving in this country in 1942 and, initially, United States Army Air Force (USAAF) aircraft were based in East Anglia. (At the time, their Army still controlled air operations, the Air Force not achieving 'independence' until 1948.) Its first bombing mission was undertaken by B-17 Flying Fortress's of the Eighth Air

Converted Whitley bombers were used at Hurn during 1942 by Army Co-Operation Command for paratroop training and glider towing. By this time their role as effective bombers had been superseded by Halifaxes and Lancasters.

Force in August 1942, but there was a new need for these bombers. The Allies drew up plans for 'Operation Torch' – the invasion of French-controlled Algeria and Morocco in north-west Africa – to relieve the pressure on the British Eighth Army in North Africa. For this, the American's formed the Twelfth Air Force under Maj.-Gen. Jimmy Doolittle, using around half of the Eighth Air Force aircraft already in England. Hurn was chosen to be the UK base for Allied troops departing for 'Operation Torch', with the first USAAF personnel arriving on 26 October 1942. The supply of aircraft and men via Gibraltar was known as 'Exercise Cackle'. On 2 November six B-17F Flying Fortress' of the 97th Bomb Group arrived to carry Army VIPs the 1,200 miles to Gibraltar. The VIPs mainly arrived from London by special train, and the party included Gen. Ike Eisenhower and Maj.-Gen. Jimmy Doolittle. The aircraft were due to set off on 3 November, but thick fog prevented their departure until 5 November – even then there was still zero visibility. The B-17s then had to fly round the coast of Portugal to reach Gibraltar. The pilot of Eisenhower's aircraft was Lt-Col. Paul Tibbets, who at the end of the war was the pilot of the B-29 which dropped the Atom bomb on Hiroshima. Thirty-nine Douglas C-47s of the 64th Troop Carrier Group (TCG) were due to follow on 9 November, but the continued threat of fog saw the aircraft fly empty to St Eval in Cornwall to collect their troops. Over the next three weeks a fleet of seventy-five C-47s of the 60th and 62nd TCG flew out supply missions, the busiest time being the departure of thirty-two aircraft in the early hours of 15 November. The C-47s were supplemented by a further fifty-five B-17s fitted out for carrying troops, plus nine B-24D Liberators. 'Exercise Cackle' saw the delivery of 2,400 aircrew and personnel, as well as large numbers of C-47s and B-17s, to the newly formed Twelfth Air Force. There was some RAF involvement in 'Cackle', with Handley Page Halifax IIs of 138 Squadron flying out on transport duties.

SUPPORTING OVERSEAS OFFENSIVES

The departure of the Americans to Africa meant that Army Co-Operation Command could return in December 1942. The Whitleys of 296 Squadrons flew down from Thruxton with many ground personnel inside the Horsas that they towed. A glider-towing demonstration for MPs on 28 January 1943 had to be called off due to bad weather, although some MPs braved a short flight in a Horsa. During January the Whitleys began to be replaced by Armstrong Whitworth Albemarles as the first stage of the command's re-equipment programme. Similar in general shape to the Whitley, the Albemarle had proved to be an unwanted aircraft. It was originally designed as a bomber of composite construction, enabling it to be built by non-aviation firms. However, it was obsolete for such a role by the time the first aircraft began to appear in early 1942. Proving to be slower than other bombers, it was decided to use them as glider tugs and special transports, with Hurn seeing the first of the tug version. Again, they could be used to carry paratroops, a hatch being provided in the floor of the rear fuselage for them to jump out of. However, on 17 April the Albemarles undertook a bombing mission on electrical installations in northern France. Unfortunately, a number of the aircraft were unable to find the target and returned home early.

Two other new units were seen at Hurn. No.3 Overseas Aircraft Dispatch Unit (OADU) was formed in January 1943 to handle the delivery of Albemarle, Halifax, Liberator and Wellington bombers to North Africa. Some of the Wellingtons were fitted with magnetic mine-sweeping loops under their fuselage for seeking out German U-boats in the Mediterranean. The bombers would fly in small groups to Gibraltar, having to fly well to the west of Portugal to avoid German aircraft. During May, eighty bombers were handled by the unit, with 148 in June. Then May saw the setting up of the Heavy Glider Maintenance Unit (HGMU), which dealt with the newly delivered Horsa gliders. During Bournemouth's Wings for Victory week in May 1943, an Albemarle towed a Horsa over the town, dropping leaflets bearing, 'A message to Bournemouth from the RAF'.

Dave Jones recalls being posted to Hurn:

It was the middle of 1943 and I expected to work on the Albemarle's Hercules engines, but found my first job was on the Merlin of a damaged Spitfire. When completed, the pilot called to collect the fighter, which I expected he would take on a test flight. But no, straight off into the sky and back to base. Another Spitfire story going the rounds at the time sounds rather suspect. When the framework of one of the new T2 hangars was being erected, a Spitfire beat up the hangar causing two of the workers to fall off into a heap of sand. The Spitfire then went into a climbing roll, the pilot fell out of the cockpit at the top of the roll, being killed as he had no time to open his parachute. The fighter then flew on over the town to crash in the sea.

Sunday 23 May saw a lunch time attack on Bournemouth by twenty-four Focke-Wulf Fw.190s which flew in low from the Isle of Wight. They crossed the coast at Southbourne and then approached the town from the north-east, providing no advance warning. Over 200 servicemen and civilians were killed during the bombing attack. The Fw.190s quickly escaped back across the Channel, although two were brought down by ack-ack fire. There had been no time for local fighters to be scrambled to intercept the attackers. This was to be the blackest day in the war for Bournemouth.

OPERATION BEGGAR

Once the Allies had regained control of North Africa, their next objective was to capture Sicily as a foothold for their return to Europe. Their plans called for paratroops to be flown across the Mediterranean from North Africa during 'Operation Beggar', making use of transport aircraft, gliders and their tugs. The RAF was to use Horsas for the first time in large numbers, but the question was how to get them to North Africa quickly. Time was pressing and consideration was given to towing the gliders out, but nothing like this been attempted over such a long distance. In May, a Halifax from nearby Holmsley South set off with a Horsa on tow en route to Hurn. However, it took ten hours to get there by flying a 1,400-mile triangular course around the country. Having proved that the idea worked, there was a rush to get sufficient aircraft ready for the planned operation date early in July. Hurn had already dispatched its squadron of Albemarles to North Africa. The Halifaxes of 295 Squadron from Holmsley South, supplemented by new ones, arrived during May for modifications before undertaking their towing task. As well as adding towing gear, their bomb bays were sealed with tape to help them float longer should they come down in the sea. The Horsas were prepared by the HGMU and, on 1 June, the Halifaxes set off to Portreath in Cornwall with their Horsas in tow, as the first stage of their long flight to Gibraltar, prior to reaching Froha near Oran. Remarkably, the flight was accomplished with only a couple of losses. The Halifaxes joined 296 Squadron's Albemarles, whose Horsas had already been positioned in North Africa. 'Operation Beggar' was on 10 July, but did not work out as planned. The RAF used Horsas and Hadrians towed by Albemarles and Halifaxes, and the USAAF used Waco CG-4s towed by C-47s. Many USAAF aircraft came down in the sea, and many RAF aircraft did not make it to main landing area. The battle was much fiercer than anticipated, but within a few days Sicily was in Allied hands. The Americans were so impressed with the Horsa, as opposed to their smaller CG-4, that they asked the RAF for 1,500 of them!

RUSSIAN AF AT HURN

Back at Hurn, there were still some Whitleys and Albemarles to be seen, plus crews from 296 Squadron who had remained behind. From June, they undertook the training of Russian aircrews onto the Albemarle, the British Government having donated unwanted ones to the Russians. About fourteen were involved at Hurn, with the Red Starred bombers making the locals look twice in amazement. Servicing was carried out by No.3 OADU and, during training one aircraft was written off when it broke its back during a heavy landing.

Roger Beach was a sergeant in charge of the Transport Section of No.3 OADU (Wng Cdr Bell was CO):

> This was 1943 and our AEC tankers would collect fuel for the aircraft from Poole Petrol Dept. Fresh aircrews were collected from Christchurch Station in Fordson coaches, stopping off at the MO before seeing the Wellington bombers they had to deliver to Gibraltar. By the end of 1943 the airfield was packed with aircraft which towed the Horsa gliders on exercises, followed in 1944 by the 2 TAF Typhoons. D-Day was a spectacle that I will always remember with fighters taking off as others retuned to rearm.

As an aside, Roger mentioned that he originally joined the RFC in 1915 to fly DH.2s.

June Troy was a WAAF during 1942–43, with quarters off Matchams Lane in Hurn Village.

> I worked in the Met Office and recall the departure of Doolittle to North Africa and also the Russian aircrew who trained on Albemarles. I was under the impression that the Russians required them as transports, as they were unloved by the RAF as bombers. The Russian crews attended a Wings of Victory dance at the station in July 1943, the WAAF's being able to hire some Russian dresses. I still have a photo of the event as a memento.

Unfortunately, no one has a photograph of the Albemarles.

OPERATIONAL MISHAPS

July 1943 saw a quick visit of some Spitfire squadrons based for bomber escort duties. Their visit was not without incident, one colliding with a Whitley on landing, and then two others collided on take-off! A 295 Squadron Whitley suffered an engine fire on take-off on 24 July, crashing into the trees adjoining Merritown Farm with all its crew being killed. The frame of the burnt-out bomber remained lodged in the trees for some while before being removed. On 9 August twenty-one RAF Bostons arrived low over Bournemouth before landing to refuel after a bombing raid over Rennes. Whilst crossing the coast to the west of the town, they were fired upon by the AA defences, luckily without suffering any hits! However, two of the already-damaged Bostons crashed before making Hurn. A similar 'greeting' befell Boston and Mitchell crews early in December, again with no hits.

There were frequent arrivals of RAF heavy bombers such as Halifaxes and Lancasters returning from bombing raids over Germany and Northern Italy. They were a long way from their normal bases in Lincolnshire and Yorkshire, from where they had departed on missions taking them across the North Sea. In order to avoid the Luftwaffe fighters, they often did not head directly home but took a long route westwards across France before heading north over the general area of the Channel Islands. Missions to Milan and Turin saw the bombers return over southern France, crossing the coast near Bordeaux before heading north over the Bay of Biscay and Brest before making it back home. Often they were low on fuel or had suffered battle damage, and so landed at the nearest available airfield to the coast. Five Halifaxes arrived on 24 September 1943 for fuel while returning from Mannheim. Early one morning in October, there were ten Lancasters of 61 Squadron which had bombed Stuttgart, a long way from their base at Syerston. Another example was a Halifax of 158 Squadron which had been so badly shot up over Evreux that most of the crew had bailed out. However, the captain struggled on homewards to land at Hurn, only for the bomber to be declared beyond repair! New Year's Eve brought thirty-seven P-47 Thunderbolts returning from B-24 escort duties, plus two damaged B-17 Fortress's. Two of a trio of Stirlings which arrived in February 1944 still had mines hung up in their bomb bays, resulting in the Navy being called in to defuse them before ground crews could attend to the bombers.

BOAC EXPANDS OPERATIONS

BOAC received the first of a large number of Douglas Dakotas in the spring of 1943. One of their routes was to Shannon to meet up with Pan American's transatlantic flying-boat service into nearby Foynes. Further long-range Liberator transports were delivered and the airline set aside a hangar for servicing the Prime Minister's VIP Liberator *Commando*. The CW-20 *St Louis* was no longer in service with BOAC, but during the autumn and winter remained based at Hurn for engine performance trials carried out by Airspeed. The airline received its first Avro York in the spring of 1944, commencing services to Cairo via Morocco on 22 April, the aircraft being fitted to carry twelve passengers in the rear with freight in the forward cabin. Later in the year, Lyneham had to be used as the terminal due to increased RAF operations at Hurn. BOAC's services catered for the military, their flights carrying many VIPs worldwide also being flown from Poole Harbour. The VIPs continued to arrive by special Pullman train from London Victoria before an early morning take-off.

As well as their passenger services, BOAC set up a Development Flight for the purpose of testing new British airliners and powerplants prior to entering service. Under its superintendent, Capt. R.G. Buck, the flight received its first aircraft in January 1944 in the shape of a camouflaged Lancaster which arrived from Croydon. It had been modified with a sealed bomb bay and no gun turrets, undertaking Merlin-engine development trials, which also took it to Boscombe Down and Lyneham. There was a need to test the Merlin for post-war, long-distance civilian operations, one flight being of 3,650 miles non-stop from Hurn to Cairo following the usual routing to the west of Gibraltar. The Lancaster was later joined by a Vickers Warwick for Centaurus engine trials.

During 1943 a number of Dakotas were diverted from the RAF for use by BOAC, all retaining their camouflaged colour scheme. However, some of them carried civil registrations with a large Union Jack, as seen here, whilst others operated in RAF marking.

FAREWELL TO CO-OPERATION COMMAND

295 Squadron returned from North Africa to Hurn with its Halifaxes, and during October 1943 they were replaced with Albemarles. 296 Squadron also returned in October, and by November sufficient Albemarles were available to form a third squadron, 570. All were involved in training exercises towing Horsas around the country, usually to Salisbury Plain. However, they were also involved in limited operational sorties, usually supply drops to SOE forces in northern France. One did not go according to plan, with arms supplies being dropped into a German encampment! Stirling glider tugs of 620 Squadron arrived on detachment in December 1943 to gain experience on supply-dropping flights.

Tony Gould was a flight engineer with 620 Sqdn:

> The crews realised that we were frequently carrying ammunition for the Resistance, and that if the Stirling was hit by gunfire there would be little chance of survival. So our crew felt lucky when we suffered little damage following an attack, only to suffer a crash landing on return due to there being no hydraulics.

A new Station Commander arrived in January 1944, Group Capt. Kenneth McIntyre, who still had an interest in the airfield forty years later when, in his capacity as chairman of Dorset County Council, he opened a new passenger terminal. The northern part of the airfield was expanded with additional parking spaces, soon being covered by large numbers of Horsas. There were to be a number of training incidents. Early one winter's morning, a Halifax departed with a Horsa in tow but the glider was unable to gain height, probably due to frost on its wings. The glider pilot cast off its tow-rope, crashing into a nursery at Kinson, thereby failing to impress the American troops on board who all ended up in hospital. On another occasion a Horsa landed in the fields at Throop, having insufficient height to make it back to the airfield. Whilst the crew walked back, an enterprising local schoolboy took command of the Horsa and charged his pals 3*d* a time to have a look around.

Early in 1944 the airfield was still used by No.3 OADU for Halifax ferry flights, again with a number of incidents. One came down just off Bournemouth Pier at the end of January when the sole pilot on board became distracted by his instruments following an engine failure. He was trying to return to Hurn but came down in the sea. Another crashed on take-off on 6 March. Then, just after midnight on 22 March, another came down at Moordown while trying to return to the airfield in the dark.

Further changes to the airfield came in March 1944 when the Albemarle squadrons moved out to enable Hurn to be transferred to 11 Group, Fighter Command.

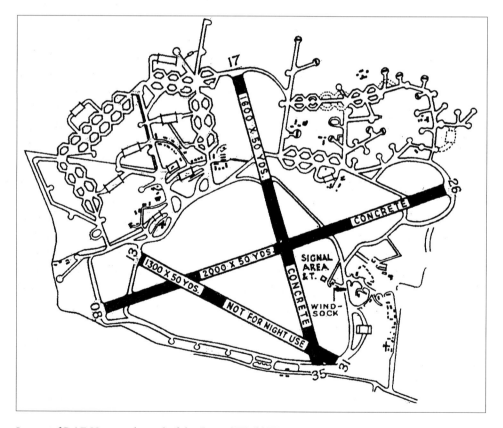

Layout of RAF Hurn at the end of the Second World War.

6

2ND TAF AND D-DAY

SECOND TAF

In autumn 1943, the RAF transferred many of its fighter squadrons to its newly formed 2nd Tactical Air Force (2 TAF) in preparation for the planned invasion of Europe. Many of these were to pass through the newly expanded Hurn. The middle of March 1944 saw the arrival, from Ayr, of three RCAF squadrons with Hawker Typhoon fighter-bombers. Many of the crews had already been to Bournemouth. When they arrived from Canada in autumn 1943, they had been billeted by the RAF in hotels around the town before being sent north for training. The squadrons were 438, 439 and 440, which from May formed No.143 (RCAF) (Fighter) Wing, operating in the fighter-bomber role. This involved ground-attack sorties, especially against the railway network in northern France. The Typhoons were equipped to carry a 1,000lb bomb under each wing, hence their nickname of 'Bombphoons'. The squadrons were declared operational at the end of May, with 438 being the first to use their Typhoons in action with an attack on V-1 sites. Three further Typhoon squadrons arrived during April, 181, 182 and 247, which jointly formed 124 Wing. Their Typhoons were fitted with rocket projectiles (RP) under their wings and they carried out rocket attacks on enemy shipping in the English Channel, as well as land targets. To extend their range for these operations, the fighters frequently landed to refuel at other bases such as Manston and Tangmere. At the time, each Wing had about ninety aircraft. Hurn also housed two DH Mosquito night fighter squadrons – 125 and 604 – which were to provide cover to the invasion forces prior to landing. Their night-time operations were known as 'Starlight' and they were controlled by nearby Sopley Radar. Accommodation for the majority of the crews were tents erected around the airfield, many being along what is now the Terminal approach road. Most of the Typhoons were parked along the southern perimeter adjacent to Parley Lane.

The Station's Operational Record Book (ORB) records 125 Squadron's first operations on the night of 13/14 April.

> They were scrambled against German raiders making their way to Bristol but unfortunately they failed to make contact. In the early hours of the 19 April a contact was made by one of the pilots but it turned out to be a RAF Wellington. Whilst landing in foggy conditions later

in the morning one of the Mosquitoes hit a hut fatally injuring one of the occupants. 125 Sqd finally had success in the early hours of the 24 April during another attack on Bristol, with three Luftwaffe bombers destroyed and two badly damaged.

The low-level operations carried out by the Typhoons were not without danger. There were a number of incidents during the latter part of May. The Commander of 143 Wing crash-landed in Normandy following engine failure, and spent his time evading capture. 124 Wing Commander Haabjoern was attacked twice, both times coming down in the Channel and being rescued by an Air Sea Rescue Walrus. A similar fate befell 181 Sqdn Ldr Keep, although on this occasion he was picked up by an ASR launch.

The 2nd TAF fighters concentrated their attacks on enemy radar sites during May, in order to put the system out of action before the invasion. These also included sites in the Channel Islands. However, flying was restricted on many days due to poor weather and haze. In anticipation of being able to move to Normandy, the squadrons had to practice landing on short, temporary airstrips. So an 800-yard section was marked out alongside Hurn's runway, which the pilots soon became adept at using. Another unit formed at Hurn housed racing pigeons to bring back messages from Normandy following the invasion – flight time seven hours. Prior to D-Day, both Mosquito squadrons had nineteen aircraft each and the six Typhoon squadrons totalled over 100 aircraft. Operations were rather busy at the airfield! There was a last-minute task for the ground crews. To provide some additional protection to the vast number of Allied aircraft flying over the Channel, it was agreed to paint black and white recognition strips around their wings and rear fuselages. The intention was that these 'Invasion Strips' would, hopefully, prevent the aircraft being fired upon by their own side in the heat of the action.

Large numbers of Typhoon fighter bombers were based at Hurn over the D-Day period. As well as its four cannons, many of the fighters carried 1,000lb bombs under their wings. Others were equipped with rocket projectiles.

Flt Lt Ellis and Flt Lt Williams, pilot and navigator of one of 604 Squadron's Mosquito night fighters. The Mosquitoes undertook missions to protect the D-Day invasion fleet and the subsequent re-supply convoys.

D-DAY

On the evening of 5 June, Poole Bay and the surrounding area appeared to local residents to be full of ships, but by next morning they had all gone. The early hours of Operation Overlord on Tuesday 6 June were marked by the vast armadas of aircraft flying over the coast en route to Normandy. There were RAF and USAAF bombers, tugs complete with their gliders all heading south – a change from earlier years when formations of Luftwaffe bombers headed north. Daylight saw many return: by 9 a.m. over 1,000 B-17s and B-24s had passed overhead.

The crew of a Halifax which had bombed German gun emplacements close to the landing beaches in the early hours flew over the Cherbourg Peninsular on their way back home. Crossing the Channel they were surprised when their radar showed up the Dorset and Hampshire coastline after only a few minutes. Visual observation showed it was the radar return of the vast armada of ships heading to the Normandy coastline. Shortly after day break a fighter pilot commented that there were so many ships sailing south from the area of the Isle of Wight that it appeared possible to reach Normandy without getting ones feet wet by stepping from one to the other.

At Hurn the three RCAF Typhoon's squadrons were the first to depart. 438 were engaged on limited sweeps, 439 bombed gun emplacements and 440 bombed German reinforcements south of Caen. They arrived over the beach-head at 7.25 a.m., just as the first landing craft were making shore, to make bombing attacks on the German gun emplacements. The other Hurn squadrons followed with 181 attacking enemy transport, 182 undertaking armed reconnaissance sorties and 247 RP attacks on and gun emplacements. Eventually the invasion was a success, although not without great losses, with Hurn's fighters having undertaken eighty-eight sorties. The long daylight hours of summer meant that, during the following days, the Typhoons could depart at 3 a.m. and continue operations until 11.30 p.m. On 7 June there were 138 sorties against German tanks and transport, with the loss of four aircraft and pilots. On 8 June 134 sorties were undertaken, but they were limited the following day due to adverse weather conditions. It was back to normal on 10 June with the RP-equipped Typhoons joining sixty RAF Mitchells for an attack on the German Panzer HQ, contributing to a total of 154 sorties. Within a few days of Operation Overlord, the Allied troops were able to construct some Emergency Landing Strips (ELS) near the beach-heads, which were intended for use by fighters, although Dakota transports soon put in appearances. Among the first users on 10 June was 181's Squadron P/O Grey, who made an emergency landing, being able to fly home later. Initially, the ELSs were only used in daylight hours, with the Typhoons returning to Hurn each evening. However, they proved to be very dusty which seriously affected the Typhoons engines, resulting in their frequently having to return to Hurn for servicing and replacement Sabre engines. Most of the pilots of 124 Wing headed back to Hurn on the evening of 24 June for this very reason. Another problem during the first few days of their use was that the ELSs were still within range of the German guns - a fact not appreciated by the pilots! The Mosquito night fighters also saw plenty of action, both squadrons being visited by Marshal of the RAF, Viscount Trenchard in the middle of June.

By way of relief after a hectic few weeks, the Station's ORB records that a Concert Party was held in the Gymnasium on the evening of the 29 June, which was greatly appreciated. There was also a knock out snooker competition, with the winner playing against Claude Faulkner (a professional), who also gave an exhibition of shots, all much enjoyed by the airmen.

The following weeks saw great activity within the various Typhoon Wings, with movements from other South Coast airfields. Eventually, by the end of June, a permanent crossing had been made by the Wings to Normandy. The majority of ground crews sailed across, although some were able to hitch lifts in Ansons.

George Bentham was an AC.2 Engine Fitter:

I was posted to Hurn early in 1944, but no one was really expecting me, so I passed my time driving the petrol bowser or bomb trolley. I received a posting to 263 Sqd in April, but had a job chasing around the country trying to find it. First I tried Harrowbeer (near Plymouth) but the Typhoons had just moved to Bolt Head. When I arrived there, the squadron had moved to Hurn - back where I'd started. I then worked on the Sabre engines of the fighters, with early three bladed propellers being changed to four bladed ones which improved performance. As the engines were so complicated, the engineers did not spend time trying to rectify faults, but replaced the complete engine. I frequently ran up the engines in the early hours of the morning so that they were warm for the day's operations, and was most impressed by the exhaust flame which reached back to the tailplane. I realised that the Invasion was almost upon us when we received our pay in francs and were confined to barracks. Along with the rest of the ground crew, I crossed the Channel by LCT.

Ken Trott was a Typhoon pilot with 197 Squadron:

I had been undertaking D-Day operations from an airstrip at Needs Oar Point, south of Beaulieu. The Squadron moved to Hurn for a few days, prior to crossing to St Croix at the beginning of July. However, after only a few days the Squadron was to return to Hurn, but this did not include myself. Prior to flying back, our aircraft were involved in a battle with Me.109's near Caen, during which I collided with one of them. Somehow I managed to parachute to what I thought was safety, but found that I'd landed in a still German occupied area! So instead of returning home, I spent the rest of the War as a PoW.

AIRFIELD CONTROL

Control of aerial activity at Hurn was slightly different from that today. What appeared to be the control tower was really the Watch Office, from which take-off and landings were watched, not controlled. There was limited contact with aircraft, with pilots receiving instructions from a Fighter Control Centre. Take-offs and landings were managed from a control caravan which was positioned at the end of the active runway, the duty controller using an Aldis lamp to give instructions to the pilots – 'Taxi to end of runway; Clear to take-off; OK to land; Go round again'. For returning pilots, there was a large letter T by the Watch Office to indicate the wind direction. The controller had no radio contact with the pilots, although there was a phone link to the Watch Office. If it was necessary to scramble the aircraft then very flares would be fired. At night-time the controller would again use a very pistol with the appropriate red or green flares. To assist returning aircraft, there was also an identification beacon (known as Pundit) which flashed Hurn's two-letter Morse code, KU, in red.

By the end of the war the Watch Office became known as Flying Control before settling on Control Tower, but use of the control van continued well into the 1950s. Although the tower now had contact with aircraft, their take-offs and landings were still under the guidance of the Federal Ground Control Approach van parked alongside the runway. Further assistance was provided by painting 'HURN' in large white letters on the roof of the hangar adjacent to the terminal area.

7

THE AMERICANS RETURN

SECOND USAAF ARRIVAL

Summer 1944 saw USAAF Ninth Air Force operations from Hurn, initially with Northrop P-61 Black Widow night fighters which arrived at the end of June for trials with the Mosquitoes of 125 Squadron. The P-61 was a new type for the USAAF. Their 'Brass' were not certain whether it was suitable for the task or whether it would even be an improvement over the Mosquito which they already operated. Six aircraft from the 422 and 425 Night Fighter Squadrons arrived from Scorton on 29 June with the crews of both aircraft types eyeing up the competition, those of the RAF thinking 'no contest'. Initially, poor weather prevented the P-61 flying at night, although the Mosquitoes continued operations, something the American crews resented. The first combined operation was on the night of 3 July over the Baie de Seine – the P-61's first operational use in Europe. However, the main activity occurred two days later when, at a demonstration, the P-61s showed themselves to be faster than, and able to out-manoeuvre, the Mosquitoes, thus surprising the assembled 'Brass'. So the P-61s returned to Scorton on 10 July having been cleared for full-scale operations. The Mosquitoes of 604 Squadron had also departed, their place being taking for a few days by 418 (RCAF) Squadron but at the end of July both 125 and 418 departed north to Middle Wallop. Most of the station personnel, including the Station Commander, moved to Middle Wallop with those few left behind moving to Holmwood Park at nearby Longham. The reason for all this movement was yet another transfer of airfield ownership.

From the beginning of August, Hurn became USAAF Station 492 for its next arrivals – Martin B-26 Marauder bombers of the 397th Bomb Group. These had been based inland at Rivenhall, but were now able to move to the coast to carry on their interdiction bombing missions across the Channel, the group having earned the title of 'Bridge Busters'. Over sixty aircraft were involved, forming the 596, 597, 598 and 599 Bomb Squadrons. Many of their B-26s were silver coloured and adorned with colourful markings such as shark eyes and teeth – a contrast to the camouflaged RAF aircraft seen previously. The group's aim was to put up thirty-six aircraft for each mission, their first from Hurn being on 7 August.

George Parker was one of the pilots:

Initially we had difficulty in getting airborne from Hurn, mainly because we had worn out aircraft. Timing was critical for formation take-offs, needing our full concentration and the whole of the runway was needed for our heavily laden bombers to become airborne. On occasions we found the main wheels would break the wire fence at the end of the runway. However matters improved when newer aircraft were received, which seemed to take-off at a bump two thirds of the way down the runway!

A mission to the Paris area on 16 August marked the group's 100th mission since arriving in England, being led by the group's commanding officer, Col. R. Coiner. The pilots wanted to celebrate the event, and the story has been 'amended' over the years. It was reported that they returned from a successful mission, whereas in fact, poor weather over France meant the morning's mission was recalled. In any event, to mark their safe return the pilots fired very flares out of their cockpit windows, which then set fire to the local farmer's wheat fields. They were not very impressed; neither were the fire brigade who commented that the Americans caused more damage than the Germans had done recently. However, the aircrew were not too concerned, and held a celebration party in the evening. Missions continued until 28 August, when preparations were made for the group to cross the Channel to their new base at Gorges on the 30/31 August.

Marvin Schultze was one of the B-26 pilots, maintaining a diary whilst at Hurn:

5 Aug:	Moved to a new field in South England (Station 492), and it's a nice place.
7 Aug:	Spent first night of leave in Ambassador Hotel.
15 Aug:	My mission No 41. Easy raid. No Flak.
16 Aug:	Mission 42 (Group's 100th) recalled because of weather. Everybody fired very flares on our way back which started grass fires.
17 Aug:	Big party to celebrate Group's 100th raid.
19 Aug:	Rained all day. Had fish & chips at best hotel in town.
23 Aug:	Nice day. Went swimming at beach near Bournemouth.
30 Aug:	Moved to Gorges, west of Caen.

END OF RAF HURN

Although the B-26s had moved out, the airfield remained under USAAF control until mid-October when it returned nominally to the RAF. However, there was no further military use for Hurn, so its active part in the Second World War commenced in August 1941 and ended in August 1944, a period of three very hectic years.

Sixty years on, there are still reminders of RAF Hurn to be seen. The RAF had built six large hangars and these remain in use – although they have been extensively refurbished over the years. The sixty or so smaller blister hangars remained for around ten years before other uses were found for them. Many of the smaller domestic and technical buildings still remain in use today, especially on the north-west side of the airfield. Originally described as 'temporary brick structure', these Maycrete-style buildings

Crews of the USAAF 397 Bomb Group take a well-earned tea break at Hurn following one of their missions. The group had an official photographer who, post-war, published a book recording the group's wartime progress.

continue to prove of use to their present-day occupants. However, the quarters in the woods around Hurn Village were mostly demolished by the mid-1950s. The 1940s-style Watch Tower still survives within the present-day Control Tower, but additions over the years make it impossible to work out the original design.

CHRISTCHURCH'S WAR EFFORT

At Christchurch the Naval Air Radio Installation Unit (NARIU) arrived in summer 1942, mainly carrying out trials with Avro Ansons in conjunction with the adjacent ADEE (later ADRE). The unit dealt with radar trials in various naval aircraft, with Barracudas, Fulmars, Oxfords and Wellingtons all being involved. Early in 1945 the Naval unit consisted of eight Ansons and six Barracudas, with one project being the early development of a guided missile. The Establishment also became involved with radio-development trials for the Army, later becoming better known as the Signals Research and Development Establishment.

Airspeed continued with Horsa-glider production, plus updating a batch of 160 Supermarine Seafires to latest service standard during 1943. A number of them suffered accidents while on test, with one ending up in a garden at Stanpit during June. (On another occasion, a visiting Fairey Battle overshot the runway, crashed onto the roof of an adjacent bungalow, and fell apart leaving its pilot still sitting in his seat on the roof.) There were plans by the Ministry of Aircraft Production, in 1943, for DH Mosquitoes to be built by Airspeeds, but production did not get underway until 1945, with only twelve having been completed by the end of the war. The majority of orders were then cancelled, although sixty-five bomber versions were completed between February 1946 and February 1948. Airspeed's name will always be associated with the graceful Ambassador airliner, where the design office commenced work as early as summer 1944 to meet the requirement for a Dakota replacement.

Although the airfield at Christchurch had been rejected by the RAF as unsuitable for fighter operations, this was to change in 1944. Part of the Allies' planning for D-Day was the requirement for a number of temporary fighter bases known as Advance Landing Grounds, with Christchurch chosen to be one of them. The original grass runway was only 900 yards long, which meant it was insufficient for fighter operations. So, land to the south-east side of the airfield was flattened during October 1943, with the RAF laying a 1,650-yard temporary steel-mesh runway. In spring 1944 Christchurch became USAAF Ninth Air Force Station 416 for use by P-47 Thunderbolt fighter-bombers of the 405th Fighter Group. There was minimal accommodation for the fliers; Bure Homage House was taken over for use as the Station HQ, although the majority of personnel had tented accommodation within the grounds. Seventy-five P-47s arrived in mid-March and the group undertook its first mission on 11 April when fifty-five aircraft were involved in sorties over north western France. For D-Day itself, the P-47s were mainly held back in reserve, undertaking some patrols over Brest and the Channel. By 13 June the fighters were able to land in Normandy to refuel and rearm, with supplies being flown in aboard C-47s. The month proved very hectic for the group, with fifteen pilots and many aircraft lost, mainly due to ground fire. However, their worst day was to be Thursday 29 June. One of the P-47s crashed on take-off early in the morning, but its pilot was uninjured. Just after 2 p.m. he set off again, suffered another engine failure, and crashed into two bungalows at the end of the runway. The underwing bombs being carried exploded, bringing down a second P-47. The combined explosions caused widespread damage and resulted in the death of sixteen service and civilian persons.

By the end of June the P-47s began to set up base at Picauville, Normandy, with the final ones departing Christchurch on 11 July. Apart from the aircraft of the NARIU, Christchurch's part in the war had virtually ended. However, it was used by various aircraft returning servicemen to Britain for rest and recuperation breaks. These included a B-17 Fortress which belly-landed in September whilst bringing in twenty-four injured servicemen from the Continent.

An RAF Gliding School was opened in 1944 to give elementary flying experience to local Air Cadets. Powered Air Experience flights were undertaken in Ansons and Oxfords, and the Cadets also had the use of a non-flying Hawker Hart.

POOLE'S WAR EFFORT

Poole Harbour was also used by RAF Coastal Command, who needed additional bases on the south coast to house aircraft to counter the growing German U-boat menace in the Bay of Biscay. Work on the former First World War Admiralty site at Lake began in spring 1942, although minimal accommodation was available. Adjacent housing was commandeered by the RAF for offices and workshops with one converted as the Flying Control. A new slipway was built but there were no hangars provided for the aircraft, only a large marquee. The first arrivals at RAF Hamworthy in September were nine Short Sunderlands of 461 (RAAF) Squadron from Mount Batten, Plymouth, to help extend the patrol coverage over the Bay of Biscay.

John Witcomb was an airframe fitter:

> I travelled up by rail with the rest of the ground crew to Hamworthy Junction station. There were problems as we had to work on the Sunderlands in the open, with our workshops being the adjacent houses. The aircrews made their dislike of the base known, not liking the cramped conditions or the lack of deep water landing areas. So a permanent move to Pembroke Dock in South Wales in April 1943 was received with glee by the Australian crews. One happy memory for me was that originally local accommodation could not be found, so I had to contact my mother who lived in Bournemouth to see if she could put me up. What a choice to make!

The Sunderlands were replaced in April 1943 by Consolidated Catalinas of 210 Squadron to continue the Biscay patrols. However, the squadron was disbanded in December 1943, mainly due to the Allies now getting the upper hand over the U-boat problem. The RAF base was officially closed in April 1944, although the quarters had already been taken over by Combined Operations in preparation for D-Day.

This is a poor-quality photograph, but provides an interesting view of 461 (RAAF) Squadron Sunderlands at RAF Hamworthy in 1943. No hangars were provided for the flying boats meaning all maintenance had to be carried out in the open. The site is now occupied by the Royal Marines.

Engine fitters at work on the Pratt & Whitney engine of one of 461 Squadron's Sunderlands. The closeness to properties in Lake Drive can be seen; most had been taken over by the RAF for accommodation and workshop purposes.

Vought Kingfisher floatplanes were among the variety of aircraft used by 765 Squadron's Basic Seaplane Training School at Sandbanks during 1941/42. Poole Park can be seen underneath this Kingfisher as it flies over Poole Harbour on a training flight.

The Royal Navy had a seaplane base at Sandbanks for a period of the war. The facilities of the Royal Motor Yacht Club were taken over in May 1940 for use by the Basic Seaplane Training School. This used a variety of Vought Kingfisher, Fairey Swordfish and Supermarine Walrus until the base was closed in October 1943. Officially known as HMS *Daedalus II*, the locals referred to the base as HMS Tadpole because the aircraft in use were so much smaller than the Sunderlands in use with the RAF at Hamworthy.

BOAC's No.4 Line at Poole began receiving Sunderlands diverted from the RAF in spring 1943, although their airline seating and equipment was rather basic compared with the Boeing 314's. They were used to improve the service to West Africa and Lagos, followed by Karachi via Gibraltar and Cairo in October, being extended to Calcutta

During the Second World War BOAC were supplied with a number of Sunderlands direct from the RAF production line. Fitted with very austere seating, they were used to build up BOAC's passenger fleet which was still struggling on with a few C Class flying boats.

in May 1944. There were many VIP flights undertaken as the Combined Operations Camp for D-Day planning was at Hamworthy; for example, Lord Mountbatten and other VIPs arrived by Boeing 314 from Canada in August 1943, escorted by Spitfires. The airline's operations had to move out of the harbour to Pembroke Dock during the period leading up to the D-Day operations, returning in September 1944. A new service from May 1945 was across the Atlantic to Baltimore by Boeing 314s which had been withdrawn from the West African services. However, their winter routing to America had to be via West Africa and Brazil, in order to avoid the unfavourable North Atlantic weather. At the end of May 1945, a Sikorsky VS.44 of American Export Airlines arrived from Foynes in connection with the airlines proposed post-war transatlantic services but, in the event, these were to be operated by landplanes. By the end of the war BOAC had a fleet of three Boeing 314s and twenty-six Sunderlands, many of which were used from September to fly home Prisoners of War, especially from the Far East.

Incidents which occurred included a BOAC Sunderland having to land off Swanage early one morning as the harbour was shrouded in fog. The pilot was then guided by a launch past the narrows of Sandbanks to the moorings off Lilliput – four hours late. On another occasion the pilot of a Horsa assault glider managed to mistake the harbour for his night-time landing site, using the flare path laid out for an expected Sunderland! The crew were picked up by launch with the waterlogged glider towed back to the slipway at Hamworthy.

8

AN AIRPORT FOR BOURNEMOUTH OR LONDON?

CIVILIAN AIRFIELD

As early as spring 1944 the RAF had been reviewing its post-war Transport Command airfield requirements, with Hurn on their list. However, in August the Air Ministry informed the Commander-in-Chief of Transport Command that the airfield had been earmarked for continued use by BOAC until a new airport at Heath Row became available in about eighteen months. At the time, construction of the airfield had just commenced apparently for Transport Command, who would use it as a UK base for war in the Far East. In fact, it was a case of the land being requisitioned under wartime needs, ostensibly as a military airfield. The real intention was to build an impressive new airport for London to replace Croydon and Heston. At the time the Air Ministry knew there would be a public outcry if the development of a civil airport was undertaken during wartime, as this was still prior to D-Day.

BOAC MOVE IN

A meeting between the Air Ministry and BOAC was held at Hurn in September 1944, concerning its exclusive use by BOAC. This detailed the transfer of its Dakota services from its No.1 Line at Whitchurch, Bristol, plus its Liberator and York services from Lyneham. The airline expressed concern at what it regarded as insufficient hangarage, bearing in mind the anticipated increase in its fleet – by the end of 1944 it had almost sixty Dakotas in service. Transport Command complained to the Air Ministry concerning BOAC's planned use of Hurn, saying it could make better use of the seven hangars and excellent accommodation. (In fact, there were only four hangars at the time, the other three only planned.) BOAC said they would settle for Hurn for the time being. However, they expected to be provided with a former Bomber Command airfield at the end of the war, as it would have better accommodation and hangarage than Hurn. Of the three runways, the main one was 2,010 yards long and the secondary one 1,615 yards long. The third runway was little used post-war and was taken out of use in the mid-1950s.

The RAF complaints did not change the plans and BOAC transferred its Passenger and Freight Traffic and Operations Sections at the end of October. At midnight on 31 October 1944, the airport was transferred from RAF Fighter Command on loan to the Director of Civil Aviation for development as Great Britain's civil air terminal. Its advantage for BOAC administration purposes was the closeness to its flying-boat services from Poole Harbour. BOAC's News Letter of the time, 'hoped the move would be the first step towards that ultimate goal of a modern up-to-date international airport worthy of British air transport'. Presumably, this was a reference to Heath Row rather than a developed Hurn. Roger Pugh was appointed as BOAC's first airport manager, with the passenger terminal set up in the former Officer's Mess at Hurn Bridge. Passengers from London arrived by train at either Bournemouth or Christchurch before being taken by coach to board their flight. Initially, the passengers found the buildings to be a nightmare, with the staff considering the airport a mess. They had great problems in trying to convert shambolic wartime buildings into a presentable terminal. The dispersal of hangars and accommodation around the airfield had been ideal for military operations, but proved hopeless for BOAC's No.2 Line. A shortage of skilled labour brought problems over aircraft servicing, not aided by the fact that only three hangars were available to house the Dakotas. Even worse, the Factories Act of the time prevented work in unheated hangars, so maintenance had to be undertaken outside whatever the weather. The Air Ministry was responsible for running the newly formed Ministry of Civil Aviation, but was too occupied with wartime RAF needs to worry about accommodation problems at Hurn.

Winifred Abraham was employed by BOAC:

> I was Mr Pugh's driver, being given the 'rank' of Inspector of Runways in order to have free access around the Airport. Even so I had to produce a pass every time I entered or departed, eventually finding an unchecked gate which saved any further hassle. At times I would drive VIP's to Poole Harbour and often managed to hitch a weekend leave trip to Whitchurch by Dakota.

Elsie Torrent also worked for BOAC:

> I was employed in their mail room initially situated at Hurn Bridge. This meant long walks to the terminal so I was glad when the mail room moved to the Airport. Whilst there some of the staff gave me driving lessons in the post van around the perimeter track, avoiding any parked Dakotas. I remember the bunches of bananas that 'fell off' the Dakotas on arrival from West Africa and the busy social life in the BOAC Club. We ate in the workers canteen with the senior officers and Customs & Excise using the staff dining room.

Scheduled services by BOAC to Madrid, Lisbon and Cairo, operated by Dakotas, commenced on 1 November 1944. The passengers found their canvas seating was very austere, more akin to the RAF paratroop version. They were kept warm by being wrapped in blankets and 'in-flight catering' consisted of pre-packed sandwiches. Flights to West Africa (Dakotas) and the Far East (Liberators and Yorks) were increased, but services still had to fly around Spain rather than overfly France. So a flight to Egypt would route Hurn–Morocco–Tripoli–Cairo. As well as BOAC, KLM of Holland moved from its wartime base at Whitchurch to Hurn, for a short while operating services to Lisbon with Dakotas. Also to be seen briefly was the Belgian airline Sabena, which used Hurn as its European terminal for mail services from the Belgian Congo, and ABA Transport of Sweden with services from Stockholm. These activities led the wartime censor to reveal BOAC's operation to the public when he described Hurn as 'Britain's finest airfield'. At the same time the Air Ministry was still saying that the new airfield at Heath Row would be for RAF Transport Command. This was despite the fact that BOAC had made it known they wanted to operate from there due to its nearness to the capital. They envisaged increasing their fleet greatly, probably requiring the use of a number of airports for their intended services to various parts of the world. Hurn would still feature with the Air Ministry, indicating that the existing main runway of 2,000 yards could be extended by a further 1,000 yards (requiring diversion of the Parley Road). The two other runways could also be greatly extended, with the possibility of a fourth being built.

SERVICES TO THE COMMONWEALTH

The new year of 1945 saw Dakotas operating thrice weekly to Cairo, twice weekly to Karachi and weekly to Madrid, Lisbon and Gibraltar. Yorks were operated to the Middle East, with the Cairo service extended to Karachi. Liberators undertook a number of flights to Sydney; Australia had been virtually cut off by air following the capture of Singapore in 1943. Limited flights were flown between Ceylon and Perth by Catalina flying boats which took thirty-two hours! So it was the Australian service that was the next to be improved with a fleet of converted Lancaster bombers ordered. Known as Lancastrians, sixty were initially ordered in 1944 for services across the North Atlantic. However, the plans were changed, with the order cut back and the aircraft used for the Australian route. For daytime services the Lancastrians were equipped with nine sideways-facing seats, each with a window, and for night-time operations the cabin was converted to house six-sleeper seats. For political reasons, BOAC wanted no publicity for this new long-range service. So the Government arranged that it would be operated with the aircraft bearing RAF Transport Command colours. The first Lancastrians arrived at Hurn early in 1945, ready for the 'Kangaroo' service. This was operated in conjunction with Qantas to 'serve the needs of the Far Eastern theatre of war'. By the time of the route-proving flights to Australia, the Lancastrians had appeared in RAF colours, with the first leaving on 23 April. The 13,500-mile flight was under the command of Capt. R.G. Buck of the Development Flight, who then flew on to Auckland from Sydney. Shortly before the service commenced there was another change of plan, which saw the Lancastrians appear in civil markings again. The inaugural service on 31 May, under Capt. Palmer, carried a crew of seven, two passengers, baggage and 500k of priority Royal Mail. The weekly service operated via Lydda, Palestine (refuelling stop), Karachi, India (change to Qantas crew), Colombo, Ceylon, then 3,000 miles overwater to Learmouth, Western Australia, and

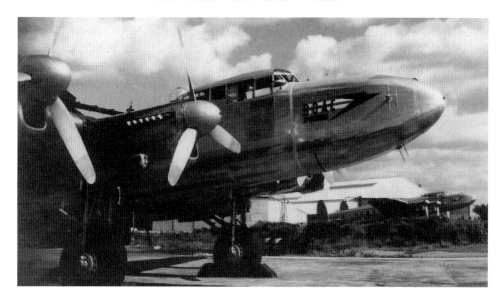

Seen outside the BOAC hangars at Hurn, these Avro Lancastrians reopened scheduled services to Australia in May 1945. Only carrying nine passengers, they were relegated to lesser duties by the introduction of Hythe flying boats from Poole in June 1946.

finally Sydney, took 67¼ hours, hence the service being referred to as 'Three Dawns to Sydney'.

BOAC were short of pilots at the time and so quite a number were seconded from the RAF. Tony Iveson had been a Squadron Leader with 617 Squadron taking part in the sinking of the battleship Tirpitz in November 1944.

> As a Lancaster pilot I was well suited to fly Lancastrians and, after training at Ossington, I was based at Hurn for three years before returning to RAF Transport Command. I consider the Government had great foresight in setting up the service before the end of the War especially as there was no end in sight to hostilities in the Far East. I would Captain the aircraft for half of the journey before handing over to Qantas crews and a round trip to Karachi with stop-overs would take about fourteen days.

BOAC also needed cabin crew, and many of these were picked from young Air Training Corps cadets who jumped at the chance to fly.

From April 1946 BOAC were able to cut out the fourteen-hour overwater section between Colombo and Learmouth. Flights now routed via Singapore and Darwin, with BOAC or Qantas crews operating throughout. Timings were reduced to fifty-six hours, which meant that if you left Hurn at midday on a Sunday, you would arrive in Sydney late the following Wednesday morning. The service to Karachi by York now took thirty-two hours, with three stops, but by Dakota it took fifty-eight hours with nine stops.

Wartime restrictions meant that these services were not available to the public, but were for Government Ministers and VIPs. In fact, the majority of BOAC's seats were reserved for VIPs until as late as July 1948. Surprisingly, the BOAC News Letter of November 1944 named some of the passengers, Count Raczynski, Polish Ambassador in Teheran; Sir George Rendel, new Ambassador in Madrid; The Maharajah Gaekwar of Baroda; Sir Patrick and Lady Duff, High Commissioner for New Zealand. There was no need for public timetables as details were available from the airline relating to flight routings and timings. Public timetables were issued early in 1946 by Bradshaws; BOAC waited until services had been transferred to London before issuing their own.

ENLARGED HURN

The Ministry of Civil Aviation (the Ministry) had major plans early in 1945 for the re-development of Hurn at a cost of £1,250,000. This was to establish it as Britain's air terminal for services to South Africa and South America. New, longer runways were to be constructed as it was felt that much larger airliners – such as the proposed Bristol Brabazon – would be required to operate these services. Contracts for construction were about to be issued when there was a change of Government in July, resulting in Labour cancelling the expansion plans. The airport's importance was revealed to the public by the press in August, with BOAC's seventy-four services a week being shown in detail. There was still some RAF activity with Skymasters and Yorks from nearby Holmsley South calling during the summer to clear customs. They were engaged on trooping flights but customs facilities were not available at their home base. At the end of September, RAF Dakotas and Yorks started bringing home Prisoners of War from the Far East, with others arriving by Sunderland flying boats at Poole Harbour. With the return to peace, the local residents expected there to be an end to aircraft activity, so there were complaints when it continued. An RAF report of September 1945 blamed transport aircraft from Holmsley South, plus BOAC aircraft from Hurn and Poole Harbour. When asked how he had been affected, the Earl of Malmesbury remarked, 'Hurn village remains much as it always has been, although large parts of my estate have been swallowed up to make the airfield'. Hurn Court had also been taken over in 1940 for use by the Red Cross, with his wife becoming president of its Hampshire Branch.

TRANSATLANTIC

The return to peace saw the Americans very keen to re-establish scheduled services to England. At the time, both American Export Airlines and Pan American World Airways were operating flying boats to Foynes, Ireland. Onward connections to London were then provided by BOAC Dakotas flying into Croydon. During the war, crews of both the American airlines had gained great experience in transatlantic operations, flying Douglas Skymaster transports on behalf of the USAAF. The airlines found that large numbers of these were available with the ending of the war, and so planned to operate landplane services to England. At the time, Croydon was the nearest airport to London, but it was too small for operations by these larger airliners. Heath Row was still in the early stages of construction and, as the RAF did not want civilian aircraft at Bovingdon or Northolt, the Ministry directed the Americans to Hurn. The Government was not happy with these planned new services as they showed up the deficiency of the existing BOAC flying-boat service from Poole Harbour to Baltimore.

Both American Export and Pan American acquired surplus Skymasters in September 1945, with Pan American undertaking a survey flight from New York on 15 September. Flying via Gander and Shannon for refuelling, it arrived at Hurn on the morning of 17 September – interestingly, landing on the shorter north–south runway. Having made history as the first landplane service across the Atlantic, the Skymaster returned home via Lisbon and the Azores. American Export undertook a survey flight later in the month, also taking in various Scandinavian airports before returning to New York. The Skymasters were fitted out for thirty-eight passengers with a crew of seven, and were equipped to a much higher standard than the Lancastrians and Yorks used by BOAC. It must be remembered that BOAC were operating wartime aircraft, whereas the Americans could start afresh. Even so, the Avro Tudor I being built for BOAC was only intended to carry twenty-four passengers across the Atlantic. American Airlines (who had taken over American Export) operated the first landplane scheduled service from America to Great Britain when *Flagship London* departed New York's La Guardia Airport on 23 October, piloted by Capt. Charles Blair. After a stopover at Shannon, it arrived at Hurn the following afternoon with ten passengers. A second Skymaster flew as far as Shannon, with its passengers being flown on to Croydon by Dakota. At the time gales were sweeping the country and it was thought the flights might have been delayed. The press reported how the Queen Mary was making heavy weather of its Atlantic crossing, having to heave to off the Isle of Wight, whereas the Skymaster captains said they coped with the 80mph winds 'as smooth as a train ride'. Reports of the successful flight referred to the arrival at London (Hurn Airport) England. American's flights were initially operated thrice weekly, taking twenty-four hours for the crossing (including stops) at a single fare of $572 plus taxes. However, the airline's timetables continued to quote London as the destination, not mentioning that passengers arrived at Hurn with a coach journey on to the capital. Pan American had intended to be first across the Atlantic with passengers, having planned their inaugural flight for 20 October. Technical delays meant that the service did not get away until 27 October, arriving at Hurn the following afternoon with eleven passengers. Operating twice weekly, Pan American ran into trouble over its proposed fares – £68 3s single and £124 return, well below what American and BOAC were charging. (It had been anticipated the single fare would have been £93 3s single.) As well as problems in America, there were strong objections from the British Government as the fares dramatically undercut BOAC's North Atlantic flying-boat fares. On the afternoon of 20 November, American's new weekly service from Chicago arrived, complete with its mayor, followed on 24 November by the first twice-weekly service from Washington and Philadelphia. Bradshaw's timetable still continued to show the arrival point as London (Hurn). Pan American had still not resolved the fare problem and, for a time at the end of the year, they terminated their flights at Shannon.

HURN: A MAJOR TERMINAL

BOAC's next major route was to South Africa, operated by Yorks. A proving flight to Johannesburg early in October 1945 took sixty-eight hours for the 6,600 miles. Operated in conjunction with South African Airways (SAA), the first service departed at tea-time on 10 November. The twelve VIP passengers had arrived from London by Pullman train; their fares were £167 single and £301 return. Lord Winster, the Minister of Civil Aviation, arrived by Anson, from Heston, to see off this inaugural flight. A second York with SAA crews took off from Johannesburg on the reciprocal flight to arrive at Hurn two days later. The Yorks were luxuriously appointed to carry only twelve passengers, the rest of the space being required for freight and Royal Mail. With night stops, the service initially took three days, being referred to by BOAC as the 'Silver York', and by SAA as 'Springbok'. So a departure early on a Tuesday afternoon arrived at Johannesburg the following Friday afternoon, allowing for stopovers. In November 1945 the Ministry announced that, 'Hurn will be a major terminal until suitable airports nearer London are available. Its use thereafter is under consideration'. However, no mention was made of the new airfield at Heath Row. On Christmas Day, the BBC sent Stewart Macpherson to Hurn to report live on activity at the airport. This included an interview with the pilot of an incoming flight from Karachi.

FIRST YEAR OF PEACE

Civilian flying in Great Britain was officially permitted again by the Government from 1 January 1946. Control of Hurn remained with the Ministry and was now open twenty-four hours a day. However, flying was restricted to scheduled services plus crew training and development flying. Group Captain W.R. Cox (formerly with Transport Command) was appointed the first Airport Commandant, a position he was to retain for ten years. Having been on loan from the Air Ministry since 1 November 1944, the airport was officially transferred to the Ministry of Civil Aviation on 25 March 1946. There were two provisions — firstly that the Air Ministry had first claim for defence purposes, and secondly that Airspeed at Christchurch could use the airport for test-flying their planned new Ambassador airliner. At the same time the Ministry confirmed that the new airport at Heath Row would officially become London's new airport and would be ready for services within a few weeks.

INCREASED SERVICES

BOAC's News Letter reported on improvements to the officers' quarters which transformed them from, 'glorified Nissen huts into a most luxurious and pleasing Ritz-Carlton-cum Country Club. If Hurn can do this, Croydon will have to look to their laurels'. BOAC's services in April 1946 were to Cairo, Calcutta, Johannesburg (all

Pan American World and American Airlines introduced Constellations on their North Atlantic services in spring 1946, followed by BOAC in July. All the airlines appeared at Hurn on diversions from London.

twice weekly by Yorks), Accra (thrice weekly by Dakota), Sydney (thrice weekly by Lancastrian) and Lydda (weekly by Dakota). The airline also commenced a flying-boat service to Sydney, in May, from Poole Harbour which took five days. Questions were asked in Parliament concerning the expense of the duplicated landplane and flying-boat services to Australia. The reply was that the Lancastrians from Hurn provided the fastest Royal Mail service, whereas the Hythe flying boats provided a slower, but more comfortable, service for passengers. A timetable of the day included a BOAC advert, but still quoted the services as being operated by British Airways.

A one-off flight to Australia was undertaken by a converted Halifax bomber in May. Purchased by Australian pilot, Flt Capt. G. Wikner, and bearing the name *Waltzing Matilda*, it carried some of his Bomber Command colleagues and families home to Sydney.

BOAC had pinned all its hopes on the new Tudor I which was originally expected to be available for transatlantic services from the summer of 1946. As well as the Tudor I, BOAC had ordered the lengthened Tudor II for its services to Australia and South Africa, with a number also intended for Qantas and SAA. Both American Overseas and Pan American ordered the improved Lockheed Constellation for their North Atlantic services. Pan American undertook a proving flight from New York on 3/4 February 1946, with regular services commencing on 11 February. These were the first landplane service to fly non-stop from the USA to England, with the flying time now under twelve hours. From April, the airline extended its services eastwards to Brussels, Prague and Vienna. American Overseas also undertook Constellation proving flights and Constellations of TWA were also seen, having been diverted from Paris. During January foreign delegates arrived at Hurn to attend the first United Nations General Assembly being held in London. Many of the US delegation returned home on 17 February aboard a Pan American Constellation which was especially renamed *UNO Clipper*. Up to now it had been customary for film stars to cross the Atlantic by liner, such as the *Queen Elizabeth*. But the opening of air services changed this, with Mary Pickford one of the first stars to arrive by Pan American Constellation in March 1946. BOAC's North Atlantic service continued to be operated by Boeing 314 flying boats from Poole, but in order to keep up with the American airlines, it was forced to order five Constellations in April 1946.

9

EFFECT OF LONDON OPENING

LONDON AIRPORT

With the official opening of London Airport on Friday 31 May 1946, both American Overseas and Pan American transferred their services from Hurn. However, there were no terminal buildings or aircraft maintenance facilities available, the only building being the Watch Tower. Wartime tents were used for passenger 'facilities', but at least the travellers now felt that they had arrived in London. American Overseas took the opportunity to introduce Constellations on its services from America. South African Airways also took the opportunity to update its fleet, introducing Douglas DC-4s from 8 July to replace their Yorks. BOAC gradually moved their services out of Hurn, most having left by 18 June. However, their Dakota services had moved to Northolt on 27 May, as there was insufficient room at London. The last scheduled departure from Hurn was BOAC's York to Cairo service on 14 June. At the same time, the Lancastrian service to Sydney was supplemented by flying boats from Poole Harbour as these were considered more comfortable. The move to London Airport did not go smoothly as the summer months proved to be very wet. So the passengers and staff were faced with a sea of mud at the country's principal airport before they could reach the never-to-be-forgotten khaki marquees.

When construction started in 1944, the airport was to be known as RAF Heath Row, after the name of a local hamlet. BOAC then referred to it as Heath Row, but on its opening for international services, the Ministry renamed it London Airport (frequently shortened to LAP). This remained in use for about twenty years until Gatwick came into being as London's second airport. So it was re-titled once again as London Airport (Heathrow) before eventually becoming the present-day London Heathrow.

WHAT USE FOR CHRISTCHURCH?

The return to peace saw Bournemouth's earlier airport at Christchurch under the control of RAF Transport Command, but there was little activity. During autumn 1945, the Glider Pick-Up Flight used the airfield for training flights. Hadrian gliders on the ground would be picked up by a hook fixed on a passing Dakota and snatched into the air. The idea was the ability to pick up small numbers of troops from the ground

Towards the end of the war Airspeed commenced production of Mosquito fighter bombers, although they were too late to see action. Production of bomber versions continued and this autumn 1947 view shows them awaiting final completion prior to delivery to the RAF.

where a powered aircraft was unable to land. The local residents complained about continued night-flying during the summer months; the RAF replied that large aircraft would continue to use Christchurch for the time being. Another complaint related to 'dirty great flying boats' flying low en route from Poole to Hythe. The reply to this was that a request had been made to BOAC for them to be clean in the future. The airfield passed to the control of the Ministry of Aircraft Production (MAP) in January 1946.

Plans for post-war airline services were drawn up by Railway Air Services during 1944, when it was anticipated they would be a major force in internal air services. One route proposed from spring 1945 was the re-opening of the Shoreham to Exeter and Plymouth route, via Ryde and Christchurch, but it was never operated. A resumption of services by Portsmouth Southsea & Isle of Wight Aviation (PS&IoW) under the name of Isle of Wight Aviation was proposed in 1945. Aircraft under consideration by the airline included Dragon Rapides and former Luftwaffe Junkers Ju.52s, but again, services were never operated. The MAP confirmed they had no objection to the resumption of civil flying at Christchurch, which it considered unsuitable as Bournemouth's post-war airport.

The Airspeed Co. undertook a one-off job for de Havilland of Hatfield by modifying the Vampire jet-fighter prototype to undertake landings on an aircraft carrier. During November 1945 the fighter had its undercarriage strengthened and a hook added to catch the carrier's arrester wire with successful trials undertaken the following month. So the Vampire became the first jet aircraft to operate from a carrier. The factory continued with Mosquito production for the RAF, with the final one of 122 built delivered early in 1948. However, Airspeed's main effort was in the design of its Ambassador twin-engined airliner, of which a mock-up was completed during the autumn of 1945. The project was overseen by the MAP who ordered two prototypes of the airliner the following spring.

PS&IoW Aviation had established Portsmouth Aviation during the war and, as such, continued with Oxford and Anson overhauls on the return to peace. The aircraft were still towed via Purewell Cross to the airfield. During 1944 the company had designed the Aerocar twin-engined, eight-seat aircraft, with plans for production to be undertaken at Christchurch. But by the time the prototype flew at Portsmouth in June 1947, the company had run out of capital and so the Aerocar project was abandoned.

POOLE'S BOAC FINALE

At the end of the war there was continued BOAC activity at Poole Marine Airport. The airline refurbished many of its Sunderlands to more luxurious peacetime standards. Known as the Hythe Class, they carried twenty-two passengers plus crew and mail. Greater improvements were made to other Sunderlands by Short Bros, now known as the Sandringham. Services were operated southwards to South Africa and eastwards to Karachi (four times a week) and Calcutta (twice weekly) – the 'Tiger' route. As from May 1945, the North Atlantic service to Baltimore was flown four times a week by the Boeing 314s. During the winter months this was reduced to once a week, operated via West Africa and Brazil to avoid the icy North Atlantic weather conditions. Fares were £142 single and £254 return, with passengers being brought from London by train. It was BOAC's intention to continue to use flying boats on its North Atlantic services. However, the airline began to realise that it would have to operate the more economical landplanes as used by the other international airlines. Being no longer viable, the Baltimore service was withdrawn in March 1946. So, for a few weeks, this left BOAC without services on the prime North Atlantic route, pending introduction of Constellations from London Airport on 1 July.

BOAC continued flying-boat services post-war from Poole, their wartime camouflage now having been replaced by silver. On a test flight early in 1946 is one of the refurbished Sunderlands known as the Hythe Class. From June they provided a luxury service to Sydney.

With the return to peace in the Far East, BOAC re-opened its flying-boat services to the region. Services to Rangoon commenced in October 1945, with Singapore added from January 1946. In February, a Hythe undertook a seven-week Far East survey flight prior to re-introduction of the Sydney service in May. Operated in conjunction with Qantas, Hong Kong was added in August. The Sydney flight was operated by Hythes (replacing the Lancastrians from Hurn) which took five and a half days for the 12,000-mile flight, with Qantas crews taking over at Singapore. A 6 a.m. departure from Poole on a Sunday reached Sydney at 5.00 p.m. the following Friday; the fare was £260 single with night-stop accommodation included. In May 1946 BOAC's based fleet consisted of twenty-three Sunderlands/Hythes, one G Class and one Sandringham. Ray Bingham was station manager at the time, receiving an MBE in January 1948 for the work he put in attending to the various VIPs. One non-BOAC flight was that of American International Airways Boeing 314 *Bermuda Sky Queen* in October 1947. This was in connection with the United Nations Conference being held in London, following which many of the American delegates departed from Poole on 12 October. The Boeing flew into strong winds over the Atlantic, running out of fuel, but it made a safe landing alongside a US coastguard warship which rescued the passengers and crew. The Boeing was then sunk by gunfire so as not to prove a hazard to shipping, and the inquiry found the incident was due to a number of irregularities in the crew's flight planning.

During 1947 a number of Short Solents were delivered to BOAC for crew training, but they did not enter service until the following spring. Flying-boat activity came to an end at Poole in spring 1948, when BOAC moved its operations back to its pre-war base at Southampton, the final service arriving on 30 March. Again, the move of base was not without problems. This time it related to finding sufficient accommodation for staff at Southampton. Increased competition from landplanes meant it was not long before the airline ceased flying-boat services altogether, with the last being taken out of service in November 1950 and stored at Belfast.

The wartime RAF Hamworthy base at Lake was only used by the RAF for fifteen months. It was used again in the early 1950s for the storage of surplus BOAC Sandringhams and Solents. They were beached adjacent to Lake Shipyard which overhauled naval craft.

Most of the surplus BOAC flying boats remained unwanted and were broken up during 1958/59. Some met their fate at Lake whilst others, such as this Solent, were moved to the beach nearer Hamworthy Quay, long since hidden by a Marina.

Once the pride of BOAC's fleet, the Sandringhams and Solents were put up for sale at £35,000 each in autumn 1952. However, they remained unsold and a dozen returned to the Poole in 1953 for further storage. A couple were eventually sold to Australia, with two others earmarked for conversion into a floating restaurant, but they ended up being scrapped along with the rest during 1958.

BOAC RETAIN PRESENCE AT HURN

Back at Hurn, the departure of the airlines to London Airport did not mean the end of activity as the Air Ministry still regarded it as a satellite base to London. As BOAC had no facilities at London, their No.2 Line also remained at Hurn. It continued with the servicing, overhaul and crew training of the fleet of nineteen Lancastrians and twenty-three Yorks used on the African and Far Eastern routes. Although these services were operated from London, the aircraft flew to Hurn between each flight for maintenance. In July 1946 the airline opened an Aircrew Club in Bournemouth for the benefit of crews based at Hurn and Poole. The airport was designated the number one diversion airport for London, and for many years the world's major airlines continued to be seen, usually on foggy winter days. The first major diversion was in November 1946 and, as there were no permanent staff, it was necessary for traffic staff to travel over from Poole Harbour. The problem for the Poole staff was that they were not used to handling such activity at their home base but they soon acquired the necessary experience to cope with all types of travellers. However, the airline decided to set up a small office near the terminal to deal with any future diversions. The winter weather proved to be very severe, with frost and snow causing major problems at the airport. Snow ploughs were unable to keep the runways clear and ice on the taxiways meant that even two tractors were unable to move parked aircraft. Other activity saw the airport used by the major airliners for crew training, flying down from London for a spot of 'circuit bashing'. As with the fog diversions, this continued until the introduction of the large jet airliners in the early 1960s.

During a diversion, BOAC staff are at work in the Long Haul Building which was situated in Hurn Village. The staff came from London and Poole; the girls are part of the Passenger Handling Staff, whilst the busy gentlemen are the Duty Room Staff.

On one occasion there was embarrassment for the captain of a diverted Pan American Constellation when he landed. His earlier radio message to say the airfield was in sight had been acknowledged although Control staff in the tower couldn't see the aircraft. The captain then advised that he was approaching the runway threshold but the tower still could not see him. The captain then said that he had landed but the airfield looked rather empty and why were there ponies roaming around? The tower controllers then realised that the Constellation must have landed at the wartime Holmsley South airfield – about five miles short of Hurn. Steps were sent to disembark the passengers and the empty airliner then made the short flight to its correct destination.

TRAINING SCHOOL

For training the large number of new crews needed, it was intended that BOAC would base its Central Training School at Hurn. Formed at Aldermaston in May 1946, the move was planned to centralise the school with the airline's other operations. What is difficult to appreciate now is that it would have been equivalent to an RAF Operational Conversion Unit with a fleet of fifteen airliners on charge. The original 1946 plan was to equip it with Tudor IIs and Yorks dedicated to the training role, as well as smaller Oxfords which were the normal training aircraft of the time. However, events did not work out as planned – the Tudor was cancelled and there were concerns over congestion and noise in the area. It had been established that a normal training circuit to the south of the airport would take the aircraft over the thickly populated area of Bournemouth. If the airliner was operating at maximum weight, or perhaps flying on three engines, it may well be that it was only flying at 1,000ft when it reached the town. Added to this was the fact that with fifteen aircraft in circuit at a time (nightmares for the control tower staff!) each one could only make one landing an hour. This was useless from a training point of view. Night-flying would also be undertaken which, during the summer months, would be between 11 p.m. and 4 a.m. Luckily, the residents of Bournemouth were probably not aware of what was in the air. In January 1947 the school's chief instructor recommended that it remain at Aldermaston due to the increased noise the residents of Bournemouth would have to suffer. He also bore in mind that they had already voiced considerable criticisms to their MP regarding existing airport operations.

DEVELOPMENT FLIGHT

Under Capt. Buck, the flight expanded its work of testing new aircraft and engines. The original Lancaster, now silver, was re-engined in 1946 with a newer version of the Merlin which was being developed for the Tudor. Flights included three trips across the North Atlantic during summer 1946 – two to Montreal and one to the Lockheed factory at Burbank. The problem of low flying and noise also included the aircraft of the flight, where the first of a number of Vickers Vikings was delivered in May 1946, plus an early production Tudor I. This did not meet the airlines requirements in many respects, and so was returned to Avro for modifications before returning in October. But there were still major problems which resulted in BOAC eventually cancelling its order for both versions and having to rely on its Lancastrians and Yorks for longer than planned. Another new airliner was the DH Dove, with the second prototype arriving for trials at the end of July 1946. Whilst undertaking single engine take-offs and landings on 14 August, it crashed at West Howe shortly after take-off. Its active engine failed, resulting in a crash in a corn field with the death of the de Havilland representative on board. A replacement aircraft arrived in January 1947 but it did not fare much better than its predecessor. The experienced crew under Capt. Buck became disorientated in fog during the late afternoon of 13 March. Although he heard flying over the airport on a number of occasions, a visual sighting of the aircraft could not be made. The Dove then flew out to sea before returning for another attempt, but crashed in the mist at Chewton Common, near Highcliffe, with the crew of three dying in the ensuing fire.

CREW TRAINING AND FOG

To replace the Tudor, BOAC ordered a fleet of Handley Page Hermes IVs in April 1947, followed by one for the Canadair Four. The prototype Canadair visited Hurn in

With the arrival of the Hermes, BOAC at last had a modern-looking British built airliner. Much development flying was undertaken from Hurn. However, it did not prove as successful in service as had been hoped, being overweight compared with the Canadair Argonaut.

A British South American Airways Tudor IV crew training at Hurn early in 1948. A number of unexplained crashes soon led to the Tudors being withdrawn. The airport's wartime control tower has now gained a glass observation area on its roof.

May during its European sales tour, the type being known as the Argonaut in BOAC service. The first Argonaut was delivered in May 1949 with the rest of the twenty-two ordered swiftly following during the year. Trials with the Development Flight included a 26,000-mile route-proving flight to Manila in June the following year. Although the first Hermes VIs arrived in summer 1949, more development work was needed before the type could enter service the following spring. The Argonaut proved the more successful of the two as the Hermes was found to be overweight. The BOAC staff also operated the Speedbird Flying Club using a number of Hawk Trainers which arrived in 1948, and were later joined by Austers and Tiger Moths. The club made use of nearby Christchurch, where they also operated a gliding section.

A number of BOAC's unwanted Tudors were passed on to British South American Airways which operated services from London Airport. The Tudors were to be seen crew training at Hurn during 1947–48. In summer 1948 the airline merged with BOAC, who did not want to take on the Tudors again, so the fleet were stored at Hurn to await their fate.

Hurn's next major diversion was at the end of November 1948, with 135 aircraft movements and 2,268 passengers. As well as Hurn, BOAC aircraft were diverted to Southampton (nine) and St Eval (two), with staff having to be sent down from London to help cope. Much of the country was affected by the fog, with some coaches taking eight hours to travel down from London. One needed two drivers – one to drive and the other to lean out the passenger door to try and see the way ahead! Luckily, the Ministry had installed Ground Controlled Approach Radar at Hurn for training purposes back in the summer, and the controllers made great use of it during the fog. The Minister of Civil Aviation himself visited the Airport to express his thanks for 'the grand job being done'. Aircraft seen included the likes of Qantas Constellations, Swiss Air and SAS DC-4s and Trans-Canada North Stars.

The prototype Bristol Brabazon circled Bournemouth on 7 November 1949 and the prototype DH Comet I jet airliner was first seen at Hurn later that evening. It had flown down from Hatfield for night-flying trials and was piloted by John Cunningham. Crew training was undertaken during 1949 on BOAC's new Constellations, followed by the larger Boeing Stratocruisers in the autumn. Complaints were again raised over night-flying, which brought the Parliamentary response, 'If BOAC is to remain efficient, night-flying is an essential part of training and economically impossible to undertake elsewhere'.

The Minister of Aviation, Lord Pakenham (wearing glasses), and BOAC chief executive, Whitney Straight, visit the crews at Hurn following a hectic diversion period in November 1948. The VIPs expressed their thanks for the crews' hard efforts in difficult circumstances.

The largest airliners in service in the late 1940s were Boeing Stratocruisers. Those of BOAC and Pan American World were to be seen at Hurn on diversions, bringing concern to the authorities that their weight might break up the runway.

In July 1949 BOAC's chairman stated that, allowing for increased activity at London Airport, the airline regarded the No.2 Line at Hurn as one of their key locations, with the future for the base being bright. During the summer they maintained twenty-six Yorks and employed 1,500 people plus a further 142 with the Development Flight. The BOAC staff and workers would arrive by a convoy of Hants & Dorset buses from Bournemouth Square to building B.50, with many others arriving by bike. As always, the summer's good news concerning the key No.2 Line was swiftly followed in November by BOAC announcing that it was now able to centralise its overhaul operations at London Airport and that its Hurn base would be vacated by summer 1950. This meant that Hurn's main role would now be that of a diversionary airport for London; the next was in November 1949 and included an Air India Constellation, Alitalia SM.95, Hellenic Liberator and Sabena Convair 240. Scrapping of surplus Lancastrians commenced in the autumn, even though some had seen less than eighteen months' service. The reason was that they were only ever intended as stop-gaps until newer aircraft became available.

10

HURN – AN AIRPORT
IN ITS OWN RIGHT

FIRST DOMESTIC SERVICES

Hurn's initial post-war operations were mainly connected with BOAC but there was other activity to be seen. From time to time there were visits by Dragon Rapides of Channel Island Airways on charters, although their scheduled services to the Channel Islands were from Southampton. The airport was also used for a number of overseas delivery flights. A brand new Bristol Wayfarer called at the end of June 1946 for attention to its radio prior to setting off for South America. It failed to make it for, whilst crossing the Atlantic between Gambia and Natal, it ran out of fuel 125 miles before making landfall. A navigation error meant the Wayfarer was flying along the Brazilian coast, not towards it! Luckily, the crew were safely rescued from the sea by a passing ship. Also South America-bound in April 1947 was a Spitfire. Equipped for aerial survey work and fitted with long-range fuel tanks, it made the long crossing between Dakar and Natal to safely reach its destination of Buenos Aires.

Post-war, a number of small airlines had commenced internal UK services, mainly using surplus RAF Dragon Rapides. At the beginning of 1947, many of these airlines were absorbed into the newly formed British European Airways. Some remained separate, but were only permitted to operate charter flights. The early summer saw a number of such charters from Hurn to Jersey by International Airways of Croydon, who operated Consuls. For the next five years there were various attempts by airlines to establish regular services to the Channel Islands.

FIRST BATH TRAVEL IT FLIGHTS

May and June 1947 saw holiday charter flights to Switzerland, the significance of which was not realised at the time. Local travel firm Bath Travel Service were agents for International Airways, who advertised, 'Luxury twin engined aircraft for travel to Jersey, Paris and Switzerland'. Bath Travel arranged a number of air tours to Basle at a price of £41 – the start of Bath's Inclusive Tour holidays which greatly expanded during the 1960 and 1970s.

A one off charter organised by Bath's was that of a Pan American World Constellation in November 1947. This carried American GI brides to the United States, for which the airliner was especially renamed *Romance of the Skies*. The Basle charters were repeated in 1948, by which time the terminal was advertised as open; 3*d* admission was charged, with teas and light refreshments available from the canteen. There was a small area in front of the canteen from which to view passengers coming and going. A proper public enclosure was provided in the 1960s when an area of grass was fenced off and chairs provided.

FURTHER SERVICES

International Airways reappeared in 1948, having obtained a BEA Associate Agreement to operate scheduled services. During the summer they operated the Croydon–Cowes–Bournemouth route with newly acquired Dragon Rapides at a return fare of £4 10*s*. Although intended to be twice-daily from August, the services were mainly flown at weekends. However, there was little traffic between Cowes and Bournemouth, which resulted in the service being withdrawn by the winter. The airline also advertised flights to race meetings at Bath, Birmingham and Folkestone, plus private charters to Jersey for £7 10*s* return. One problem for the intending passengers was the Ministry police check they had to go through on entering the airport. This was until Group Captain Cox pointed out to the police that the passengers were entitled to use the airport and should not have to endure their questions. Of note is that International Airways used the name Bournemouth Airport and not Hurn.

In January 1949 supporters of Bournemouth Football Club chartered a Dakota to fly to a match at Manchester. Their enthusiasm was short lived as the Dakota suffered engine problems shortly after take-off and had to return, with a relief plane appearing in due course. The first recorded royal visit saw a King's Flight Viking arrive in September 1949, carrying the Duke of Edinburgh en route to Christchurch. Further attempts at scheduled services were made by Flightways of Southampton in 1950, again promoted by Bath Travel. They operated a Saturday-morning service to Jersey between April and September, flown by Dragon Rapides at a fare of £6 12*s* 6*d* return. Bath's also offered fifteen-day Air Tours to Jersey from £23 2*s*. At the time, the Ministry advised potential visitors by air, 'Customs, Immigration and Met briefing on request, limited hangarage, marshalling, restaurant, no maintenance and no transport'.

Mid-September 1950 saw a diversion from London with a more substantial one at the end of November – forty-two aircraft arriving on 26 November. After a few days there were well over fifty airliners to be seen parked in the gloom – Air France, BOAC, KLM and SAA. April 1951 saw a prototype de Havilland Comet arrive for six months route proving and crew training with BOAC's new Comet Unit. By the end of the year early production aircraft arrived for further crew conversion training. BOAC's first Comet was officially handed over at London Airport in February 1952, but the jets were not favoured by the local residents due to the noise of their night-time training. The next major diversion was in December 1952. With smog all over the Home Counties,

Hurn was the starting point of the *Daily Express* South Coast Air Race in September 1950. Aircraft ranged in size from a converted Halifax bomber down to a Comper Swift ultra light. Seen prior to the race, this Gipsy Moth was one of two entered by local pilots.

almost 100 aircraft were handled during the month, including a number of Comets. This showed that Hurn could handle the new breed of jet airliners.

HURN TO HERNE AIR RACE

A major event in 1950 was the South Coast Air Race held on the afternoon of Saturday 16 September. Sponsored by the *Daily Express*, its course was along the coast from Hurn to Herne Bay, Kent. The event had been threatened by unsuitable weather during the previous week, but this finally cleared for the race. The public were admitted to the airport at a charge of 1*s*, and it was estimated that 6,000 arrived to see the aircraft. Prior to the race, the huge Brabazon prototype flew past the airport and town while on a test flight from Filton. Locally, the course took the aircraft westward from the airport round a pylon in the grounds of Canford School. It was then south to Poole Power Station and Sandbanks before heading off eastwards along the coast. The aircraft ranged in size from a Comper Swift to a converted Halifax bomber, with a Percival Proctor winning the Race Trophy and a prize of £1,000.

Allen Rustall had recently joined the Royal Observer Corps:

> Our members had been tasked with monitoring the Race Course from various observation posts. I was pleased to be allotted to Poole Power Station where I had to ensure that, in addition to logging each aircraft on a score sheet, they passed to the west of the chimneys and did not cut the corner en route to Sandbanks. Normally ROC members would be looking high in the sky for aircraft but those in the race approached very low over Holes Bay.

Royal Navy capital ships would visit Bournemouth on goodwill visits, including the battleship HMS *Vanguard*. On this occasion in the early 1950s, it was the aircraft carrier HMS *Theseus* whose Sea Fury fighters came under public inspection.

This was confirmed by his colleague Tony Needham, who was stationed on top of the Haven Hotel adjacent to the Sandbanks Ferry. He was able to take some photographs of the competitors, all looking down on their wing tops.

SCHOOL OF AIR TRAFFIC CONTROL

Spring 1948 saw the arrival at Hurn of the School of Air Traffic Control from Aldermaston, where it had been set up the previous year by the Ministry. The school was housed in a number of wartime wooden buildings on the south-east side of the airport as well as in part of the control tower. Here it continued its role of training civilian air traffic controllers and assistants. The Ministry had a Flying Unit at Gatwick which was tasked with training and testing commercial pilots in instrument-flying rating checks and blind-approach techniques as well as airfield radio-aid calibration. Their fleet of Avro Ansons and Airspeed Consuls (later Doves and Princes) visited Hurn to act as 'blips' on the schools trainee's radar screen. They would then give the pilot the, hopefully, appropriate landing instructions. Over the years the work of the school expanded, proving to be the longest user of the airport. Modern buildings for the school were opened in October 1962, and in January 1963 they were joined by the ATC Experimental Unit from Heathrow. The unit evaluated new techniques and systems, simulating their use in various operational situations and undertaking any modifications prior to future service.

HELICOPTER MAIL FLIGHTS

A local experiment was the use of civilian helicopters for GPO mail deliveries. BEA had established an experimental helicopter unit at Yeovil at the end of 1947 and was seeking a commercial use for them. So a five-week trial service, carrying dummy mail sacks, commenced with Sikorsky S-51s at the end of January 1948, flying a twice-daily route around Dorset from

Yeovil. Locally, the helicopters called at Wimborne, Poole and Wareham; the Poole landing site was on the south of Turbary Common, adjacent to Wallisdown Road. Later in the year more permanent GPO services were operated by the airline around East Anglia.

TRYING TO INCREASE SERVICES

Jersey Airlines had been formed in December 1948, but regulations prevented it undertaking scheduled services at the time. However, it flew frequent charters from Jersey to the south coast and northern France. Following a change of Government and regulations in 1951, the airline underwent swift expansion during the spring of 1952. Scheduled services with Dragon Rapides were soon established across the Channel to Exeter and Southampton. Hurn soon followed, and this proved to be the start of continued services to the Channel Islands. From Hurn, the service was extended northwards to Manchester in June, and Coventry in August.

Walter Lucas was an early passenger:

> I lived in Manchester, getting married in June 1952. Although expensive at the time, my bride and I decided on a honeymoon in Jersey finding that there was a direct air service. We did not realize how new it was and found ourselves as the only passengers on the Sunday flight. We stopped off at Hurn for further passengers but there were none – the pilot explaining that he had to comply with the advertised timetable. So we had a cup of tea before walking back to the Rapide after an hour and headed south. From what we saw we liked the look of the area and the following year moved down to live in Bournemouth where I found employment with Vickers-Armstrongs.

From summer 1952, the signboard at the airport's entrance proclaimed, 'Bournemouth (Hurn) Airport' but it took fifty years before the Hurn part was forgotten. The name was officially amended the following spring, which annoyed Christchurch Council. As in the 1930s, councillors were unhappy that Bournemouth was claiming an airport which did not lie within its area – at the time it was within Ringwood & Fordingbridge Rural District. Work was undertaken to modernise the Control Tower, with the latest flying aids installed as well as a large glass cupola on top. This gave the controllers a greatly improved view around the area. A Consultative Committee was formed, whose first task was to try and attract further services with routes suggested to Manchester, Edinburgh and Glasgow. To emphasise the need for services, the month of May 1952 saw only eight transport movements with sixteen passengers. This had improved by October, with twenty-three movements resulting in 234 passengers. Another problem was the lack of a permanent Customs Office at the airport, which meant an officer had to travel by taxi from Poole Quay, with resultant delays for passengers. The committee also wanted the public to visit the terminal but admitted there was little to be seen. The locals realised that better views of the aircraft could be obtained from the various lay-bys that existed at the time along Parley Lane.

Private flying took some time to be re-established at Christchurch after the war. Following a number of attempts, the Christchurch Aero Club was established by Tommy Marshall (left) in June 1952, remaining until 1964, just before the airfield closed.

The airport was used during the 1950s and early 1960s for summer camps by members of the Women's Junior Air Corps who pitched their tents for a fortnight near the terminal area. For a payment of 7s 6d, Air Experience flights were undertaken by the girls in the Corps' Fairchild Argus *Grey Dove*. Following its retirement in 1957, the Corps brought along an Auster or Tiger Moth for these flights.

Gillian Tong was one of these youngsters:

> I was a member of the Hythe Unit and recall an interesting day at the airport in 1952. Armed with a letter of introduction to the Airport Commandant, a friend and I cycled across from Hythe to see what activity there was at Bournemouth. We were given permission to cycle around the perimeter track to the far side (making sure we observed the traffic lights before crossing the runway), where our letter gained us entry to the hangars to see aircraft under construction. We had brought sandwiches for lunch which we ate under the wings of one of the stored BSAA Tudors. The driver of a passing fire engine stopped to chat and then took us aboard the Tudor which was airless and hot due to having been parked outside for some months. The only air activity we saw was a BOAC Argonaut which came down from London to undertake a few training circuits. It was then time to bid farewell to the fireman and start our long cycle ride home.

Gillian feels certain that youngsters would not get away with such an adventure today.

PRIVATE FLYING FROM CHRISTCHURCH

Christchurch airfield did not see airline services again and attempts to re-establish the Bournemouth Flying Club by, now Sqdn Ldr, Fisher, in May 1946, failed. He purchased four surplus RAF Hawk Trainers but the MAP prevented the club from operating. As a result, the trainers just gathered dust in the old club buildings. However, some private aircraft did appear and club flying finally returned with the formation of the South Hants Ultra Light Aero Club (SHULAC) in spring 1948. The members built a Heath Parasol ultra-light but, despite the best efforts of Airspeed's test pilot, it failed to become airborne due to it being underpowered. It left by road for Hurn, where members of the Speedbird Flying Club coaxed it into the air. The SHULAC ran into financial problems and closed down in October 1950, with the Christchurch Aero Club formed as a replacement. The new club operated a fleet of Austers and Tiger Moths, as did the majority of flying clubs in the country at the time, with flying rates of £2 per hour. In June 1952 the club was reformed by Tom Marshall who took over the derelict pre-war club pavilion. This was then destroyed during a gale in December 1954, and replaced by an equally ancient building. The pilot of one of the Tiger Moths decided to take a close look at the aircraft carrier HMS *Indefatigable*, which was moored off Bournemouth Pier in early June 1953. Lack of concentration resulted in the Tiger ending up in the sea with the pilot safely swimming to the pier.

Glider-flying instruction was also undertaken with both civilian and military operations. As well as a few private owners, there was the BOAC Gliding Club in the late 1940s with pilots hoping to benefit from thermals from the nearby cliffs at Mudeford. Cadets from local ATC Squadrons continued to be provided with gliding experience by No.89 Gliding School, based in a hangar adjacent to Warren Avenue. Only basic gliders were provided for the cadets, sufficient to give them the feel of an aircraft whilst undertaking a circuit of the harbour and airfield.

Basic glider flying was available to local Air Cadets at Christchurch. Instruction was given on Cadet gliders; in this case the instructor was also one of BOAC's Comet crew from Hurn. BOAC also had a gliding club at Christchurch.

11

LOCAL AVIATION INDUSTRY – 1

AIRSPEED CHRISTCHURCH

During 1945–46 the Airspeed factory proceeded with design work on the Ambassador. The Ministry of Aircraft Production indicated that there would be a possible order for thirty plus fifty of a proposed Ayrshire military version. The prototype Ambassador flew on the evening of 10 July 1947 with George Errington at the controls, and the lack of problems enabled it to appear over the town's regatta the following month. At the time the airfield still retained its pre-war 900-yard grass runway. This proved valuable to flight testing on a number of occasions as the airliner suffered various undercarriage problems. As early as November 1947, it was forced to make a wheels-up landing, although suffering little damage, with a similar incident occurring in July 1950. However, the most memorable occurred on the morning of 13 November 1950, when an unintentional heavy landing was made during centre-of-gravity trials. This resulted in both engines breaking clean off their mountings, with the aircraft bouncing upwards before making its final 'landing' as a glider. Luckily, the aircraft suffered little damage as the incident occurred on grass. It returned to the hangar where the engines were soon re-attached to enable it to fly again within a short time. Despite these incidents, a £3 million order for twenty was placed by BEA in September 1948, but these were the only production aircraft built. Airspeed also designed the Ambassador II, powered by turbo-prop engines, but this version was not proceeded with.

A contract was received in 1948 to overhaul sixty Horsa assault gliders for the RAF, who still considered them effective for airborne operations. The gliders arrived by road, and then departed by air behind a Halifax bomber. In May 1948 the de Havilland Aircraft Co. purchased the remaining shares of the Airspeed Co., looking for additional production space for its own range of aircraft. At the time, this involved Vampire and Venom fighters for the RAF and export, Dove feeder airliners and Comet jet airliners. Despite the potential for further development, de Havilland decided to limit production of the Ambassador to those for BEA. It decided against spending further time and money on the airliner, thereafter concentrating work at Christchurch on its own designs. First off was the Vampire Trainer, the original Vampire fighter having flown from Hatfield in September 1943. This was followed by a two-seat night-fighter, which formed the basis of the new Trainer. The Christchurch site was entrusted with

The prototype Ambassador one summer's evening in 1947, with the flight test crew in discussion. Of interest are the Mosquitoes in the background awaiting delivery, plus a visiting Warwick. One had previously been used by Airspeed for Centaurus engine development trials.

The early Ambassador trials were noteworthy for the number of landing accidents. This was one of the first in 1947, the grass runway preventing serious damage to the aircraft. A more 'interesting' landing occurred in 1950 when both engines broke away from the wing.

The Airspeed factory was entrusted by de Havilland in 1950 with the design and development of their Vampire jet trainer, the prototype of which is seen outside the flight shed. The trainer was built in large numbers for the RAF, Royal Navy and many overseas air forces.

its design and development, followed by construction of the prototype which flew on 15 November 1950. The new jet had already been taken by road to Farnborough to appear at the Air Show in September, before returning by road for completion. Large numbers were ordered by the RAF and overseas air forces with production also undertaken by de Havilland at their Hatfield and Chester factories.

AMBASSADOR

As mentioned, Airspeed undertook test flying of the Ambassador from the grass at Christchurch, but it also made use of the hard runways at Hurn. This had been one of the conditions back in 1944 when the airport was released for civilian use. The prototype was joined in August 1948 by a second, which undertook overload weight trials at Beaulieu late in 1948. This was because test equipment was available there and not at Hurn. The airliner suffered another accident at Hurn on 13 March 1950, whilst taking-off with one engine stopped. George Errington quickly retracted the wheels but the aircraft failed to gain height and sank back onto the runway, where it skidded along for about 300 yards. The fire crews had been watching and with a sixth sense anticipated problems, which meant they reached the aircraft almost before it had come to a halt. Again, damage was not too great and it was patched up at Hurn and flown back to Christchurch for a full check over. George Errington commented, 'It is one of those unfortunate mishaps which must be expected when engaged on extensive testing work. The fuselage has stood up remarkably well to the gruelling belly-slide under full load conditions'. (Although the fuselage proved to be strong, the design team had to undertake a major strengthening of the wing before full production could get underway.) There was another accident four months later, on 13 July, when the undercarriage collapsed on landing at Hurn, again with little damage. Note how all the accidents occurred on the 13th!

A view of the Airspeed factory in the early 1950s. Following its absorption by de Havilland in 1951, it lost its Airspeed titles, now proclaiming 'De Havilland Aircraft'. The closeness of the airfield to Mudeford can be clearly seen.

An early production Ambassador climbs out to the west over Christchurch Priory, the congregation of which had to put up with plenty of noise over the years. Local residents will note the absence of the Christchurch bypass which was not built until 1958.

With BOAC moving out of Hurn, Airspeed took over one of their hangars on the north side of the airport in spring 1950. This became their flight-test base, being used for production Ambassadors which began to appear the following spring. By then, the hangar had also seen the prototype Vampire Trainer which visited during its maiden flight from Christchurch and was soon based there for further trials. Production Vampire Trainers were followed by Venoms in 1952 and Sea Venoms from 1953. There was a fatal accident on 11 May 1954 when one of the Sea Venoms suffered engine problems on take-off. It failed to gain height, killing a passing motorcyclist as it crossed Parley Lane before coming to rest in the adjacent farmer's field.

VICKERS-ARMSTRONGS

In 1950 Vickers-Armstrongs (Aircraft) Ltd had a major production site at Weybridge. The year 1951 was to see the firm arrive at Hurn, initially using the airport as a temporary Flight Test Base. Production of Viking airliners and Valetta transports and trainers was undertaken at Weybridge, being followed by the new Varsity trainer for the RAF. Flight testing was undertaken from Wisley, which only possessed a grass runway at the time. Vickers had just completed the prototype Valiant V-bomber, which made its first flight from Wisley's grass runway on 18 May 1951, piloted by Mutt Summers. It had been agreed that a hard runway was needed at Wisley, this being proved by the ruts made by the new bomber on landing. So the Valiant's fourth flight on 1 June took it to Hurn, which was to be its temporary base until Wisley's runway was completed. Vickers initially leased two former BOAC hangars on the north side, also using the base for testing the Viscount airliner as well as production testing of Valettas and Varsities from Weybridge. The Viscount 700 prototype arrived on 31 May, and was followed by the earlier 630 prototype, with Vickers' test pilots Jock Bryce and Brian Trubshaw undertaking most of the flying. (Bryce had just been appointed chief test pilot for Vickers. Trubshaw became chief test pilot of BAC in 1965, being remembered for his later test work on Concorde.) The Viscount 700 was flown to Farnborough early in September for the Air Show before departing at the beginning of October for tropical trials at Khartoum, returning at the end of November. The unique jet-powered Tay Viscount also arrived at Hurn but only undertook minimal flying during its stay, as both engines needed overhaul by Rolls-Royce during autumn 1951.

VARSITY AND VALIANT

In 1951 Vickers had a full order book from the RAF for Varsity trainers and the new Valiant, as well as increasing orders for Viscount airliners. In fact, a number of RAF Valetta transports had been cancelled to make way for the additional military orders. At the time there was a real fear in the country that another world war might break out, precipitated by the Korean conflict. However, Vickers solved their capacity problem by sub-contracting much of the Valiant work. Then they switched Varsity production to Hurn, using two

The prototype Valiant V-Bomber was based at Hurn during the autumn of 1951. Seen parked outside the former BOAC hangars, the bomber was lost in a spectacular crash in January 1952, which was witnessed by many local residents.

additional former BOAC hangars with further staff transferred from Weybridge. Initially, only wings and tails were produced locally, with fuselages arriving from Weybridge. Soon, complete aircraft were produced at the Hurn site so as to leave Weybridge free for Valiants and Viscounts. The first Hurn-assembled Varsity flew on 29 November 1951, piloted by Jock Bryce, and the type was to be part of the local scene for the next two years. Of the 163 Varsities built, 146 were from Hurn, although further orders were cancelled late in 1952.

The Valiant was flight-tested by A&AEE crews who visited from Boscombe Down early in September 1951, following which it was displayed at the Farnborough Air Show. The Valiant then flew to Wisley for new engines before returning to Hurn just before Christmas. Fuel leaks were noted prior to resuming test-flying in the new year. Whilst airborne on 12 January 1952 undertaking engine shutdown and relight procedures, it suffered instrument failures with the crew deciding to return to Hurn. They then discovered that there was an uncontrollable engine fire which rapidly spread to the wing. The crippled bomber was clearly seen at height over Bournemouth early in the afternoon, with flames pouring from the starboard engines and wing whilst trying to lose height. Turning over the bay, Jock Bryce considered trying to make Boscombe Down but, before crossing the coast near Highcliffe, large chunks of the wing were seen to be falling off. The immanent danger of the wing breaking off forced the crew to bail out, regrettably with the RAF co-pilot being fatally injured in the process. The Valiant exploded with the pieces falling around Harrow Farm, near Bransgore, and the crew coming down between Highcliffe and the crash site. Following Jock Bryce's 'Mayday', the controllers in the tower at Hurn saw the black smoke from the crash site 5 miles away. Fearing the worst, they were surprised to receive a telephone call from Jock Bryce. He had found a telephone box close to the site of his landing, and was able to report back with news of the crew. The fire was traced to a faulty fuel supply in the early version of the Avon engines.

The second prototype Valiant, which flew from Wisley during April, had a modified fuel system. This meant that there was not too much delay in test work for the bomber, which had been placed on 'super priority' production for the RAF. Other trials work undertaken by Vickers from Hurn during 1951–52 included a couple of English Electric Canberras for guided-missile development work, and later, two Boeing Washingtons.

VISCOUNT

The Viscount marked a milestone in civil aviation in July 1950 by being the world's first turbo-prop airliner to carry fare-paying passengers. BEA placed its initial order in August 1950, with the first of its fleet flying in August 1952. At Vickers' AGM in May 1952, it was stated that, 'Production of the Viscount can only be small due to the heavy demands of service types, it being impossible for Vickers to reap the full rewards'. The solution reached by Vickers was to expand their Hurn depot (as it was referred to) to undertake Viscount production. As well as increasing the area of the production hangars, a full design office and flight test centre was established. The pressure on Vickers was eased when the RAF cancelled the final fifty Varsities on order. The initial Viscounts to be produced were the basic series 700 aircraft which suited the requirement of short-haul airlines such as BEA, Air France and Aer Lingus. The fuselages were produced at Hurn but the wings were built by Saunders-Roe at Cowes.

Vickers-Armstrongs took over the former BOAC hangars for production of Varsity trainers and Viscount airliners. This July 1954 view of a Trans-Australian Airlines aircraft was prior to the hangar being lengthened to double the production area.

BEA was the first airline to put the Viscount into service. Although this is a Weybridge-built aircraft, it spent some time crew training at Bournemouth during autumn 1952 prior to entering service with the airline the following April.

With the second production line being set up at Hurn, Vickers was able to expand the variants of Viscount. This included a longer-range version with additional fuel tanks in the wings, which led to an order from Trans Australian Airlines in June 1952. It also caught the eye of Trans-Canada Air Lines. However, to meet the stringent North American requirements, changes were needed for the aircraft, and over 250 modifications were made. This hard work resulted in an initial C$11½m order for fifteen from TCA in November 1952, followed by additional orders for a further thirty-six. So, as well as production, Hurn became involved in design and flight testing, and in due course became the main production centre.

Dennis Cailes joined the design office in autumn 1953:

> The first Viscounts were nearing completion. There had been delays as the production drawing supplied by Weybridge was not 100% accurate. This was a time when aircraft were still being individually finished, with minor modifications made on the production line. These did not always appear on the drawings – hence the need for the Hurn staff to update them. It was even more necessary for us to make sure the drawings were accurate in order to satisfy the North American certification regulations.

Other Viscounts to be seen visiting Hurn were early production aircraft for BEA used on intensive crew training from London Airport during the spring of 1953. Towards the end of the year, Hurn's first aircraft for BEA and Aer Lingus were taking shape. BEA's first flew on 1 December piloted by Jock Bryce, with Hurn's final Varsity appearing a few days later. In November, Vickers announced that it had commenced production of the last of twenty-four Viscounts to be built at Weybridge and that thereafter all production would be at Hurn. It was the intention that their production level could be increased to 100 a year, and that that at Weybridge would taper off by the end of 1955. However, this was not to be. Weybridge had already developed the larger series 800 in 1952, which sold in large numbers, so production at both sites continued. At a peak in the late 1950s, seven or eight Viscounts per week were rolling off the Weybridge and Hurn production lines.

As in BOAC days, one thing common to both Airspeed and Vickers was the need to transport workers to the factories. There were few cars in those days, so they either cycled or arrived in a convoy of Hants and Dorset buses from different parts of the area.

AIRSHIP *BOURNEMOUTH*

Another local project was the brainchild of airship enthusiast Lord Ventry, who lived in Poole and was the only certified Aeronaut in the country. He had flown aboard the Graf Zeppelin during its 1932 visit to England and, post-war, he still promoted airship travel, designing a small airship for demonstration purposes. Resembling a lengthened Second World War barrage balloon, it carried a gondola underneath for a crew of three. It was propelled by a Salmson engine at the rear of the gondola, hopefully to give it a speed of 40mph. Lord Ventry had formed the Airship Club of Great Britain in 1950, with local meetings held at Boscombe. Its members undertook construction of the gondola, together with engine tests, the following year in a shed at Hurn. They were then taken to Cardington, where the 45,000cu.ft envelope was completed the following spring. The hope was to fly over Bournemouth during the Festival of Britain celebrations that June, as Bournemouth Council had provided finance towards the project. The enthusiasm of the small team was not matched by the performance of the airship. It did not make its first flight (or more of a bump) until May, followed by a more successful one on 19 July. This revealed control problems which continued during the initial flight trials, and resulted in the envelope being enlarged during the winter. Further trials at Cardington during 1952 revealed more problems, so there was no hope of an appearance over Bournemouth during that summer either. Enthusiasm was renewed, with more successful flights undertaken during September. Unfortunately, the project came to an end in April 1953 when the envelope was irreparably torn whilst in the hangar; the surplus gondola eventually turned up in a hangar at Christchurch in the late 1950s. Lord Ventry maintained his interest in airships and returned to the Hurn in summer 1980 for a flight in the visiting *Goodyear* Airship.

$67 MILLION VISCOUNT

Following the introduction of Viscounts into service in Canada, the next boost for Vickers-Armstrongs came in June 1954, with an initial order for three aircraft from Capital Airlines of Washington. This was followed two months later by an order for a further thirty-seven to make a total order value of $67 million. This was a major breakthrough into the American market, and proved to be Britain's largest dollar-earning contract at the time.

1. Airwork was one of the major aviation firms based at Bournemouth Airport. As well as operating a Fleet Requirement Unit, it also undertook overhauls on civil and military aircraft. Seen outside their main hangar is a Hunter Trainer from Boscombe Down.

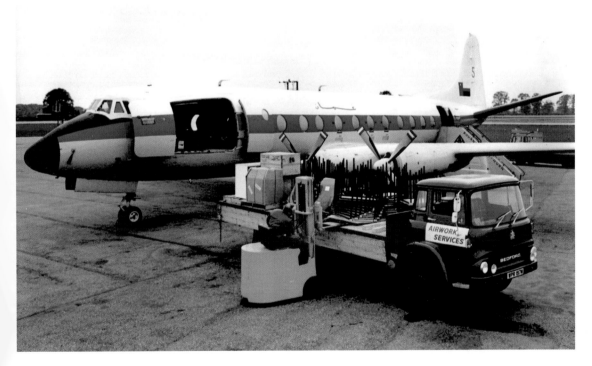

2. The Viscount has two connections with Bournemouth. Firstly, almost 300 were built by Vickers-Armstrongs. Secondly, as one of Britain's best-selling airliners, it was used by a large number of operators into the airport. This freighter version is from the Sultan of Oman Air Force.

3. Over the years a variety of airliners have been used on holiday flights to the Mediterranean. Comets, Coronados and One-Elevens were regulars in the past. Caravelles were not so frequent, but the Spanish airline Hispania used them during the mid-1980s.

4. A selection of airline names seen at Bournemouth over the years, going back to BOAC in 1945. Some are still well remembered, such as Cambrian, Dan-Air and Jersey Airlines. Others, such as Air Wales and Aviation West, only operated for a few months.

5. Not immediately obvious, but this is one of Ryanair's Boeing 737s bringing a splash of colour to the apron. In the mid-1990s a number became flying billboards, this one advertising Hertz Car Rentals. It proved to be an additional income for the airline.

Above: 6. The Mediterranean is still the main holiday destination from Bournemouth. This Airbus A320 of Spanair is representative of the various airlines currently serving this market. Tour operators are now seeing a change from the old package holiday to internet-booked ones.

Overleaf: 7. This shows the teamwork that is needed in supporting airline operations at Bournemouth. Even though Palmair European and Thomsonfly only operate two 737s each, their frontline and backup crews are ably demonstrated, along with the necessary airport's ground services.

8. Thompsonfly set up a low-cost airline division in 2004. Services commenced from Bournemouth the following spring, offering travellers seven destinations daily. The airline is part of the German Tui Group, whose logo is carried on the tail of this 737.

9. The first major airline user of Bournemouth was BOAC. Aircraft of its present-day successor still visit the airport. They may be on diversion from London or, as in this case of a Boeing 737, on a holiday charter to the French Alps.

10. During the 1980/90s, Jet Heritage was widely known for the overhaul work it undertook on Hunter fighters for the jet warbird collectors. The ground crews prepare two of the aircraft for a practice air–display routine in 1997.

11. The public know the Red Arrows for their outstanding and not to be missed displays. In between these it is necessary for the Hawk aircraft to be checked over and refuelled. Seen here, the pilots are referred to as 'The Reds' and the ground crews, 'The Blues'.

12. For a number of years the airport was known as Bournemouth International Airport. This title appears on the passenger steps by this Air Europe Boeing 737 which is preparing to depart to Palma with another full load of holidaymakers.

13. A regular visitor over recent years has been this VIP Boeing 747 'Jumbo Jet'. Its Middle Eastern owner finds it easier to park the aircraft at Bournemouth whenever he is visiting London. Lighter then a normal 747, the VIP version adequately copes with Bournemouth's runway.

The Viscount order placed by Capital Airlines in 1954 was a major boost for Vickers. This is their first aircraft shortly after roll-out in May 1955. It was mainly used for crew training by Capital pending delivery of their main order for thirty-seven aircraft.

The Viscount was the first British airliner to fly internal routes in the USA since converted DH.4s in the 1920s. The US airworthiness requirements were mainly met by the TCA modifications, although nose radar was fitted to the Viscount for the first time. Capital later placed additional orders but by early 1957 had run into major financial problems which resulted in further deliveries being suspended. Vickers were forced to seek payment for the aircraft already delivered. This led to a number of the undelivered aircraft being stored outside the factory covered in protective paint prior to resale.

The year 1956 saw the visit of the Soviet Minister of Aviation Industries, Mr Dementier, accompanied by Sir George Edwards. As well as touring the production line, lunch was provided at the Carlton Hotel, but whether there was any real expectation of selling the aircraft is uncertain. April 1958 saw a visit by the Duke of Edinburgh, who arrived by a Viscount which he had piloted down from Wisley. The Duke was to visit the factory on a number of occasions to see progress on the airliner.

As mentioned, the Weybridge site had developed the series 800, commencing production in summer 1956. The Hurn design office also worked on the series 790 Local Service Viscount for short-distance services. Despite a demonstration to various US airlines in spring 1958 there were no orders; airlines preferred the cheaper, twin-engined Fairchild F.27. As a follow on to the Viscount, Vickers designed the larger Vanguard in the mid-1950s. In order to make way for its production at Weybridge, Hurn undertook production of Viscount 800s from the end of 1958, with the final 700 delivered in the spring of 1960. The improved and strengthened series 810 prototype first flew from Weybridge in December 1957, and the type followed the series 800 down the production line at Hurn. Those for All Nippon of Japan were unique at the time (1960) because they had flight entertainment in the form of TVs mounted in their luggage racks. Production rate of the Viscount had slowed down by the end of the 1950s. In order to keep the workforce fully employed, overhaul work was undertaken on Valiants and Varsities. The Valiant contract covered a three-year period commencing in June 1959.

The final Viscount order came in December 1961 for six for China (Peking) – the first communist China airliner order from Britain. Of the 444 Viscounts built, 279 appeared from the Hurn production line and were sold to forty countries. The final series 810 was delivered from Hurn to China in April 1964.

12

LOCAL AVIATION INDUSTRY – 2

DE HAVILLAND CHRISTCHURCH

In July 1951 Airspeed became fully merged into de Havilland Aircraft to become its Airspeed Division. This incorporated an enlarged design office with staff transferred from Hatfield. Delays with the Ambassador meant that the first for BEA was not ready to be handed over until August 1951, with the final one delivered in March 1953. In service, the airline referred to the airliner by its fleet name, *Elizabethan*. Production of Vampire Trainers was also undertaken for a number of overseas air forces, including New Zealand, South Africa and Sweden. However, the company was not pleased to be informed by Christchurch Council in February 1952 that they did not approve of jets flying from the airfield. They wanted it closed within ten years; ministerial intervention from London was necessary to smooth matters with the council members. By the end of 1952 production had also commenced on Venom night-fighters (an improved version of the Vampire) for the RAF, followed in spring 1953 by Sea Venom fighters for the Royal Navy and the Royal Australian Navy. At this time, 2,600 workers were employed by de Havilland. With an increasing amount of jet testing, the airfield was provided with a wider, 1,500-yard concrete runway during summer 1954. Vampire production ceased in March 1955 (242 were produced) and Sea Venoms in January 1956.

The factory space at Christchurch was only a part of that used by de Havilland around the country to cope with their large number of military orders; production was also undertaken at Chester and Hatfield. Even before the first Sea Venom had flown, the Navy had issued a requirement for its replacement. It chose the DH.110, which had already been built by de Havilland at Hatfield in anticipation of a possible RAF order. The Christchurch design office undertook a major redesign of the DH.110 to make it suitable for carrier operations, and a navalised prototype flew in May 1955. Being armed with Firestreak guided missiles, the new fighter did away with guns and proved to be more than twice as heavy as a Sea Venom. Early flights revealed few problems and the prototype was able to undertake deck-landing trials on HMS *Ark Royal* in the English Channel in April 1956. The new fighter received the named Sea Vixen, and the first production aircraft flew from Christchurch in March 1957. As with the Vampires and Sea Venoms, the majority of flying was undertaken from the flight test hangar at Hurn. This was not without incident. One of the early Sea Vixens had its main wheels fold up on landing in July 1957. The initial order was for seventy-eight of the all-weather fighter, and was soon increased by a further forty.

Following on from the Vampire, the de Havilland factory turned its attention during the mid-1950s to Venom and Sea Venom fighters for the RAF and Royal Navy. Seen here on a test flight early in 1954 is one of the first Venom NF.3s destined for the RAF.

Again, the factory was entrusted by de Havilland with the design and development of the DH.110 as a naval fighter, the new naval prototype flying in May 1955. Seen here on an early trials flight in 1957 is the first production aircraft, prior to the type being named Sea Vixen.

In 1960 de Havilland Aircraft became part of the Hawker Siddeley Group. They confirmed production would continue at Christchurch as the lease of the factory ran until December 1978. However, their Portsmouth factory was closed in August 1961, followed in November by major redundancies at Christchurch prior to full closure of the factory in July 1962. This was said to be necessary in order to redistribute work around the other former de Havilland sites in the country. Despite local protests, further production of the Sea Vixen was switched to Chester, with the last of one 118 built at Christchurch flying away in August 1962.

With the impending departure of de Havilland from Christchurch, there was a glimmer of hope early in 1962 that aircraft production might continue. Beagle Aircraft announced that they were interested in taking over the site for production of their Beagle B.206 executive twin aircraft. However, they soon pulled out, stating that it would cost too much to move into Christchurch and that the factory was too large for their requirements. So ended twenty years of aircraft production at Christchurch, with over 1,900 aircraft of all types having been built.

BRITISH AIRCRAFT CORPORATION

BAC came into existence when the Conservative Government insisted on a reduction in the numerous UK aircraft manufacturers of the late 1950s. In January 1959 Vickers-Armstrongs and English Electric received a contract to develop a new strike bomber for the RAF (TSR2), so the two companies were obvious choices for an amalgamation. Along with Bristol Aeroplane and Hunting Aircraft, the companies became part of the newly formed British Aircraft Corporation on 1 July 1960. Viscount production at Hurn was not affected, although it was not long before a new airliner was announced by BAC as its replacement. Vickers was producing the VC.10 airliner at Weybridge to meet BOAC's requirements, also proposing the smaller VC.11 for BEA. However, BAC decided to drop the VC.11 in March 1961 in favour of the H.107 project which it inherited from Hunting – soon to be enlarged as the BAC 111 – with Government launch-funding switched to the new airliner.

The One-Eleven 'bus stop jet' was officially launched in March 1961 followed in May by an order for ten from Freddie Laker's British United Airways at Gatwick. As well as being the design centre, Hurn undertook final assembly with major parts built at other BAC sites at Filton, Luton and Weybridge. As with the Viscount, the North American market was soon broken into with an initial order in October 1961 for six from Braniff Airways of Dallas. This was followed by a $40 million (£14 million) order for fifteen by American Airlines in July 1963. All this before the maiden flight! The prototype was completed by the middle of July 1963 and made its first flight on the evening of 20 August, piloted by Jock Bryce and Mike Lithgow. At the time, the production hangar still carried the name Vickers-Armstrongs (Aircraft) Ltd, which one would have thought would have been changed with the launch of a new BAC project. The Vickers name did not officially disappear until 31 December, and documents show that the initial One-Elevens were built by Vickers-Armstrongs (Aircraft)

Roll-out of the prototype BAC One-Eleven in July 1963, with the aircraft in the colours of the first customer, British United. It is definitely a low-key event compared with the present-day fanfares that accompany the appearance of a new airliner.

Ltd, not BAC. The workers had been waiting all day for the flight and were joined along the surrounding roads by many local residents (the author included). Most of the early test flying was undertaken from Wisley and it was from there that the prototype took off on a routine test flight on the morning of 22 October. Whilst undertaking stall tests over Wiltshire it entered a flat spin, from which the test crew were unable to recover. It crashed at Chicklade with the loss of all six crew, including Mike Lithgow. The news of the crash was initially met with disbelief by the workers at Hurn, and a sense of gloom fell over them. The reason for the crash was soon understood, which allowed the necessary modifications to be under way before the flight of the second aircraft in December. Unfortunately, there were two further major accidents in the flight test programme during 1964, which delayed the new airliner receiving its Certificate of Airworthiness.

AIRWORK

Although not involved in aircraft production, Airwork was a well-known name in the aviation world, having been formed at Heston in 1928. It became one of the major companies to be based at Bournemouth. At the end of 1951 it announced the formation of a civilian-operated Fleet Requirements Unit (FRU) on behalf of the Royal Navy, advertising positions for former service aircrew. The unit operated second-line naval aircraft to act as 'targets' over the English Channel for naval gunners on radar direction exercises and ship's gun alignment sorties. A similar unit was already operated by Airwork at St David's, South Wales; the new one at Bournemouth replaced a Naval manned FRU at Ford in Sussex. The 'Airwork Fleet Requirement Unit (Hurn)' occupied two hangars at the western end of the airport by the following June, and soon received its first aircraft in the shape of DH Sea Mosquitoes. These were only a temporary measure as the first of about twenty DH Sea Hornets arrived in spring 1953. This was just in time as two of the Sea Mosquitoes had been written off in landing accidents during the spring.

An additional contract obtained by Airwork in spring 1953 was to operate RAF Oxfords in conjunction with the radar station at nearby RAF Sopley. The aircraft again acted as targets, but this time for the trainee radar operators. Five aircraft were involved and operated three-hour training sorties in the morning and afternoon, plus occasional night sorties. The Oxfords were taken out of service in 1955, reputedly to be replaced by Ansons the following year.

Hawker Sea Fury fighters arrived for the FRU in 1955, again just in time as the Sea Hornets were found to have decomposition in their wooden airframes and were hastily grounded in October. A few Supermarine Attacker jets also arrived to make up numbers. A slight change of name occurred in January 1957, when Airwork Services was formed to distinguish itself from the airline business of Airwork. Although jets, the Attackers were not liked by the FRU pilots. One reason was that they only had an hour's endurance, compared with the piston-engined Sea Fury's three hours. Another was that the Sea Furies were almost as fast as the Attackers. So plans to replace the Sea Furies with more Attackers were changed to introduce the Hawker Sea Hawk jet, plus further Sea Furies. In due course the Sea Hawks proved ideal for FRU duties, as they were well liked by both pilots and ground crew. After a short time they received a special black colour scheme as an aid to visual identification by the warship crews. So that the naval gunners could have something to fire at, the first of twelve Fairey Fireflies arrived in February 1957. These towed a sleeve target attached by a wire to a winch on the aircraft's wing, which enabled the target to be towed a long way behind during live firing exercises. It was then winched back towards the aircraft before being dropped over the airport prior to the aircraft landing. The ground crews could then count the number of hits.

In June 1957 the first of fourteen Boulton Paul Balliols arrived at Airworks instead of the anticipated Ansons. These were for operations in conjunction with trainee trackers and plotters at RAF Sopley, where the School of Fighter Control had arrived from RAF Bolt Head in South Devon. As with the Oxfords, sorties were flown early morning and early afternoon with the aircraft normally operating in pairs. Balliol operations by Airwork Services continued until the spring of 1960 when, as the only Balliols still flying, they were withdrawn from service.

The Airwork Fleet Requirement Unit operated a variety of former Royal Navy fighters. The Sea Fury first arrived in 1955 and over twenty were used before they were withdrawn in 1962. By this time the elderly fighters were beginning to show their age.

The pilots of the Fleet Requirement Unit were fond of the Sea Hawks that were in use between 1957 and 1968. During this time about thirty aircraft passed through the unit. Their overall black colour scheme was unique to the FRU aircraft.

The Fireflys did not remain long in service as target tugs as they were replaced in May 1958 by Armstrong Whitworth Meteor TT.20s. The FRU was the first unit to receive this new mark of Meteor. As before, the target was controlled by a wind-driven winch above the wing with the used target being released over the airfield prior to landing. For controllers to distinguish between the aircraft types they used individual call signs, Sea Furies being 'Broadway', the Sea Hawks 'Radium' and the new Meteors 'Acorn'. Other call signs used at the time included 'Netball' and the not too glamorous 'Dribble'. The last of the Sea Furies were taken out of service in spring 1962, with a number of them later being preserved.

AIRWORK SERVICES HEADQUARTERS

During its existence, Airwork had undertaken aircraft maintenance and overhaul at various sites around the country. With the completion of a number of military contracts in the 1950s, this work diminished. The period also saw the closure of many airfields used by the company. So in summer 1959, Airwork Services moved their Headquarters Base and Overhaul Facility to Bournemouth. This enabled them to close down their operations at Langley (headquarters), Lasham (engineering) and Blackbushe (overhaul and sales). A new office block was erected at the western end of the airport the following spring, with the aircraft housed in a hangar recently vacated by de Havilland. Some aircraft flew in but others, including two Marathons and an Oxford, arrived by road.

A hive of activity in the Airwork Services civil maintenance hangar. Seen undergoing overhaul in this summer 1960 view are three Dakotas, a Cessna 310, Dove, Marathon and Viking. Major aircraft overhauls continued until the early 1990s.

With various airline amalgamations at the time, both Airwork and Airwork Services became part of the British United Group in June 1960. Overhaul work brought in a number of airliners. The years 1960–61 saw Sudan Airways Doves and Dakotas as well as various Skymasters and Vikings. Military types included DHC Chipmunks and Hiller UH-12s from the Army Air Corps at Middle Wallop. Airwork also undertook the delivery flights of Fairey Gannets to Indonesia, as well as handling the new range of Cessna light aircraft as part of their newly awarded UK Cessna Agency.

The Airwork FRU's Sea Hawks were now becoming dated and were replaced by Supermarine Scimitars, with the first arriving in December 1965. However, it was some time before further aircraft were received as pilot training had to be undertaken by the Royal Navy at Lossiemouth. The Scimitar was a large and complex fighter which required more attention by the ground crews and extra concentration by the pilots. The Scimitar did not prove well suited to the job and so in March 1969 the first of ten Hawker Hunter GA.11s arrived; this fighter was well received by all the crews. The ageing Meteor target tugs were replaced around the same time with English Electric Canberra TT.18s, and again, the FRU was the first unit to receive this new version. Operations with the Hunters and Canberras continued until October 1972 when the Airwork Services FRU merged with the Air Direction Unit at Yeovilton to form the Fleet Requirements and Air Direction Unit (FRADU). The Hunters departed in two waves on 20 October, with the final Canberras departing on 28 October. Although a loss to the airport, their departure did not disappoint many of the local residents who had suffered from their noise levels.

13

AIRLINE SERVICES EXPAND

JERSEY AIRLINES AND INDEPENDENT AIR TRAVEL

The mid-1950s saw a gradual increase in airline services at Bournemouth. With a fleet of seven Dragon Rapides, Jersey Airlines introduced modern fifteen-seat DH Herons during summer 1954. Their publicity and timetables mentioned that Herons were also used by the Queen's Flight. The Herons allowed the introduction of air hostesses, which had not been possible on the Dragon Rapides. Fares on their Duchess Service to Jersey were available from £5 12s return and at peak summer times the airline was flying one hundred passengers a day through Bournemouth. The airline found that by removing the small toilet they were able to add two further seats. Various other airlines called at Bournemouth to clear customs en route to the Channel Islands. These included Dakotas of BKS from Newcastle, Derby Airways from Burnaston and Starways from Liverpool. At the time, unlike Bournemouth, not every airport in the country had customs facilities – hence the extra visitors.

A new name was Independent Air Travel which expanded from being a London travel agency into the airline business at the beginning of 1955. The managing director was Capt. Marian Kozubski, along with two Bournemouth businessmen. Initially operating two Doves, the mayors of Bournemouth and Christchurch were present in April to officially name the first one *Hurn*. Cross-Channel charters were undertaken with more ambitious ones to Majorca planned. New directors early in 1956 brought a change of direction for the airline, seeing the acquisition of a number of Vikings. Capt. Kozubski, being a 'hands-on' managing director, frequently flew the Vikings which operated holiday charters from Blackbushe and Bournemouth. The summer of 1957 saw the first of three Skymasters arrive which enabled longer-range flights to be undertaken. One made headlines when it caused a diplomatic incident following being forced down by Mig fighters whilst overflying Albania on 31 December 1957. After negotiations the Skymaster was released to return home four days later. Independent also operated a Bristol Freighter on behalf of a French race-horse owner to fly his horses between meetings. Whilst setting off on a freight flight from London Airport in the early hours of 2 September 1958, one of the Vikings crashed at Southall following an engine failure. The crew thought they were in the vicinity of Blackbushe whereas in fact they were over London Airport. The resulting Court of Inquiry in March 1959 showed that the crew were tired and lost in fog with the

Viking overloaded. Capt. Kozubski stood down as director straight away but the airline was unable to continue full operations, struggling on until the autumn of 1959.

Capt Kozubski had achieved some notoriety in aviation circles, having served with Bomber Command during the war, for which he was awarded the Polish VC. He then served in the Berlin Air Lift, later joining William Dempster Airlines as chief pilot. After Independent, he went on to form Falcon Airways, again frequently flying their aircraft but falling foul of the law in March 1961. Returning from the West Indies he deviated from the flight plan. It was then discovered that the flight had been operated with insufficient rafts, resulting in a fine for Capt Kozubski at Bournemouth Court in September 1961.

COMETS AND BRITANNIAS

BOAC retained their wartime association with Bournemouth throughout the 1950s. At the beginning of the decade they undertook crew training with Hermes and Argonauts, followed by Comet 1 jets in 1952. With the grounding of these original Comets in 1954 the airline was forced to use propeller airliners once again, Constellations, Stratocruisers and new DC-7Cs all appearing. Sixty former Comet crews were retrained on Constellations during the summer and autumn of 1954, appropriately using an aircraft named *Bournemouth*. January 1956 saw the arrival of the first of the airlines Bristol Britannia turbo-props, with two based at Bournemouth for crew training. They proved to be much quieter than the earlier propeller airliners, earning the nickname *The Whispering Giant*. Whilst waiting on the end of the runway on the evening of 20 April 1958, one of the Britannias was instructed to swiftly take-off. Unknown to the crew, a Proctor had declared a 'Mayday' following engine problems. Unfortunately, the Proctor just failed to make the end of the runway, ending up on its nose in the marshy ground between Matchams Lane and the airport. The first Comet 4s appeared in August 1958 but, as with the Comet 1s in 1952, they were not popular with the local residents due to their noise. Training was switched elsewhere, resulting in less frequent appearances at Bournemouth. BOAC finally broke its ties with the airport in April 1959 with the closure of the Britannia Training Unit.

Other major airlines such as Pan American and Qantas used Bournemouth for training in between their flights to and from London. In the early 1950s there would be a few hours, if not a day, before the return flight home. So this spare time was taken up with training flights to possible diversion airports in England. Bournemouth was also used for training by Bristol Aircraft at Filton, with Freighters appearing in the late 1940s and early 1950s. These were followed by Britannias from the late 1950s, which included those of Cubana and El Al.

A fatal crash befell one of BOAC's Britannias on Christmas Eve 1958 whilst flying in fog in the area. On a flight out of London, not Bournemouth, the crew were flying on instruments when the altimeter was misread by 10,000ft. Whilst making an approach to Bournemouth, it flew too low and crashed into the grounds of Sopley Park at midday, killing nine of the twelve on board. It had seen less than one year's service with the airline.

From 1956 two Britannias were based at Bournemouth with the BOAC Britannia Training Unit. The training of crews at London with flight simulators was still some way off. Note the runway marker boards for establishing the runway visual distance during periods of fog.

DIVERSIONS

Bournemouth remained a major diversion airfield for London throughout the 1950s, at which time the capital and surroundings had to contend with horrendous smogs. Douglas DC-6/7s, Stratocruisers and Super Constellations of the world's major airlines were to be seen at these times – Air India, BOAC, El Al, KLM, Pan American, Qantas, Sabena, Swissair, TWA, Trans-Canada. The last large diversion of major international airlines was in October 1961. By this time many of the airlines had acquired Boeing 707 jets which could not be handled at Bournemouth, having to go to the likes of Manchester or Prestwick.

'Chappy' Chapman was one of Bournemouth's controllers at the time:

I recall being asked by London Control if Bournemouth could handle a large number of diversions. I replied that there would be no problem as long as the airliners arrived at regular intervals. This they did so safely and the reason for my request became obvious when it was found I was the only one on duty in the tower! Staff had to be rushed it to deal with the passengers still stranded in their aircraft. There were often VIP's amongst the passengers – one occasion seeing the Shah of Persia. Unable to travel on to London by road because of the fog he was booked in to the town's Royal Bath Hotel. The Shah insisted on being driven from the aircraft direct to the Hotel but regulations prevented a taxi driving out onto the apron. So I was volunteered with my old Ford which was turned away by the Hotel doorman who was expecting a VIP who surely wouldn't travel by Ford!

AIRPORT OF THE SOUTH

Following the 1954 Sea Venom crash, traffic controls were introduced at the end of the runways. Initially this was one of the Ministry policemen stopping the Parley Lane traffic, but in due course traffic signals were installed. Wartime wooden huts were still in use as Bournemouth's terminal. These were supplemented in 1956 by some prefabricated building brought down from Blackbushe where a new terminal had been built by the Ministry (only for them to close the airport in 1960!). Group Capt. Cox retired as airport commandant in July 1957 and was replaced by Mr E.D. Cooper. Then Mr F.W. Hilton was appointed by the Ministry as commandant in June 1960, having previously been at Blackbushe.

During winter of 1956/57 the grass runway at Eastleigh became rutted and waterlogged, forcing airlines to use Bournemouth for a while. These included services by BEA Dakotas, Cambrian Herons and Silver City Superfreighters. There were similar problems the following winter. Jersey Airlines had a fleet of seven Herons, also purchasing, rather belatedly, a further Dragon Rapide in February 1958. Mainly used on inter-Island services, it visited Bournemouth during 1961, retaining its connection by being preserved at the Aviation Museum forty years later. Increasing passenger numbers led Jersey to look for new aircraft, having already received a demonstration of the original Handley Page Herald in October 1956. From Bournemouth it visited both Alderney and Guernsey and, to this day, remains the largest aircraft to land on Alderney's short grass runway. The Herald was re-engined with Dart turbo-props, and in this new form was demonstrated to Jersey again in April 1958. Whilst making a decision they introduced Dakotas (referred to by the airline as Dakmasters) in May 1959, so increasing seating from fifteen to thirty-two. Jersey Airlines obtained a contract from the UK Atomic Energy Authority to fly personnel between Winfrith and Harwell. So the Heron or Dakota on the Manchester service would pick them up at Bournemouth and drop them off at RAF Abingdon (no alighting for normal passengers). The airline finally ordered six Dart Heralds in September 1960 with the first delivered in May 1961. The aircraft were soon brought into service, their first route being Jersey–Bournemouth. The first passenger-carrying flight was on 16 May – a Dakota acting as back-up – with the first official service operated three days later. The new aircraft were soon showing impressive passenger load factors of 85 per cent.

Above: Ground and maintenance staff had to be brought down by road from London during diversions as there were no local staff. Here, BOAC's engineering crews happily pose under the nose of an Argonaut in the autumn of 1954.

Right: Slightly behind the times. By 1960 the Ministry of Aviation had still not caught up with the fact that the airport should be Bournemouth-Hurn Airport. To the present day, the airport is still frequently referred to as Hurn by those who used to work there.

Opposite: During times of diversion it was often necessary to undertake maintenance in the open. Here the engine of a BOAC Hermes has been giving problems. Other airliners parked by the terminal can be seen under the nose of the Argonaut.

In the spring of 1959 the Ministry announced expansion plans for Bournemouth, favouring it over Eastleigh for future development. The plans for the 'Airport of the South' included a new £250,000 terminal on the north-east side, increased control tower facilities, a new fire station and even talk of a rail link to the main London–Bournemouth line. The Ministry explained that this would make Bournemouth 'a very important provincial airport', designed to handle sixteen flights and 400 passengers an hour at peak times. The Ministry also said that it would relinquish control of Eastleigh in March 1961, at which time it was expected to close.

SILVER CITY

With the threatened closure of Eastleigh, Silver City moved their car ferry operations to Bournemouth in March 1959. A car terminal was added to cope with the additional business which saw services to Cherbourg, Deauville and the Channel Islands. Silver City estimated that it would be operating thirty-six return services a day and anticipating a 50 per cent increase in business. Their Superfreighters carried three cars plus their passengers, with the cars driven up ramps into the aircraft nose through two large doors. Silver City's boast was they could carry anything from Bentleys to bicycles, the latter for 5s, the former slightly more! If there was not a full load of cars for the return flight the empty space would be filled with cheese, although this delayed unloading of the cars on return to Bournemouth. Summer 1960 saw three Superfreighters based at Bournemouth but during the winter this was reduced to one aircraft which flew two flights daily.

Cambrian operated their Cardiff/Bristol to Paris service through Bournemouth as from March with Dakotas, although BEA continued to use Eastleigh for the time being.

PALMAIR

Local travel firm Bath Travel Service took over the running of two holiday flights to Majorca in October 1958. The original London travel operator had backed out but Bath's soon found enough people to fill the flights. Operated by Independent Vikings, the fifteen-day fully inclusive holiday cost 45gns. Encouraged by this local enthusiasm, two similar flights were undertaken by BEA Viscounts in October 1959 under the now familiar *Palmair Holidays* name, the flights being repeated in 1960. Since then Bath Travel have not looked back with their range of holiday flights.

GOVERNMENT SELL-OFF

Bournemouth suffered a setback in summer 1960 when the Ministry of Aviation announced that the new terminal had been abandoned on financial grounds. Then a Government White Paper the following year announced that the airport was

Many local residents will recall the Bristol Superfreighters of Silver City droning backwards and forwards across the Channel during the 1960s. Before the days of drive-on/drive-off cross-Channel car ferries, their flights greatly boosted traffic at the airport.

being put up for sale. This did not appear to cause any immediate concern as there were still plenty of services with more expected when Eastleigh closed. As it turned out, Eastleigh did not close but was sold by the Ministry into private hands in May 1961, ostensibly for property development. However, the uncertainty over its future had resulted in the airlines moving to Bournemouth en masse in March 1961. BEA took the opportunity to replace their faithful Dakotas with Viscounts on their services to Jersey. During the summer of 1961 the Ministry contacted Bournemouth Corporation and Hampshire County Council to see if they were interested in taking over the airport. The Ministry had assumed that the airport was within the Borough of Bournemouth, whereas it was, at the time, within Ringwood & Fordingbridge RDC. Although passenger numbers were about to double, a problem relating to the sale was that the Ministry were unable to provide any airport accounting or operating figures.

AIRLINE SERVICES

Air Safaris was a Gatwick-based airline which operated holiday flights during 1960, also setting up overhaul facilities for its fleet at Bournemouth. The directors introduced scheduled services during 1961, the majority operating from Bournemouth. A twice-weekly service to Ostend and Amsterdam commenced in April, with the usual civic guests being carried on the inaugural flight. This was soon followed by Dublin and Belfast, with Newcastle–Birmingham–Bournemouth–Exeter operating from June. Flights were operated by Viking with fares being £14 6s to Amsterdam, £13 to Dublin and £12 4s to Newcastle. Wishing to introduce newer aircraft, a demonstration of a Herald took place during April but no order was placed. The airline also had a number of Hermes which were used on holiday flights out of Gatwick. Scheduled services from Bournemouth to Edinburgh and Glasgow via Birmingham were planned for September, but rapid expansion resulted in financial difficulties related to their holiday flights. The Newcastle service finished at the beginning of September although the airline began advertised fishing holidays to Ireland at the end of October. However, the relevant

BEA used Viscounts on their services from the Channel Islands. Other airlines to use this classic British airliner on services into Bournemouth were British Midland, British United, Cambrian, Channel and Dan-Air.

Dublin service was withdrawn on 27 October with all flying ceasing four days later. The Hermes and Vikings were then parked on the north side of the airport, most ending their days as scrap – £360 for a Hermes and £130-£325 for a Viking.

British United was a major new airline formed in July 1960 out of the merger of a number of well-known airline names – Hunting Clan, Airwork, and Transair. The new group then took over a number of other airlines, including Silver City in January 1962, and Jersey Airlines in May. There were no immediate changes locally, although in due course British United titles appeared on the Superfreighters, Dakotas and Heralds. During the summer Silver City were operating up to twenty-three return trips to Cherbourg.

A new local airline, Bournair, was formed by flying club members in 1962 with a Dragon Rapide. Really an extension of their air-charter operations, a short-lived service was operated during June to Sandown at a fare of 25s single. Later, Bournair sought support from local businesses for a service to London, but it never saw the light of day.

For the benefit of the increasing passenger numbers, a further extension to the terminal building was brought into use for the 1962 summer services. The temporary structure remained for twenty years. However, in the autumn the Ministry announced that it was withdrawing twenty-four-hour watch cover at the airport. They reduced opening hours to 7 a.m. to 10 p.m., saying that the airport was no longer required for bad weather diversions from London. At the time there was still not any real concern amongst the airlines.

Despite the reduced hours there was increasing holiday-charters business from Bournemouth during the early 1960s. Ambassadors operated by Dan-Air flew to Basle (£35 8s) as well as Palmair flights to Majorca (47gns). They also flew pilgrim charters to Tarbes during the spring of 1963. For 1965, Bath Travel went bang up to date with the introduction of British United One-Eleven jets on its fortnightly Majorca holiday flights from April; the type had only just entered airline service. The directors felt justly proud to use a new local product on the service which now became known as *Palmair Express*. Only seventy-four passengers were carried instead of the maximum of ninety-four. This was so that the jet could take off with a full fuel load from Bournemouth's relatively short runway. Whilst away on holiday, it was possible to park cars with Chubb's Garage at the airport for 15s a week.

British United were operating to the Channel Islands four times daily (£3 7s single) with Viscounts introduced in 1965 to supplement the Heralds. However, their Dakotas continued to be seen, along with Heralds, on the Dublin/Belfast, Coventry, Manchester and Glasgow (£6 13s) routes. Superfreighter were operating less frequently than before, down to eight flights daily to Cherbourg and twice daily to the Channel Islands. Here there was less demand due to competition from the Sealink ferry operating out of Weymouth. A couple of Herons were retained for use on Alderney's short grass runway. Cambrian replaced their Dakotas with Viscounts in the spring of 1965 which meant that BEA, British United and Cambrian were now all operating Viscounts through Bournemouth.

MILITARY TRAINING

As well as airlines, the RAF would undertake crew training at Bournemouth. Varsities from Thorney Island were seen in the late 1950s – there were six one morning in April 1959. Britannias and Comet 2s then began to appear in the early 1960s from their base at Lyneham. On a smaller scale RAF Ansons and Chipmunks visited to provide air experience flights to local Air Cadets. The aircraft came from their bases at Old Sarum and Hamble. The airport was also used by aircraft from A&AEE at Boscombe Down clearing customs, such as their Valetta and Bristol Freighter. There would be a selection of Dakotas/C-47s from various countries, Canada, Germany, Norway and USA included.

Some visitors had military connection from an earlier time. Sir Douglas Bader of Fighter Command fame now flew for Shell Aviation, and would arrive frequently in their Miles Gemini to clear customs. By now he was accustomed to climbing in and out of aircraft with his tin legs. The company upgraded to a Beech Travel Air in the early 1960s. Neville Duke had also been a wartime pilot, receiving many decorations; he is probably best remembered by the public for winning the world air-speed record in a Hawker Hunter in 1953. He later became pilot for the Dowty Group flying their executive Dove and, again, would land at Bournemouth to clear customs.

Bournemouth was also used from the mid-1950s by Air Service Training of Hamble to train airline pilots using a fleet of Chipmunks and Oxfords. A reorganisation saw it become the College of Air Training early in 1962, introducing a new fleet of Piper Apaches, which were in turn replaced by Beech Barons in spring 1968. Other similar organisations at the time included Airways Training from Gatwick and CSE Aviation of Oxford, usually operating Piper Twin Comanches for commercial pilot training.

JERSEY AIR RALLY

This was an important event in the Channel Islands' social calendar, taking place during the first weekend in May. Many light aircraft would call at Bournemouth to refuel and clear customs prior to crossing the Channel. In the 1960s and 1970s these would include a number of elderly aircraft such as Austers, Messengers and Tiger Moths. So it was customary for the RAF to provide a safety escort in the shape of an Anson or Devon. Aircraft would still call in the early 1990s but the more modern aircraft had sufficient range to cut out Bournemouth and there was no longer the need to clear customs. However, the 1989 Rally did see four Tiger Moths pass through.

MINISTRY APATHY

Despite the apparent buoyant services at Bournemouth, problems were raising their heads again in the early 1960s. Nat Somers, the new owner of the now Southampton Airport, managed to retain passenger services and construct a concrete runway. He advised the airlines that it would be ready by summer 1965. Talks between the Ministry and Bournemouth Corporation failed to progress and the post of airport commandant was done away with in May 1965. With no apparent interest in its future, the Ministry seemed to be happy to let the airport run down, saying it would close if agreement was not reached on its future ownership. With this uncertainty it was not surprising that the airlines agreed with Southampton's new owner request to return there as from April 1966, apparently leaving Bournemouth with little future as an airport.

CHRISTCHURCH CLOSURE

Mention needs to be made of Bournemouth's former airport at Christchurch where the Aero Club was thriving, along with the Air Cadets gliding school. The gliders continued to provide elementary flying for the cadets who also had the use of the fuselage of a worn-out Tiger Moth to sit in.

Ron Hayter was the commanding officer of the gliding school:

> Having been a wartime ATA pilot, I arrived at Christchurch as an instructor and remained post war, also giving instruction on powered aircraft with the Aero Club. I acquired an old Tiger Moth in 1959 and with the help of some of the senior cadets restored it to an airworthy condition. I was pleased to get a personalised registration for the Tiger which flew again in 1961, often with a cadet as passenger.

By the early 1960s the Aero Club moved on from Austers and Tiger Moths to newer Piper Tri-Pacers. Advanced training was undertaken on Oxfords with pleasure flights and charters using Dragon Rapides. (The author had his first pleasure flight round the

Contact! A classic scene which could have been taken anywhere over a forty-year period. In fact, this is a summer 1959 view at Christchurch at the time when the Tiger Moth was coming to the end of its training days with the Aero Club.

The year 1961 and the final days of the Aero Club. There are still Austers and Tiger Moths, but a Tri-Pacer has arrived for modern training. In the top view the former Airspeed factory can be seen in the background, whilst the wooden club house still just stands in the lower view.

bay in one of these during August 1959 for 12s 6d.) Flying rates were £6ph in an Oxford and £7ph in a Tri-Pacer. The airfield was also used by RAF pilots on weekend leave in the area, parking up the likes of Chipmunks and Provosts for the weekend. However, the future of the airfield had been under threat for some while and the departure of de Havilland in 1962 meant that time was running out. The Aero Club had unsuccessfully used Bournemouth during the summer of 1960 and eventually closed in the autumn of 1963. The gliding school moved to Old Sarum in July 1963 and the remaining private aircraft moved away, some to Bournemouth and others to a farm strip at New Milton. Refuelling facilities were withdrawn in 1965, although one or two aircraft still crept into the airfield during the late 1960s.

As with many former airfields, Christchurch was developed into an industrial estate and for housing. Much of the development was undertaken by Barretts which brought visits of their Agusta 109 helicopter in the early 1980s. Memories of former times are to be found in the road names: de Havilland Way, The Runway, Comet Close and so on. A more fitting memorial arrived in December 1984 in the shape of a Sea Vixen which was towed by road from Bournemouth Airport on a quiet Sunday morning. It was then mounted on a plinth adjacent to the main road and in front of the former de Havilland building. After fifteen years on display the elements, and vandals, took their toll on the fighter, so in June 2000 it departed by road to the Tangmere Aviation Museum. February 1998 saw a plaque unveiled to commemorate the airfield, with the event being overflown by a Venom and two Vampires. June 2002 saw the erection of a memorial at Purewell Cross War Memorial dedicated to all those killed in operations from Christchurch Airfield.

14

GLOOM OF THE 1960S, THEN NEW LEADERSHIP

HURN TO DIE

31 March 1966 was a black day in the diary of Bournemouth Airport, with the local *Echo* newspaper's headline reporting, 'Hurn Airport starts to die'. It was the last day of major services by the airlines before returning to Southampton where the future was now looking very bright. Token services remaining at Bournemouth were British United Viscounts to Jersey on Saturdays and Sundays, and Cambrian's Viscount to Paris on Sundays. The Palmair holiday flights also remained, being operated by British United One-Elevens during the summer and BEA Vanguards in the winter, plus various charters to France and Rotterdam. Not surprisingly, passenger figures were to plummet, summer 1965 seeing: 195,000, 1966 only 45,000, and 20,600 in 1967! Southampton saw the reverse: 60,000 for the summer of 1965 and 250,000 for 1966. The Ministry had Bournemouth for sale at £1 million but the local authority was only interested at a figure nearer £300,000. (At the end of 1963 Derby Council bought RAF Castle Donnington site for £37,500 – look at Nottingham East Midlands now!) Negotiations were now under way with a consortium of Bournemouth Corporation, Hampshire County Council and Dorset County Council. Even though the airport was in Hampshire, Dorset realised its commercial importance in connection with its own economic development. (The airport 'moved' to the Borough of Christchurch and the County of Dorset with the county boundary changes of April 1974.) Then, in July 1966, the Ministry announced that, as from November, opening hours would be reduced to 9 a.m. to 5 p.m. on weekdays. But it would be closed altogether at weekends (the only days it had scheduled services) due to operating losses – there being insufficient movements. As a result, both British United and Cambrian were forced to pull out. So Bournemouth had no scheduled services for the first time in fourteen years. However, the Sunday ban was broken by a BEA Comet in September 1967. Shortly after take-off from Heathrow, an engine fire warning light showed and the captain decided to land as quickly as possible. This meant using Bournemouth where the Comet landed safely, the warning being a false alarm. The Ministry's comments regarding this 'violation' are not recorded.

RESUSCITATION

In order to promote the airport the Hurn Airport Development Association was formed in April 1967, with Sir Alan Cobham as its president. He reminded members that in the early 1930s, when asked for the best site for Bournemouth Municipal Aerodrome, he concluded that Hurn was a natural site. The association promoted the airport's potential as a regional airport, whether in council hands or private ownership. It pointed out that Portsmouth only had a grass runway and Southampton, situated within a residential area, had a torturous road system and difficult car parking. But Bournemouth had none of these problems. (How different today.) Sir Alan urged 'a quick purchase in order to get into business'. The district valuer placed a figure of £750,000 for the airport, less than the £1 million being sought by the Board of Trade (BoT) who had taken over from the Ministry. Bournemouth were still interested, but with losses estimated at £70,000 p.a. Hampshire pulled out of the negotiations at the eleventh hour in May 1967. Fearing a lost sale, the BoT agreed on the £750,000 figure. It would provide Air Traffic Control facilities free of charge for seven years but pointed out that if the airport failed within a twenty-one-year period, it would revert back to their ownership. On this basis, Bournemouth and Dorset indicated that they were happy to proceed, with agreement finally reached by all parties in July. However, many months were to pass before completion was made with the aid of a loan from Bournemouth Corporation. Now to get some scheduled services back.

NEW SERVICES

In spite of the airport's problems, local travel firm Kentways announced early in 1967 a new fortnightly holiday flight to Majorca. Flights commencing at the beginning of April initially operated by Douglas DC-7s of Spanish airline Trans Europa. The logo 'Kentways to Majorca' soon became well known around the area, whilst other holiday flights were organised by Swift Travel Services. Palmair continued with their fortnightly flights to Majorca, still operated by British United One-Elevens.

In January 1967 both Dan-Air and Channel Airways made application to operate a number of new routes, both including Bournemouth to the Channel Islands. Dan-Air was planning a number of services to link the north and south of the country but in the spring withdrew their plans for the time being. Channel were thinking along similar lines, talking of a 'bus stop' service from Aberdeen–Southend. Intended to be operated by One-Eleven bus-stop jets, there would be a link to Bournemouth from East Midlands. Channel's request to operate at weekends was turned down by the BoT as there was still not enough business to warrant re-opening at weekends. The basic application was approved, enabling Channel to introduce a Southend–Bournemouth–Channel Islands service on 12 June. It was operated twice daily by Hawker Siddeley 748 turbo-props at a fare of £3 18s single. The service was extended northwards to the East Midlands in November, with Channel announcing that HS Trident jets would be used the following summer. In spring 1968 Channel advertised that the Jersey route would be operated by

One-Eleven, taking only twenty minutes with up to twenty services a week. This was objected to by British United (who had moved to Eastleigh), resulting in Channel being restricted to ten services a week operated by Viscount or HS.748.

Passenger figures showed an increase at Bournemouth, from 20,653 in 1967 to 37,959 in 1968. Another set of figures showed that although Bournemouth was an airport, actual airliner movements comprised the least! June 1968 showed ninety-eight commercial airliners, 554 BAC test and training flights, 820 club aircraft, 472 private and business, 252 Board of Trade and 441 military (mainly Airwork FRU).

On the holiday flight front, Palmair increased their number of services in 1968. The government's restriction of the time on foreign currency spending money did not have much effect at Bournemouth. One flight in May 1968 was not operated by the usual One-Eleven but a much larger Vickers VC.10. On the return flight the captain announced that he was lined up for approach to Bournemouth at a time when the passengers were noting Lands End passing beneath them, good weather enabling the captain to make a long approach. In March 1968 Kentways switched to Convair Coronado jets of Spantax. The large jets, similar to Boeing 707s, looked most impressive, with smoke-like exhaust coming from their engines on take-off seemingly indicating power.

On one early occasion the Coronado was piloted by the airline's owner. Prior to take-off he examined his airport manual relating to Bournemouth and informed the control staff that he intended to take-off on the shorter runway. They queried this, but he confirmed he was going to take-off to the north. As feared, the Coronado was still on the ground at the end of the runway but managed to climb into the air after using a short section of the overrun area. When questioned on his next visit, the owner explained that when he examined the manual, he assumed that runway lengths were quoted in metres, not in feet. This meant that he had to take-off in a third of the anticipated distance. He swiftly learnt a lesson about English airports and manuals!

BOURNEMOUTH'S AIRPORT

If March 1966 was a black time for the airport then 1 April 1969 was to be a red-letter day. It was the date when airport operations were taken over by the two local councils from the BoT. The event was marked by flights to Jersey in Channel Airways Viscount and Trident for 170 VIPs and guests. The official handover took place on 2 April when William Rogers from the BoT presented the necessary documents to the chairman of the new Airport Management Committee (and Mayor of Bournemouth) Alderman Michael Green. Guests at the event included Sir Alan Cobham who was pleased to see that at long last Bournemouth had its own airport. The purchase price was £757,500 5s, mainly funded by a loan from Bournemouth Corporation, which it was anticipated would be repaid within a fairly short time. Initial running costs were funded 50/50 by the councils, with an anticipated profit being made within five or six years. Finances did not work out as planned with continued losses meaning no income for the councils plus an increase in the loan debt.

Harry Longhurst was appointed airport director at a salary of £3,000 p.a., having previously been at Leeds Airport. He explained that he caught the flying bug from Cobham's Flying Circus as a youngster in Swansea, where he received his first flight in an Avro 504. So the connection with Cobham remained, with Sir Alan welcoming him to the area. Operating hours were extended to ninety-six per week, resulting in increased business. The hard standing area in front of the terminal was extended during the winter and the year's end saw a change of name to Bournemouth-Hurn Airport, together with a new logo. The new director confirmed that he was happy with the additional opening hours, considering that full twenty-four-hour operations would not be cost-effective. Even before taking up his new post he faced complaints from local residents' associations, most recently over noise from One-Eleven crew training. He confirmed that the airport intended, 'to give priority to the problem of aircraft noise', adding that a runway extension would be needed for the airport to reach its full potential. The problem for the director was that the local residents now had someone they could direct their complaints at.

Pleasure flights at £1 were introduced from the summer of 1969 by Cannon Aviation, from the viewing enclosure in front of the terminal, initially operating a Piper Cherokee.

SERVICES RETURN

The spring of 1969 saw the first visits by Dakotas and Skyvans of Exeter-based South West Aviation which were used on Channel Islands freight and flower flights. This business soon increased and was to become an important part of the airport's traffic over the following years. Then, on 31 May, BUIA commenced daily summertime services from Jersey operated by Heralds, in addition to those flown from Southampton, with their Dakotas being used on freight work. Channel proposed a thrice-weekly service to Paris Le Bourget with One-Elevens or Viscounts, but it was never operated. They applied again to use One-Elevens on the Jersey route, but once more this was turned down. As it turned out, traffic fell off during the winter and the end of the year found that Herons were sufficient for the Channel Islands traffic. Viscounts returned in spring 1970. Bath Travel introduced flights to Tenerife in October 1969 with BUA One-Eleven 500s. Again, the length of Bournemouth's runway meant that they could only take off with ninety-four passengers out of 109 seats and needed a fuel stop in Portugal en route. It was the same problem for Swift Travel Services, so Dan-Air Comets were introduced for their new service to Faro in September 1971. Football traffic saw a Norwegian team from Trondheim fly into Bournemouth in September 1969 for a match at Southampton. The following month the Southampton team flew out to Oporto by BEA Comet. For some reason, the teams were unable to use Eastleigh. Similarly, in November a BoBMF Spitfire used Bournemouth for a Remembrance Day fly-past over Southampton, Bournemouth Airport having waived its landing fees (of £3 12s!). The passenger terminal was expanded for the benefit of the Customs Office and examination hall, but it was still only a wooden extension.

From summer 1970 Cambrian operated to Paris with Viscounts three times a week (in addition to Southampton) at a fare of £21 10s return. Then, in July, Westward Airways of Plymouth introduced a twice-weekday service from the Isles of Scilly–London Heathrow. Operated by a BN Islander, it included a stop at Bournemouth, from where the fare was £4 10s single. A separate Bournemouth–London service was planned for November, but Westward ceased flying in the middle of October due to lack of capital.

The new year of 1971 commenced with diversions from London due to fog, eighteen aircraft arriving on 3 January and fifteen the next day, totalling 4,500 passengers. The aircraft types involved were One-Elevens, Comets and Viscounts, and it was the first major diversion for the new owners. In the end no more aircraft could be handled due to lack of space and the staff being worn out as they had been unable to get breaks. There were more diversions the following weekend which included Bournemouth's first Boeing 707 which arrived from Toronto. Channel Airways had run into financial difficulties by the end of 1971 due to a drop in passenger numbers and a receiver was appointed on 1 February 1972. The airline was forced to suspend the majority of its scheduled services, although that from Bournemouth–Channel Islands continued for a few weeks. The airline finally ceased all services at the end of February. This was a blow to the Airport management but there were soon a number of bidders keen to take over the former Channel Airways routes. As a temporary measure, it was agreed that British Midland would operate the Bournemouth–Channel Islands services with Viscounts.

DAN-AIR

Dan-Air were already known at the airport as their Ambassadors, Comet 4s and Dakotas had operated holiday flights for a number of years. The airline considered there was more business to be obtained through Bournemouth than Southampton, and drew up plans at the end of 1970 to operate scheduled services. These eventually came to fruition in the spring of 1972 with a Link-City network. The initial service operated northwards to Birmingham, Liverpool, Manchester and Newcastle, flown by HS.748s from 10 April. Sample fares were £11.60 return to Birmingham and £20.30 return to Newcastle. Dan-Air were also interested in the former Channel Airways routes to Guernsey and Jersey, and were

A Spitfire outside the Second World War VIP hangar. It was so named because it housed the Prime Minister's VIP Liberator transport during 1943. To the right can be seen an earth bank which provided additional protection to the hangar. However, this is a November 1969 view.

Dan-Air was to be one of the longest serving airlines to use Bournemouth. Their services were operated by a fleet of HS.748s and Viscounts. This 748 carries Dan-Air Skyways titles, being seen in the summer of 1972 shortly after the two airlines had merged.

Dan-Air Comets were used by Bath Travel and Swift Travel for their holiday flights from Bournemouth. However, the two seen here had been diverted from Gatwick in December 1972 due to bad weather around London.

granted permission to operate these instead of British Midland as from 1 July. Again the services were flown by HS.748s. From the summer of 1973 they offered a Coach-Air service from London Victoria via Bournemouth to Jersey at £14.10 return. Their Link-City service was extended northwards to Leeds and Glasgow in November 1974.

OPERATION REDSKIN

Bournemouth was seeing an increase in freight traffic to and from the Channel Islands. In spring 1971 Jersey flowers were flown into Bournemouth for markets at London, Birmingham, Nottingham and Manchester. The majority were carried by Dakotas of British Island, Intra Airways and South West. In the past the flowers had been carried by sea into Southampton or Weymouth, but this changed in spring 1972. BR Sealink switched their service from Weymouth to Southampton which the Channel Islands growers said did not provide a guaranteed or regular service. Then a seaman's strike in July resulted in a backlog of freight at both ports with a growing mountain of tomatoes in Guernsey. At the beginning of August the Guernsey Tomato Marketing Board set up Operation Redskin in order to fly the tomatoes to the mainland. Being a heavier cargo than the normal flowers flown across, larger aircraft were needed to assist the local Dakotas. Four Armstrong

Operation Redskin took place during August 1972, bringing tomatoes across the Channel from Guernsey during a seaman's strike. Argosies, Dakotas and even a Hercules were employed to bring the tomatoes to Bournemouth before they rotted on Guernsey's dockside.

Whitworth Argosies and a couple of Bristol Freighters arrived at Bournemouth to help out, with the Argosies undertaking fourteen flights a day. A most unexpected arrival was a civilian Lockheed Hercules from the United States which carried twenty-one tons – twice that of an Argosy. Despite being an expensive way of getting tomatoes to the mainland, the Marketing Board considered it worthwhile in order to retain customer confidence. One problem with the larger aircraft was soon evident as their greater capacity meant they could carry more tomato boxes. But on arrival at Bournemouth it was found that the top boxes loaded inside the Hercules had crushed all the lower ones, so providing instant tomato ketchup! Less damaged boxes, whilst not suitable for sending to the London markets, soon disappeared to local homes via the busy loaders. Also arriving were Jersey potatoes, whilst going in the other direction were fresh food and cigarettes.

'Operation Redskin' lasted four weeks, by which time the seamen had returned to work. However, the operation had demonstrated to the island growers the benefit of air transport in getting their produce to the mainland markets faster, although ships continued to be used for a few more years. Flights from Bournemouth were now carried out by Dakotas of Intra and, from August 1972, Carvairs of British Air Ferries (BAF) who also operated car-ferry services. Much of the return business was carrying flowers on behalf of Carpenters Air Services in Guernsey, more of whom later.

LAKER'S SKYTRAIN

4 December 1972 was a round-the-country flag-waving day by Freddie Laker, with his first Douglas DC-10 visiting Bournemouth in the afternoon for a demonstration flight for the travel trade. This pleased the director as it showed that the airport could handle the new breed of large jet airliners even with the existing runway length. It was stated that holiday destinations could now be reached without the need for a full fuel load, but passenger demand for a 350-400-seat aircraft from Bournemouth was never sufficient for such operations. However, other Laker DC-10s arrived with passengers in later years having been diverted from Gatwick due to fog. By then the airline had commenced its cheap Skytrain services across the Atlantic which was to cause so much bother for Sir Freddie.

BARON BOTHERS

Having used Bournemouth for some years, the Beech Baron training aircraft of the College of Air Training set up base in February 1971. Students at the college undertook ground training in a new building provided near the terminal. Their Hamble base had proved unsuitable for a number of years as it frequently became waterlogged which resulted in cancelled flights. Basic training with Chipmunks remained at Hamble but the twelve Barons of the Advanced Flying Unit arrived at Bournemouth where they were maintained by Airwork Services. From the very beginning the complaints started coming in from residents about circuit training until 11.30 p.m. when the airport closing time was 9.30 p.m. The Management Committee explained that when they accepted the college it was anticipated that the majority of flying would be away from the local area, as the course did require students to fly to the likes of Hamburg and Nice. This proved not to be the case and, with complaints increasing, the airport was forced to place restrictions on night-flying from October 1971.

There were further outcries from local residents in March 1971 when their MP's comments in the House of Commons were misinterpreted. He expressed his view that Bournemouth was ideally placed to be an international airport which residents took as meaning he felt it should become London's third airport! The period 1972-74 was taken up with opposition over the proposed runway extension which led to the formation in the autumn of the Hurn Airport Action Group (strongly against the airport). There was wonder the local papers had any room for any other news with the amount of column space taken up by articles and letters. After three years in the job, poor Harry Longhurst was wondering what he had let himself in for:

> Obviously my position made me a target for press interviews but from the start I was never happy with their coverage. Half of my first report for the local press had been fabricated, and when I complained the explanation was that due to the short time available for the interview the reporter had expanded the story with his own words! On another occasion I mentioned that I felt Concorde would be a great success. This was translated into my supporting services from Bournemouth!

The Barons remained based at Bournemouth until 1975, when they returned to Hamble. However, they continued visiting on training flights until the College of Air Training closed in April 1982.

CARPENTERS

The wartime VIP hangar close to the terminal became the freight terminal from summer 1973 with the adjacent apron area being expanded. BAF had been operating their car-ferry service with Carvairs to the Channel Islands, also using the aircraft for freight work which included flowers from Guernsey. However, they lost this major flower-carrying contract in July 1973, pulling out of the airport in October and leaving the Channel Islands business to the Dakotas of Intra Airways. There were further changes at the end of 1973 when Carpenter Air Services arranged for Guernsey's flower crop to be flown to Bournemouth by BIA Cargo. It was anticipated that Bournemouth would now be handling 80 per cent of Guernsey's flower exports. Their onward transportation to inland markets was handled by Carpenter Transport who set up a small office in the freight hangar. BIA replaced their Dakotas with Heralds in June 1974, being the last regular Dakota service through Bournemouth. However, Dakotas continued to be seen at the airport for almost another thirty years. Frequently returning empty to the Channel Islands, the aircraft needed some form of ballast, resulting in the crews 'borrowing' concrete blocks that were lying around the apron area for use as tie-down blocks. They were never returned! BIA were operating about 140 flower flights a month, with Intra operating around thirty.

FUEL CRISES

The Arab–Israeli War in October 1973 brought about a world fuel crisis which resulted in the Government declaring a national fuel emergency. This affected the availability and price of aviation fuel with a resulting cutback of some services. Having only reopened services to the Channel Islands on 1 November, BIA were forced to suspend them at the end of the month until the following spring. It was a similar situation for Cambrian with their Paris service, although Dan-Air were able to continue their services. Holiday flight passengers were forced to pay a supplement prior to take-off from 1 December to cover these higher fuel costs. The crisis provided major problems for local tour operators. Swift Travel Services went out of business in February 1974, with Kentways only continuing until November when it became insolvent. Bath Travel came to the rescue of the majority of the travellers in both cases. There had been plans by Horizon Holidays and Thomson to use Bournemouth during 1974, but the crisis meant they were put on hold. Bath Travel had been using British Caledonian One-Elevens on its Palmair flights but the soaring fuel prices brought a change. Dan-Air Comet 4s were introduced in 1974 on the Corfu and Tenerife routes, where all 119 seats could be filled. As Swift Travel had found, the Comets took off easily within Bournemouth's runway limits due to the power of their four engines. One-Elevens continued to Benidorm and Majorca.

Dan-Air promoted their Channel Islands services at the beginning of 1977. Having carried 37,500 passengers the previous year, they hoped to increase this by a further 15,000. People were cutting back on continental holidays at the time and so flights to the islands were promoted from £28 return. At the same time Bath Travel were forced to cut the number of its IT flights, this being in line with the national trend. The last year that they used One-Elevens was 1977, as economic factors saw all services operated by Dan-Air Comets from October. Thomson Holidays operated from the airport from spring 1978 with holiday flights to Majorca by Britannia Boeing 737s, but the number of holidaymakers was not as high as anticipated.

15

GOVERNMENT PLANS

A report for the BoT was issued in July 1970 by the South Hants Plan Advisory Committee, concerning airfields in the county, concentrating on Bournemouth and Southampton Airports. It pointed out that Bournemouth was well established, containing BAC, Airwork and the College of Air Traffic Control. As such, it could be developed as a regional airport at a cost of £6 million over a ten-year period. The committee recommended that Southampton Airport should be run down by 1974 so that it could be replaced by a new one to the east of the existing site. It felt that with two regional airports in operation, Bournemouth would be handling 50,000 passengers by 1979/80, but if Southampton was not developed numbers would reach 75,000. An alternative scheme involved the wartime Stoney Cross airfield to serve both Bournemouth and Southampton. The open area would have been easy to develop, there was good access via the A35 trunk road, but the idea of such a development in the New Forest was not practical. The report's recommendation was that the needs of south Hampshire would be satisfied by the expansion of Bournemouth, favouring the early extension of the main runway eastwards by 500 yards. Further development could entail the extension of the secondary north–south runway southwards into the grounds of Hurn Court (to be demolished!) and the further extension of the main runway westwards. This would result in the closure of Parley Lane, necessitating a new commuter road south of the River Stour. Naturally, the report brought forth howls of protest from local residents associations and parish councils alike (including the Christchurch Branch of the Women's Gas Federation!). In the event, the reports conclusions were not put into practice.

Runway extension possibilities were considered by the Management Committee in October 1971 and details were given in their report to the councils the following September. Their report also anticipated that Southampton would be closed by 1974. The runway extension plans were: (i) extend 675 yards westwards at £2.2 million or (ii) extend 600 yards eastwards and 80 yards westwards at £3 million. Either would enable the expansion of holiday flights to Europe and North America. The plans were put on display at Bournemouth Town Hall in September 1972, with the Management Committee recommending option (i), where work would hopefully commence the following autumn. (Gatwick had just announced a 365-yard extension for £1.2 million.) Application for funding was made in July 1973 to Bournemouth and Dorset Councils as owners, but their problem was working out how to raise the money from their ratepayers.

The expansion plans were to be argued over for the next twenty years. The local parish councils would disapprove ('We're not having another Gatwick'), the local residents feared a further increase in noise and, finally, who was going to provide the finance? There was even a bid in October 1972 from Nat Somers of Southampton Airport to purchase Bournemouth as well. He was told, 'no deal'. Undeterred, he bid again in June 1976, but received the same reply. During 1973/74 it was still widely thought that Southampton would close due to planning problems, but this was not the case. In July 1974 Bournemouth's councillor Bill Forman replaced Michael Green as chairman of the Airport's Management Committee. A strong supporter of the airport, he had to admit in November that there was no money for the runway extension and that many locals would not live to see the airport's expansion. The airport's future was complicated again in July 1974 when the Government announced that it was not proceeding with a proposed 'Third' London Airport at Maplin. It concluded that passengers could continue to use existing airports in the south. (A follow-up report in the autumn of 1975 recommended a fifth terminal for Heathrow, a second one for Gatwick and the expansion of Stansted to the size of Gatwick. Heathrow waited until 2006 for its terminal, Gatwick got its, and Stansted's expansion was delayed many years). Bournemouth was optimistically mentioned as able to handle 15 million passengers a year by 1990, assuming the runway was extended to 10,000ft. The airport's management were only planning for 1.2 million passengers with a 7,400ft runway! However, being a time of soaring fuel prices and with a lack of local council backing, the Government's plans came to nothing. Matters were not helped by the fact that the airport was still operating at a deficit, not making a profit as anticipated. Added to this, following the 1974 county boundary changes, the airport came under Christchurch Council who turned down the initial plans for the runway extension.

Another twist came in August 1975 when the Civil Aviation Authority revealed its study of airports in the South West, as it considered there were too many. It concluded that, although Bournemouth and Southampton had useful roles, Bristol served the area best, 'there being no need for Bournemouth as well, due to its associated high running costs'. The *Bournemouth Echo* predicted in September 1975 that, 'Hurn Airport will close by the 1980s' and the local residents, 'would be able to relax without any jet noise'. But this was countered by yet another Government study in November which confirmed it was still considering Bournemouth as an overflow airport for London! Then in June 1976 the Department of Trade announced its airfield strategy for Great Britain. Again it confirmed that both Bournemouth and Southampton had useful roles. Bournemouth's existing terminal could cope with 600,000 passengers each year with scope for expansion taking the total to 5 million by 1990. In spite of all these conflicting reports, the airport's immediate problem was that it still needed to raise capital. A December 1974 plan was to turn surplus land on the north-east side into a major industrial estate served by a connecting road from the A338. This would provide extra rental income for the airport and by 1980 the plan had progressed into a £20 million estate providing 3,000 jobs. Two years later it was to be a £100 million science park providing 10,000 jobs, but by then the plan had become too large a proposal for acceptance by the local councils. The plans had their ups and downs over many years, never to be realised.

Yet another Government White Paper appeared in February 1978, recommending that Southampton should have preference over Bournemouth for services to the Channel Islands. They regarded Southampton as a local airport on a par with Bristol and Exeter. Bournemouth was only considered suitable for general aviation in line with Biggin Hill. This did not please the Management Committee who showed that the airport had reduced its operating losses from £288,343 in 1976/77 to £71,386 in 1977/78. They did not mention the loan debt. Dan-Air commented that they found it cheaper to operate from Bournemouth where their passenger numbers had increased.

COLLEGE OF AIR TRAFFIC CONTROL

The School of Air Traffic Control was redesignated a college in 1968 with its Experimental Unit becoming the Evaluation Unit. The college instructed potential ATC officers from many countries (over 150) and students were trained for both airfield and area sector control. In September 1972 the college had thirty-five staff, and the Evaluation Unit, 300. The college moved into the computer age at the beginning of 1975 with the students undertaking training on simulators. This did away with the need for Doves to fly circuits of the airfield in order to show up as blips on the student's radar screen, with the last Dove being used in February 1975. Two HS.748s had been introduced from the summer of 1969. They still visited Bournemouth, but were now used to check airport approach radar systems around the country. Students had also received flying training on the aircraft but now made use of flying club aircraft. Some overseas students arrived by air, bringing the likes of Algerian Government An-12s and Greek AF Hercules in the 1970s. A £2 million college extension was opened in October 1990 by the Transport Secretary. At the time the 240 students a year under training would only be sufficient to meet UK needs. Eighteen months training was undertaken, followed by a further eighteen months 'on the job'. The Evaluation Unit became Air Traffic Management Development Centre in November 1995, undertaking research and development work for National Air Traffic Services, including a new surveillance system to monitor aircraft outside existing radar range, such as across the North Atlantic.

1970S MISCELLANY

Diversions from London continued to be seen, although the weather was not as disruptive as twenty-five years earlier. The 1970s brought the likes of BEA Tridents, BEA Airtours Comets, Britannia 737s, BUA and Caledonian One-Elevens and Swissair Coronados. Moving to the 1980s, there were British 737s, Laker DC-10s, Dan-Air Comets, One-Eleven and 727s, Lufthansa 727s and 737s and SAS A300s and DC-9s.

A typical diversion scene in the early 1970s. These included Lufthansa Boeing 737s, SAS DC-9s (seen here) and Swissair DC-9s, as well as BEA Tridents, British United and Caledonian One-Elevens and Dan-Air Comets.

RAF Hercules were seen from the mid-1970s, initially crew training from Lyneham. Later years saw them also calling to collect Royal Marines who had arrived by coach from Hamworthy for parachute drops in Poole Bay; this continues until the present day. Excellent views of the Marines parachuting out of aircraft can be had from Bournemouth's cliff tops. They are then picked out of the sea by their colleagues and returned to camp.

On a lighter note, a DH Fox Moth biplane arrived in spring 1976 to undertake pleasure flights from in front of the terminal building, later being joined by a Piper Tri-Pacer. 'Capt. Johnny' continued these flights until September 1983 when the Tri-Pacer was damaged beyond repair when it was blown over in front of the terminal during a gale.

'Capt. Johnny' – John Lewery – became a familiar figure around the terminal area:

I offered people a flight in the Fox Moth 'hansom cab', an expression I used as the four passengers sat inside the cramped cabin whilst I sat in the open cockpit behind the cabin area. I knew the local area well as I was also a professional ice skater, having appeared at a number of summer shows in Bournemouth. Whilst at an Ice Show in the late 1950s I purchased the wreck of a Tiger Moth at Christchurch for £50, slowly rebuilding it during 1957/58. In the following years I undertook pleasure flights at Blackpool and Southport before moving south again. I gave up flying from Bournemouth following the damage to the Tri-Pacer, the majority of which I felt was caused whilst trying to right the aircraft.

POOLE HARBOUR FINALE

Poole Harbour was to see its final flying-boat operations in August 1976 with the arrival from the Virgin Islands of a Short Sandringham of Antiles Air Boats. Flown over at the request of local enthusiasts, it caused the harbour master some concern as it landed within the harbour, not in the open sea off Studland as expected. For the next two weeks it carried out pleasure flights for the enthusiasts from Studland Bay, before returning across the Atlantic.

BOURNEMOUTH'S AIR SHOWS

The year 1977 saw Bournemouth's first Air Pageant staged by businessman Jock Maitland, and sponsored by the *Evening Echo* on 11/12 June (£1 entry, 50p child), being preceded by the South Coast Air Race on 9 June. The race was sponsored by Southern Television, the idea being similar to the 1950 race, but on a smaller scale. Due to be flown from Hurn to Herne Bay and returning, torrential rain put paid to the return leg. The rain and winds also affected the weekend Pageant, where the display included the RN *Blue Heron* Hunter aerobatic team, B-17 Fortress *Sally B*, The Tiger Club and Wallis WA.116 autogyro *Little Nellie*. A similar Pageant was held in July 1978, which included the Red Arrows, but still suffered wind and rain. The show also included aerobatics from Philip Meeson in his Pitts Special (also in 1979), who returned to the airport in 1983 as owner of Channel Express. The 1978 show also brought problems for the RAF's Buccaneer pilot and a local horse.

Flt Lt John Myers (as he was then) was the RAF Buccaneer display pilot:

> Naturally I concentrated on my display to the public, but during the low level demonstration with full engine power a prize Arab stallion owned by almost name-sake Doug Meyer of Parley panicked and injured itself. I was unaware of this at the time, but later found out that the vet's bill was sent to Jock Maitland for payment. This was my introduction to Bournemouth, as I returned a few years later as the Director of Flight Operations for FRA's fleet of Falcons.

The 1979 Air Pageant also included a shorter Air Race, plus a noisy display by a Vulcan bomber. 1980 saw a demonstration by Richard Noble of his Thrust II land speed record car, as well as B-17 Fortress, B-26 Invader, Vulcan and Battle of Britain Memorial Flight. The Pageants were expanded in later years, the shows becoming important events in the aviation calendar until the early 1990s. They resulted in the first public appearance of Concorde at Bournemouth with a low fly-past during the 1982 Pageant whilst operating a charter for local residents out of Heathrow. This had been arranged by the *Bournemouth Echo* and John Plank Travel, giving a just under three-hour round trip for £310.

For a number of years Bournemouth hosted very successful air shows. The first Air Pageant was held in 1977, with one participant being the preserved Flying Fortress *Sally B*. At the time it was new to the air-show scene and was flown in a silver colour scheme.

With its distinctive nose lowered, Concorde makes a slow fly-past at the 1982 Air Pageant whilst carrying local residents on a charter out of Heathrow. Such practises were soon to be banned by the Ministry for being too dangerous.

Jock Maitland was unable to organise a show for 1984, so the arrangements were taken over by International Air Tattoo (of Greenham Common fame), with sponsorship from TeleVision South (TVS). Held in August, the show was much larger than before, now including more military items. From the RAF there were Harrier and Nimrod, with the USAF providing A-10 Thunderbolt, F-4 Phantom, C-141 Starlifter and a fly-by of a huge C-5 Galaxy. However, the show was memorable for its live 'demonstration' of an ejection from a RAF Phantom. One of a pair taking off, it suffered a main-wheel problem, veered off the runway onto the grass, whereupon the pilot ordered (correctly) 'eject', which the navigator did. The pilot then realised the fighter was heading for various helicopters and Hercules, plus ground crews, so he engaged full reheat which somehow blasted the Phantom off the grass and into the air. The pilot then made a slow flight to Lyneham for a successful emergency landing. The navigator required hospital treatment, but the incident could have been a disaster. The shows were now biennial, with 1986 similar to 1984. However, it included a couple of German F-104 Starfighters and a USAF F-111 fly-past. The year 1988 continued in the same vein, including two U-2 spy planes and a NATO E-3 Awacs. The show also commemorated the twenty-fifth anniversary of the One-Eleven's first flight. Optimistic thoughts of there being twenty-five aircraft on display ended up with only four on the day.

The 1990 IAT show was originally planned for Bournemouth, but IAT switched it to Boscombe Down, as there was much greater capacity. New organisers stepped in for Bournemouth Air Day 1991 which was held over the August Bank Holiday, admission now £7.50. Entitled 'Back from the Gulf', it saw demonstrations by soon to be retired Buccaneers and Phantoms, plus eight RAF Tornados (not all together). Also billed was 'Hurn Airport 50th Anniversary Display', but there was little on show in this connection. The show included further public 'landing accident demonstrations', with a Seneca whose wheels collapsed on landing. This was followed by a burst tyre on a Canberra resulting in it veering off the runway towards Parley Lane and a line of spectators. Luckily it slowed down and stopped in time. The 1992 show was planned for May, but in the event was cancelled, due to the recession and rising costs leading to low attendances. So 1991 was the last of Bournemouth's well-loved shows, as thoughts for a 1993 revival were abandoned in February 1993.

16

BAC/ONE-ELEVEN/AIRWORK

BRITISH AIRCRAFT CORPORATION

Early in 1964 BAC erected a further large hangar to house a second One-Eleven assembly line, increasing their site to an area of 800,000sq. ft. Although production of the One-Eleven appeared fairly straightforward there were various problems, often financial, which affected it over the years. There were also a number of replacement projects which could have followed it down the production line from what BAC continued to refer to as its Hurn site.

ONE-ELEVEN

After the unfortunate start to the One-Eleven flight test programme, production got under way during 1964. A renewed effort by the 3,500-strong workforce saw the airliner awarded its Certificate of Airworthiness on 5 April 1965. Early series 200 production aircraft were soon delivered to British United and Braniff, with the aircraft entering service with British United from Gatwick on 9 April and with Braniff from Dallas on 25 April. As an indication of its flexibility, British United used their One-Elevens on routes as diverse as Gatwick–Jersey and Gatwick–Accra. The prototype of the more powerful series 400 version for American Airlines flew on 13 July 1965, with the first aircraft handed over at the end of the year. BAC had received a severe blow in April 1964 when the TSR2 strike bomber was cancelled by the Government. This was due to be produced at their Weybridge site, which consequently suffered financial problems due to lack of work. Despite the orders it had, BAC announced in November 1965 that there was a high probability that the Hurn site would be closed by the end of 1967, with production being switched to Weybridge or even cancelled. Matters were not helped by the Ministry trying to dispose of Bournemouth Airport around the same time. However, the problems were eventually resolved and production continued at Hurn. A small number of One-Elevens were also completed at Weybridge to take up spare space, so enabling six aircraft a month to be produced at peak capacity.

During the 1960s the BAC design office was involved with a number of One-Eleven-related projects. They developed a lengthened version of the One-Eleven – the series 500 – with BEA placing an order for eighteen in spring 1967. The airline ran a competition for a name for the new version, resulting in the imaginative winning entry of 'Super One-Eleven'! The prototype series 400 aircraft returned to the hangars to be lengthened into the new BEA version, first flying as such on 30 June 1967. BAC had also designed the Two-Eleven airliner by 1967, a 200-seater competitor to the HS Trident 3. BEA indicated that they were interested in a fleet of thirty with the new Laker Airways also showing interest. The project was dropped in summer 1967 when the Government advised that funding was unavailable as it was supporting the early European Airbus airliner proposals. Undeterred, a further lengthened version of the One-Eleven was proposed in 1968, with improved engines. This was the time that Rolls-Royce ran into financial disaster over the design of its large RB.211 engine. As a result, there was no money for them to develop an improved engine for the One-Eleven and this was to hinder its sales over the following years. Another design which emerged in 1969 was the Three-Eleven, which was a 245-seater wide-bodied airliner. Powered by two Rolls Royce RB.211s, it was smaller than the proposed Airbus A300B. BEA made a commitment in September 1970 for a fleet of twenty with Laker requesting three. As there seemed to be more hope for this design, BAC drew up plans for a new £4 million factory site at Hurn for its production. Once again it was not to be, as any surplus Government finance was still needed to support the new Rolls-Royce aero-engine company. So the Three-Eleven project was cancelled by BAC in December 1970, resulting in some job losses at Hurn.

FACTORY FUTURE IN DOUBT

In April 1971 the BAC board had once again considered ending One-Eleven production and closing one of their factory sites. To boost work, the Hurn site undertook the overhaul of Viscounts, Pembrokes and earlier One-Elevens, whilst the paint shop handled a number of new Islanders from Bembridge. Hurn was also involved in the building of Concorde's droop noses for the final assembly line at Filton. In autumn 1971 BAC purchased the former Long Haul Terminal buildings at Hurn Village with the intention of clearing the site and building a sports complex for its employees. However, the financial climate delayed these plans for some years. On the afternoon of 7 September 1972 Concorde 002 made a fly-past of the airport for the benefit of the BAC workers, many of whom were involved in building parts for the supersonic airliner. By autumn 1972 One-Eleven production was virtually suspended and it appeared that production would end with three for the Sultan of Oman AF (SOAF). Despite their financial problems, BAC remained upbeat. If Bournemouth's runway was lengthened, they would expand their site and increase the workforce from 3,000 to 8,000 in order to undertake major airliner reconditioning work.

As local residents knew, the Spey engines of the One-Eleven had always been very noisy. This resulted in BAC and Rolls-Royce joining forces to develop a 'hush kit' for the Spey in order to meet new international noise regulations. The 'hush kit' was fitted to BAC's trials aircraft during the spring 1974, first flying on 14 June. Although the boffins were able to prove that there was a reduction in the number of decibels on

The first production Super One-Eleven (although shown as one-eleven on the engine) for BEA during pre-delivery testing in spring 1968. BEA was well behind the likes of British United and Caledonian in placing an order for the airliner.

take-off, this was not readily apparent to people who lived near airports served by the airliner. One repair job was almost delivered direct to BAC's doorstep. Whilst flying from Birmingham on 4 December 1974, a British Airways One-Eleven developed problems with its nose wheel, which would not lower. So it was flown to Bournemouth where a successful emergency landing was made by the pilot. There was little damage to the aircraft which was soon moved the short distance to BAC for repairs. A more substantial repair job was needed on one of the SOAF aircraft which had been delivered to Oman in October 1975. A few days later it was badly damaged as a result of an oxygen bottle fire in the cockpit, followed by a flash fire in the cabin. This resulted in it almost being declared a write off. However, as it was a brand new aircraft the Omani Government decided it should be rebuilt, the aircraft being dismantled for shipping home by sea via Poole. The lengthy repair involved fitting a completely new forward fuselage and cockpit. Frequent One-Eleven crew training was being undertaken at the time, which led to further complaints by local residents. This resulted in advertisements placed in the local papers by BAC explaining why the training was necessary, and the times when flying would be undertaken. In the late 1970s there was the possibility of an order from Japan where there was a requirement for a short-haul airliner with exceptional short field performance. The One-Eleven 670 was proposed, with BAC's prototype being modified once again to test a new braking system that had been developed. Trials during autumn 1977 involved flooding the runway with the One-Eleven landing at different weights and speeds but, although successful, there was no Japanese order.

BRITISH AEROSPACE

In the mid-1970s the whole of the British aircraft industry was suffering from over capacity and lack of orders. As a result, the Labour Government decided the industry should be nationalised as the newly formed British Aerospace (BAe). So on 1 January 1978 the two aircraft firms of British Aircraft Corporation and Hawker Siddeley Aviation became the major part of this nationalised company. There was no immediate change locally, though in due course the British Aerospace name appeared on the side of one of the hangars, and also on the trials One-Eleven.

As part of an agreement with the Government whereby they could buy Boeing 737s, British Airways also ordered three further One-Elevens at the end of 1979. At the same time BAe proceeded with two further aircraft on speculation of future sales. These were to be the final batch of British built One-Elevens, with the final (and Hurn's 222nd) aircraft delivered in August 1980.

ROMBAC DEAL

The Romanian airline Tarom had received six One-Elevens back in 1970. As part of the Romanians desire to work closer with Western countries, a major deal was concluded in June 1978 for the production of the One-Eleven in Romania, the Rombac Deal. The contract signed by the President of Romania initially covered twenty-five aircraft, with the first three to be completed at the Hurn site by Romanian workers. The rest would follow on from a new production line set up in Bucharest. Originally, it was anticipated that the Romanians would complete about eighty One-Elevens over a fifteen-year period. The deal resulted in the then unusual sight of Antonov freighters calling at the factory from summer 1979 to collect parts for the Romanian production line. Also involved were Boeing 707 freighters and the Airbus Guppy which was able to carry complete fuselages to Bucharest. The first One-Eleven to be completed by the Romanians flew at the end of 1980, with the first from Bucharest in August 1982. The final One-Eleven built at Hurn was handed over to the Romanian Ambassador in March 1982. Financial, political and production problems beset the One-Eleven programme in Bucharest, with only nine aircraft having been completed by 1989. In the end the production line was abandoned, with BAe withdrawing from the Rombac agreement in July 1993.

END OF BAE HURN

In June 1981 British Aerospace produced a booklet to mark their thirty years at Hurn, noting how over 1,000 aircraft had passed through the works. This included newly constructed Varsities (146), Viscounts (279) and One-Elevens (222); the remainder were rebuilds and overhauls. The booklet commented on new building being erected, but in the event they

The One-Eleven Rombac Deal had been preceded by a number of aircraft built at Bournemouth for the Romanian airline Tarom. Seen in final production, these Series 500 aircraft were delivered during 1977.

were not required. Redundancies from among the 2,400-strong workforce were announced in spring 1982. However, BAe announced in September that, 'existing work would carry factory through to middle of decade' and that a 'decision on the Airbus A320 was crucial to BAe Commercial Division'. There were hopes to revive the One-Eleven production line with a version powered by Rolls-Royce Tay engines where a prototype could be flying by summer 1986. Once again, this One-Eleven development was not to be and on 6 July 1983 British Aerospace announced the closure of the Hurn site, 'due to the depressed state of the worldwide civil aircraft market'. There was very little One-Eleven work, and possible sub-contract work on the proposed Airbus A320 was still not forthcoming. This resulted in the loss of 2,000 jobs, with other cuts by BAe around the country, plus the loss of local ancillary jobs. Rundown of the site commenced in autumn, with final closure the following June. The two speculative One-Elevens were made airworthy in February 1984, with one registered to mark the 'Last Hurn Delivery' and departing with a low fly-past of the factory on 30 May. In due course new use was found for the empty hangars and it was by no means the end of Bournemouth's association with the One-Eleven.

AIRWORK SERVICES

Although nowhere near as large as BAC, Airwork Services was still a major employer at the airport, spread between its HQ buildings and maintenance hangar. In May 1966 Airwork received a valuable contract from the Royal Saudi Air Force to provide technical support and training. This was in conjunction with a much larger contract obtained by

Although it had major contracts with Oman and Saudi Arabia, Airwork Services handled a variety of aircraft for other Middle Eastern air forces. These ranged from the ever-faithful Dakota (South Arabian AF version seen here) through Islanders to Strikemasters.

BAC to provide new fighter and trainer aircraft for the expanding Air Force, some of which passed through Bournemouth. First to be seen were two Hawker Hunters at the end of May, followed by a number of Cessna 172 trainers. However, Airwork's involvement at Bournemouth was mainly the supply of equipment which resulted in the visit of Britannia, CL-44 and DC-6 freighters over the next few years. Three Constellations were used in September 1966 – the last to be seen in service at Bournemouth. Aircraft were also handled prior to delivery for the Abu Dhabi AF (Caribou, Islander), Qatar Police (Gazelle), Singapore AF (Strikemaster), South Arabian AF (Bell 47G, Dakotas), SOAF (Dakota, Skyvan, Strikemaster, Viscount) and Sudan AF (Jet Provost).

In February 1971 the Baron training aircraft of the College of Air Training arrived with their maintenance being undertaken by Airwork. December 1978 saw the arrival of the Scottish Aviation Bulldogs of Southampton UAS and the DHC Chipmunks of No.2 AEF to be based with Airwork who undertook their hangarage and maintenance. The trainers had endured the frequently flooded grass airfield at Hamble for long enough, finding the move to Bournemouth beneficial with less flying hours being cancelled. The Bulldogs provided initial training for prospective RAF pilots at Southampton University (often using Lee-on-Solent airfield) and the Chipmunk basic trainers gave air experience flights to local Air Cadets.

From 1 January 1980 Airwork Services reverted to its original title of Airwork Ltd. This had been the name of the airline part of the group, but it had merged into the British United Group of airlines back in 1960. Many contracts were held around the country – the FRADU at Yeovilton, flying school at Perth and civilian maintenance facilities at Exeter. They obtained the FRADU contract in April 1988 to overhaul their Hunters at their Bournemouth base, where they had taken over an additional hangar from BAe. Short Skyvans also appeared to be a specialty of Airwork. A damaged one from SOAF returned for repair to Bournemouth inside a Belfast freighter in the summer of 1982, much quicker than the old way of returning by sea. A similar return by air occurred in November 1989, representing the end of the SOAF contract. Four damaged Ghana AF ones then returned by sea to Poole in September 1990 for major overhaul. In 1991 Airwork was joined by the former Britavia design office from Southend. So as well as its HQ, the Aircraft Engineering Division was situated at the airport, with spares provision at its Supply & Logistics Division in nearby Ferndown. There were 220 staff were employed at the airport, with 3,500 worldwide.

AIRWORK TAKE OVER

In October 1993 Airwork Ltd was acquired by Short Bros of Belfast, thereby becoming one of the Bombardier (of Canada) Group of companies. Initially this did not bring any changes to the work at the airport, where the FRADU Hunter contract had recently passed to FLS. In April 1995 Shorts moved the No.2 AEF Chipmunks to a separate hangar on the south side of the airport. However, this was only until the following March when the Chipmunks were taken out of RAF service, resulting in the hangar being vacated. RAF Bulldogs were still being overhauled during 1996 but in due course their hangar on the north side was taken over by European Aviation for storage, the Airwork name virtually disappearing into history. However, it is still used in the Middle East in connection with the continuing Oman contract. From the beginning of 1998 the new Administration HQ building carried the name Bombardier, but following a take over by the Vosper Thorneycroft Group in June 2000, the name became VT Aerospace. The building is now the Headquarters for a number of companies within the VT Group.

SHACKLETON AND GLOS AIR

These two companies both chose Bournemouth in 1973 to expand their businesses, also being the first to erect new hangars at the airport since the war.

Shackleton Aviation was a well-established company dealing in the sale of secondhand aircraft. They constructed a large hangar on the north-east side, moving their stock of aircraft down from Coventry during August. They handled a full range of aircraft – Cessnas to Boeing 707s – with there usually being a stock of thirty aircraft on display. May 1978 saw Shackletons purchased by Via Nova, who continued in the same line of business. From the 1980s the hangar has seen a variety of companies and uses.

Glos Air erected their hangar in the autumn on the south-east side for the overhaul of Islander and Trislander aircraft, initially of its subsidiary company Aurigny Air Services. An increase in business saw the hangar size doubled in 1976. One unusual project undertaken in summer 1980 was the fitting of a harness to the top of the fuselage of a German Islander. This was to enable an 'intrepid' aviator to cross the Atlantic from Germany to New Jersey during October, whilst standing on top of the aircraft! Glos Air became part of the Brencham Group in October 1983, later acquiring further hangars on the north side of the airfield. Mike Carlton became Brencham's chairman in 1984, using the hangars to house his Hunter One collection. August 1987 saw the arrival of the Bamberg Group who were UK agents for the Beechcraft range of aircraft. Initially trading as Eagle Beechcraft, and then Eagle Aircraft Services, aircraft sales did not reach expectations, resulting in the company moving out of the hangars at the end of 1988.

17

1980/90S UPS AND DOWNS

The 1980/90s were times of highs and mainly lows for both the airport and its airlines. Plans were in hand for the Terminal Replacement Building, 'to merge in with the picturesque surrounding rural landscape and provide a pleasant atmosphere for all travellers and visitors'. Main airline services at the beginning of the period were those of British Island Airways with Heralds, Dan-Air with HS.748s and Viscounts and Express Air Services freight flights also with Heralds. Air UK, who had just taken over BIA, then dropped their Channel Islands services at the end of October 1980 to concentrate their local operations at Southampton. Dan-Air were operating twice daily to the Channel Islands (from £18.50 single) and northwards to Manchester and Newcastle with their Link-City service. There were also the Bath Travel holiday flights, although passenger numbers had dropped by about 50 per cent due to economic conditions. The majority of their flights were operated by Dan-Air Comets, but they were withdrawn in March 1980 and replaced by Boeing 727s. To mark the final day of service from Bournemouth, Bath Travel sold seats on the Comet's return evening leg to Gatwick for £8.50, finding that the seats could have been sold three times over. Dan-Air operated the Comet's last ever commercial service on 9 November 1980 with an enthusiast's flight from Gatwick on a round trip which took in Bournemouth. Bath's introduced Dubrovnik from spring 1980, Sun Blessed Holidays operated to Algarve/Faro with Air Portugal 727s, Horizon Holidays operated Orion 737s during winter 1983/84 to Ibiza and Unijet Holidays used Hispania Caravelles to Malaga during summer 1984.

FREIGHT AND ROYAL MAIL

The 1970s had seen increases in freight traffic to and from the Channel Islands. Flights were operated by ABC Argosies, and Dakotas of Air Atlantique and Intra carrying mainly flowers and tomatoes. Freight handling and forwarding at Bournemouth was undertaken by Carpenter's with an associated company, Express Air Freight, formed in summer 1976. Express moved into aircraft operations in spring 1977 when two Dakotas were chartered from Intra, integrating their services with those of ABC. Express Air Freight introduced Heralds of its own in January 1978. The Heralds were acquired not only for the freight flights but also passenger charters. During the summer these were undertaken on behalf of Dan-Air and Intra. To reflect this, the company title was amended to Express Air Services, passengers not wanting to think they were only baggage! Attempts were made to try and keep two Heralds dedicated for these passenger duties, but this did not always work out. One problem related to a fresh-fish contract, for which a passenger aircraft sometimes had to be used. This usually resulted in a fishy odour remaining in the cabin for some days after, much to the annoyance of passengers. The increased business saw the airport handle 9,000 metric tonnes of freight during 1978 compared with 875 in 1971.

There were hopes of a gas and oil bonanza developing off the south coast in the 1980s. October 1979 saw Norwegian workers arrive at Bournemouth to be flown to a British Gas rig off the Isle of Wight by helicopter, with supplies being taken by boat from Poole. Similar operations continued for a few years, but no financially viable gas or oil finds were made locally. Express Air Services applied to operate an oil workers' service from Aberdeen, later planning to build a £0.5 million freight complex at Bournemouth. Neither event took place as the oil bonanza of the 1980s did not reach the south.

Express Air Services commenced an important contract in February 1980. The Post Office had decided that a greater amount of Royal Mail would now be carried by air. So it invested £2 million in the setting up a central hub at Liverpool Speke for these flights, known as the 'Spoke from Speke'. Aircraft would arrive from around the country, swap their mail and then return home. Initial details of the nightly flights were announced in November 1979 when it was intended that the service from Bournemouth would be operated by Dakotas. This brought a howl of protest over nightly 'noisy Dakotas', although the protesters were more concerned at future expansion of night-time flights. In the event, EAS Heralds were used, commencing the nightly letter service to Bristol and Liverpool from February. Departing each weekday at 10.30 p.m., the Herald returned home at about 2 a.m. The number of flights needed from Bournemouth increased over the years, reaching five by 2005.

Ken Halls was a senior captain with EAS at the time:

> I frequently flew the mail flight, but this was a cold occupation during the winter months due to the lack of cockpit heating. Two of the Heralds had been acquired from Israel where the system had been removed. Extra layers of thick clothing were required by the crews, but the best way to get warm was to personally load the mail bags as quickly as possible. I found that three or four tonnes in ten minutes usually did the trick!

RUNWAY AND TERMINAL PLANS

Plans to divert Parley Lane away from the end of the main runway to provide a safety area finally received Dorset County Council's approval in October 1978. However, a condition was that the airport withdrew its plan to extend the runway. The logic behind this was to appease the local anti-noise brigade, but there were still objections and delays. Having been awaited for some years, Phase 1 (of a planned eight) of the terminal building was brought into use in spring 1981. Officially opened as The Sir Alan Cobham Lounge in June, it acknowledged the vital part he had played in the past.

The first visit of an Airbus A300 in May 1981 proved an embarrassment to Bournemouth as the airport's steps would not reach their doors. Boxes had to be provided for passengers to step onto first before descending to the ground.

Having handled BOAC aircraft in the past, Bournemouth now saw airliners carrying the British title. This is one of a line up of Tridents diverted from Heathrow. Other British airliners seen in the 1980s were Boeing 737s and One-Elevens.

The facilities had been made use of by a number of diversions from Heathrow during May, including the airport's first Airbus A300. However, it was found that the airport's steps were 18in short of reaching the doors of these SAS aircraft. Another problem was that although diversions now included less aircraft than thirty years before, they carried more passengers. It was reported that 4,000 passengers were handled on 1 May, with a further 2,000 on 3 May. The terminal had been planned to cope with airliners then using the airport, such as fifty-seat Heralds and HS.748s, not Laker DC-10s with 300 seats. April 1983 finally saw the completion of the Parley Lane diversion at the western end of the runway, thus providing an improved safe overrun area. This was 'tested' later in the year when a Hunter ran off the runway onto the grass overrun when its braking parachute failed.

Bournemouth Council came up with a plan in November 1983 which would 'move' Bournemouth Hurn Airport from the Borough of Christchurch to Bournemouth. To do this they proposed to purchase land – which included the airport – from Christchurch. Naturally, such an audacious 'land grab' was rejected! The following January saw new check-in and baggage facilities completed at the terminal, with a departure area and lounge brought into use in September 1984. This first half of the planned terminal was officially opened by Kenneth McIntyre, chairman of Dorset County Council and strong supporter of the airport. Expenditure during 1981/85 totalled £1.5 million, but the freezing of funding at council level prevented any further work. When the contract had been agreed the council only authorised development in stages, so delaying progress. Had the contract initially been signed for full development, it would have meant that Bournemouth would have gained the terminal it required. Passengers have had to put up with an inadequate arrivals area ever since. An Open Weekend was held in January 1985 to try and convince locals to use the airport, not to suffer the inconvenience of travelling elsewhere. Pleasure flights were available at £10 on one of Dan-Air's 748s, and visitors on the Sunday saw the airport coping with eleven aircraft diverted from the London area due to snow.

As an aside from normal airline operations, the airport had to contend with an uproar over grain storage during 1985. One of the former British Aerospace hangars had been leased out for storage of 25,000 tons of the EEC Grain Mountain which existed at the time. At the end of 1984 application was made to use a second hangar and at this stage Christchurch Council got wind of what was going on. They informed the airport that the grain storage was illegal as there had been no planning application for change of use of the hangars. It was then discovered that one of the buildings at the old de Havilland factory at Christchurch was storing 40,000 tons of grain. Christchurch Council continued to snipe at the airport, but Bournemouth Council backed it. The local Conservative MP backed Christchurch, but was then embarrassed when the local Conservative Association rented office accommodation in one of Bournemouth's hangars. The matter died down by the end of the year, and in due course the grain was moved out.

Bournemouth saw its first BAe 146 airliner in December 1982 when one arrived from Hatfield to undertake route proving trials prior to being granted its C of A. Flights to Germany under airline conditions with BAe staff were undertaken as part of these trials. During 1983 both Dan-Air and RAF versions visited Bournemouth for crew-training duties, with Bournemouth CCF cadets receiving a flight in January 1984.

Not all British visitors were airliners. This Chinook appeared for crew training in March 1981 prior to entering service on North Sea oil rig duties. At the present time there are still frequent visits by Chinooks, now RAF ones crew training from Odiham.

AIRLINES COME AND GO

The 1980s was a frustrating time for services. Small airlines came and went, often without operating any services. This section covers the saga of some of them.

Alderney Air Ferries commenced operations to Alderney in July 1979 with Islanders offering day trips for £19.50. Originally the airline was very much a one-man band – with owner Ron Ashley acting as booking clerk, check-in and luggage handler, and general gofer. One of the Islanders suffered the ignominy of running out of fuel whilst inbound to Bournemouth in August 1980. It made a forced landing in a barley field 2 miles short of the airport – now the site of Bournemouth Hospital. The barley was cleared and the Islander safely flown out the following day to continue operations, more than can be said for its pilot who resigned later that evening. Alderney Air Ferries added Cherbourg to its network in July 1981, followed by a twice-daily Gatwick service (£35 single) to tie in with intercontinental flights. With new management, the airline re-equipped with twenty-seat DHC Twin Otters in March 1982, also taking the opportunity to rebrand itself Metropolitan Airways. In addition to their existing flights, they entered into an agreement with Dan-Air to operate their Link-City flights to Manchester and Newcastle with the Twin Otters. The reason was that Dan-Air were faced with rising costs, but static passenger numbers. For example, as well as utilisation costs of its 748s, it was necessary to pay three lots of landing fees during the flight – and these were rising. Operating costs of the Twin Otters were much cheaper. Changes in 1984 saw Aurigny taking over the daily Alderney service in February at a fare of £27.50 single. Metropolitan introduced Short 330s during the spring to supplement their Twin Otters, concentrating on the twice-daily Link-City services (Manchester £61 single and Newcastle £87 single). August 1984 saw new owners acquire the airline with ambitious plans to set up a second hub at Manchester where two One-Elevens would be based. From April 1985 the airline took over the operation of the Link-City services in their own right, not on behalf of Dan-Air who were now free to concentrate on their Channel Islands routes. Then, out of the blue, Metropolitan ceased flying and went into liquidation on 31 August. The new owners said that after one year's operations the airline was not financially viable, mainly due to falling passenger numbers. One of the 330s quickly disappeared into the hangars to have a new registration applied in order to avoid repossession.

Air Wight set up a short-lived weekly freight service to Bembridge in September 1984, using an Islander. The aircraft was then available for charter work. In autumn 1986 the airline proposed a twice-daily service to Manchester with Piper Navajos, but the route was never operated.

Aviation West/Air Camelot commenced services from Bristol through Bournemouth to Alderney and Cherbourg from April 1986, with Islanders and Trislanders. At the end of the year it was announced that they were being taken over by Regency Airways who would also operate Islanders and Trislanders. Their inaugural service was planned for Friday 13 March 1987, with local dignitaries turning up early at the airport for the flight to Alderney. But there was no aircraft as it had been impounded at Liverpool following the bankruptcy of its legal owner. It finally arrived in May but the advertised services were never operated.

Dan-Air's monopoly of the Guernsey and Jersey services was challenged at the end of 1986 by Jersey European, who proposed commencing services on 1 April 1987. Objections from Dan-Air were over-ruled, resulting in the airline saying it would immediately withdraw from the routes, only operating on summer weekends in the future. This meant that Jersey European had to act swiftly to commence their twice-daily services on 4 January. These were initially operated by Short 360s with fares of £56 return, plus a £21 stand-by single. Dan-Air operated their 1987 summer services with HS.748s, but these ended on 24 October. At the time it was not realised that this would be the end of Dan-Air's twenty-five year association with Bournemouth, the airline deciding not to return for summer 1988. So the routes were left to Jersey European who introduced Fokker Friendships in May 1988.

Newcomer Air Metro announced plans in spring 1988 to operate Swearingen Metros twice daily to Amsterdam and Paris at £180 return. The company made much publicity of the fact that it needed air hostess's less than five foot high due to the compactness of the Metros, the first of which was delivered in August. However, as approval was still awaited to operate the routes they took over Air Wight's unused license to fly to Manchester. In November Air Metro announced its merger with Ellan Vannin Airlines, which then announced it had taken over Air Metro, removing its former Director in the process! Although intending to keep the Metros on order, the Manchester service would now be operated with ten-seat Navajos. The airline also planned services to Amsterdam, Paris and the Channel Islands, operated by BAe Jetstream 31s. Orders for further Metros and two Boeing 737 were announced by Ellan Vannin, whose managing director then fell out with the airport board over administration space. The thrice-daily Manchester service finally commenced in March 1989, but the airline soon ran into financial difficulties with its aircraft being impounded by the autumn.

Another airline of this period was Air Sarnia, which commenced services to Alderney and Cherbourg with Islanders and Trislanders in June 1989 at a fare of £20 single. Aurigny countered with £19! Then, in November, Air Sarnia purchased the Ellan Vannin name, saying that they would introduce Embraer Bandeirantes to Manchester. The aircraft never appeared as Air Sarnia ran into financial problems itself and struggled on until June 1990. Air Sarnia were taken over, its former director saying in late August, 'this take over has given the company a new lease of life and saved it from liquidation'. Two weeks later the new buyers withdrew from the deal, saying there were financial irregularities which meant they could not continue services.

Finally a new name which received a fair amount of press coverage was Southern Airlines with proposed services to Glasgow and Brussels with Saab 340s from summer 1990. By January 1991 the plan was to use Friendships on the services, with the press commenting, 'Airport to get new airline' – obviously having not consulted their own back issues. In April 1991 one of the directors was arrested on suspicion of fraud and from thereon things just seemed to die.

A common theme was the various airlines' desire to serve Manchester, replacing the former Dan-Air service. None of these comings and goings were good for the airport or passenger numbers, with less than 200,000 handled in 1990 compared with Southampton's 500,000 plus.

CHANNEL EXPRESS

Luckily, events proved different for Express Air Services although it, too, had run into financial difficulties by the end of 1980. Its freight side was suffering from competition by the Sealink Ro-Ro ferry service into Weymouth. Its passenger operations were running at a loss – it was estimated that the airline lost £5 for each passenger it carried! By the autumn it seemed that it was going to disappear, but at the eleventh hour it was purchased by a business entrepreneur with a make or break proposal to concentrate on flowers and freight. The fleet was cut back to just two Heralds, operating improvements were made and the airline finances were slowly pulled around. One example of how was when the new owner acquired an old fuel tanker and informed Shell that if they did not give him the lowest prices, he would fill the tanker up elsewhere and refuel the Heralds himself! By summer 1982 the Channel Islands business had improved, and the nightly Post Office service was carrying 50,000 items of mail from the Wessex area.

In September 1982 the airline revamped itself as Channel Express to reflect its main area of operation, and was acquired by businessman Philip Meeson in April 1983. Well known at the time as the UK aerobatic champion, he had displayed at Bournemouth's recent Air Pageants. Channel Express expanded its road distribution network from Bournemouth and constructed a cool store. This enabled their specialised fleet of temperature-controlled vehicles to deliver flowers and produce swiftly to thirty-four markets around the country. A children's competition was held to choose names for the two Heralds, which also brought publicity for the airline, so much so that when one of the aircraft suffered a wheels-up landing in Guernsey it received get well cards from the local children!

July and August 1984 saw another dock strike hit the Channel Islands and an airlift was set up to bring tomatoes and other produce to the mainland. The airlift included a couple of Hercules, one from France and one from Botswana (it was already on charter duties in the country at the time). By now the handling staff were used to the Hercules which were bringing in tomatoes faster than the lorries could take them away. A further strike in September affected Southampton Docks with the *QE2* and *Canberra* liners forced to use Cherbourg. The passengers and luggage were flown into Bournemouth to be taken on to London by coach.

Channel Express expanded its operations in the late 1980s and increased its fleet of Heralds. The airline had obtained contracts for express parcel deliveries into Europe for multinationals such as Federal Express and TNT. There were also the early-morning flights delivering papers and Royal Mail to the Channel Islands. These provided the local residents with a 5.30 a.m. wake-up call. By now the majority of tomatoes were being shipped by a subsidiary company by sea using the Ro-Ro ferries, thereby freeing up the aircraft for other duties. For greater capacity, the first of a number of Lockheed Electra freighters entered service in December 1988. Although able to carry a record 3,200 flower boxes, they were only used for a few months on the Channel Islands routes. The Electras were switched to Channel Express's parcels operations where their capacity aided the expansion of business. By summer 1994 it was obvious that the Heralds were not going to last forever and so Friendships began to appear as replacements, with two normally based at Bournemouth.

The freight aircraft of Channel Express were based at the airport for many years. They operated the nightly Royal Mail flights to Liverpool and the produce and newspaper flights to the Channel Islands. Seen landing is one of their F.27 Friendships.

When the Electras first entered service they were flown by their former American crews who drew breath at the site of the 'short' runway at Guernsey. The Channel Express pilots soon had them landing in half the length with the use of reverse pitch on the engines. However, the Americans were still heard to comment that some of their Navy carriers had longer decks than Guernsey's runway!

In May 1991 a new holding company was formed, Dart Group Plc. This became the parent company for the expanding Channel Express operations.

ONE-ELEVEN EVENTS

In December 1986 the first of a number of One-Elevens was repainted at the airport for a new Irish airline, Ryanair. At the time, no one realised what that was going to lead to! August 1988 saw the commemoration of the twenty-fifth anniversary of the One-Eleven's first flight from Bournemouth in 1963. A special flight was laid on for invited guests, including test pilots Jock Bryce and Brian Trubshaw, operated by a Ryanair One-Eleven. It fell to Jock Bryce to cut the anniversary cake. Early in 1990 Australian businessman Paul Stoddard purchased two former Australian AF One-Elevens, which were registered to his company European Aviation in September. One was stored at Bournemouth for a few months before being sold on to Nigeria. This was later to lead to the start of another airline for Bournemouth.

18

AIRPORT FOR SALE

AIRPORT SELL OFF

The Government's Airport Bill of 1986 stated that airports could no longer be run by local authorities, now having to be in private ownership. So the two local councils incorporated Bournemouth Hurn Airport Plc in November 1986, both taking a 50 per cent shareholding. Valued at £6 million in November 1985, tenders were invited from the private sector the following November for operation of the airport as from 1987. Interested parties included British & Commonwealth Shipping (Airwork), Bamberg Group, FR Aviation, Ogden Aviation and P&O Group. Losses for 1985/86 were £273,000 and, tied in with possible sale plans, any further terminal extensions were put on hold. The 1969 loan debt of £750,000 had risen to £2.8 million, with the local authorities having underwritten the annual deficit over the years. These figures were not good for any potential purchaser. The new Airport Plc commenced business on 1 April 1987, paying £16.2 million for the various assets on the 970-acre site and introducing the operating title of Bournemouth International Airport. (The airfield site consisted of 470 acres related to flying, 200 acres of industrial use and 300 being designated a Site of Special Scientific Interest.) The bidders to run the airport management had been reduced to Ogden Aviation when, in May, the Plc announced that operations would remain 'in house'. Efforts were made to attract new business but the problem was not so much attracting the airlines as getting passengers to use Bournemouth. It was estimated that 400,000 people in the local catchment area had undertaken holiday flights during 1986, but only 25,000 had used Bournemouth. Gatwick was considered to just about have reached saturation point, with the need for its holiday flights to go elsewhere. Bournemouth remained upbeat about some of this coming its way, but in the end Gatwick coped. Application was made to the EEC in summer 1987 for the release of monies from their regional development fund to finance the further extension of the terminal buildings. However, no payment was available as the EEC informed the directors that Bournemouth was not in the right part of England to qualify! The sudden 'first' retirement of Harry Longhurst after eighteen years as airport director occurred on 13 December 1987:

> It has been more like a hobby than a job and for that I could not be more grateful. When I arrived there were three services a week to the Channel Islands plus three local holiday firms operating flights to the Mediterranean. Despite improvements, there is still a problem

of not being to offer a wide range of flights and destinations, with some local travel agents not supporting holidays from Bournemouth. Hence the reason for the likes of Thomson and Horizon only operating for short periods, compounded by the extra costs of operating away from base. Bournemouth should be the south's regional airport as it has superior facilities to Southampton and could soon see 1m passengers a year triggered by capacity problems at Heathrow and Gatwick.

The director's post was advertised in February 1988, offering a total package commensurate with the standing of a major International Airport! This resulted in 115 applicants but no immediate selection of a replacement. In March the councils made it known they were considering selling part of their shareholding. In September they confirmed that they intended so sell their 50 per cent holdings in the airport, requesting merchant bankers to advise on the sell-off. The plans were thrown into disarray in October when millionaire Peter de Savary bought Southampton Airport, announcing expansion plans which included a new terminal and industrial complex. This unexpected development reduced the saleability of Bournemouth so it was back to square one for a while. The P&O Group later said they could not understand why their 1987 bid had been turned down, as their plan was to purchase both Bournemouth and Southampton. The latter would have been closed and developed as an industrial park with all air traffic sent to Bournemouth.

WHO IS IN COMMAND?

With no director, the airport's board chairman came to the fore as spokesman for airport business. Frustrated by restrictions over further expansion, he resigned in November 1988 and moved to Exeter Airport as commercial director. A replacement director was finally appointed in January 1989. However, he only lasted until December when his contract was prematurely terminated; he was asked to clear his desk one morning and leave! On top of this the operations director had accepted early retirement in August 1989. Following the short tenure of his replacement, Harry Longhurst was recalled in April 1990 to the post of temporary airport director. After twenty-five years of service to the airport, Harry finally retired in spring 1992, having been replaced by Doug Wilson who arrived from Belfast Airport. He saw the potential of the airport site, not only for air services but for the surrounding aviation-related companies.

RUNWAY PROBLEMS

A Civil Aviation Authority report early in 1989 recommended that a 'new' runway would be needed in south-east England fairly soon. Instead of at Heathrow, Gatwick or a new airport this should be at an existing one, with Bournemouth and Stansted mentioned as possibilities. In spring 1989 the Airport Board considered plans to increase passenger numbers to 3.5 million within ten years, up from the current 160,000. However, Dorset

Council objected, saying they would not allow the airport to become a second Luton. The CAA followed up in July 1990 by saying it considered Bournemouth, with a new terminal plus runway extension, could handle twenty airliner flights an hour and 3 million passengers a year within ten years. The recession at the time meant that these proposals could not be followed through.

In April 1990 the two councils decided not to proceed with the sale of their shareholdings (estimated value £50 million), hoping to introduce industrial expansion on the northern side of the airport, aided by the closure of the secondary north–south runway. It was considered the closure would not affect the economic viability of the airport, and would help preserve the Site of Special Scientific Interest at the north-eastern side of the airport. There was opposition to the closure from operators both large (Bath Travel) and small (Flying Club). (The runway was eventually closed without ceremony during 2003.) The councils considered that development of a business park would be more financially beneficial than airport operations, which could be turned over to a specialist operator. The 200 acres allocated to the business park were described as a 'multi-million pound property goldmine', but the downturn in the economy prevented any such development. The airport wanted to be regarded as the south's airport, not, as suggested by the South West Regional Planning Conference, a sub-regional airport for the south-west. Unfortunately, figures did not support this: 1989/90 passenger numbers were Bristol 878,800, Exeter 228,000 and Bournemouth 194,000. The airport frequently seemed to be stuck in the middle; was it south-east or south-west?

WARTIME MINES

A matter of some concern in the early 1990s was that many airports still had wartime defence mines, usually situated under their runways! Examples in the south included Exeter, Plymouth and Southampton. The Army were called in to undertake surveys, resulting in Southampton being closed for a weekend in February 1990 for the mines to be dealt with. Luckily, there had been no problem in 1964 when the concrete runway was laid. Bournemouth's turn came in 1991 with the Royal Engineers finding a number of pipe mines in the vicinity of the runways – all were safely defused.

FURTHER HOLIDAY PROBLEMS

Palmair introduced a Princess Air BAe 146 for a number of its flights from April 1990; at the time they were flying 25,000 passengers annually from Bournemouth. Other flights were operated by Air Europe with Boeing 737s. However, Princess Air ran into financial problems, appointing a receiver at the end of February 1991 and going out of business in early March. The 146 was due to be repossessed by BAe, but at the time was in Palma ready to fly holidaymakers back to Bournemouth. Luckily, BAe agreed that their aircraft could make this one last flight before being repossessed. Bath Travel had only received three hours notice of the problem, and hastily arranged for Dan-Air and Trans European

A number of south-coast airports had a scare in 1990 when it was discovered that a number of them – Bournemouth included – still had wartime pipe mines around their runways. The Royal Engineers safely removed Bournemouth's in spring 1991.

This Air 2000 Boeing 757, diverted from Gatwick in February 1991, proved to be Bournemouth's first non-stop flight from the USA for many years. Up to then larger aircraft had been used across the Atlantic, proving too big to use Bournemouth 'short' runway.

Airways to operate subsequent flights. In March 1991 Air Europe went out of business, in June there was a civil war in Yugoslavia and in September Trans European Airways went bust. Not a good year for Bath Travel! It was followed by Dan-Air going out of business in October 1992. Having suffered problems with various airlines over recent years, the directors finally decided to set up their own airline in the spring of 1993, with a BAe 146 Whisper Jet of Palmair Flightline introduced on their flights from May.

February 1991 saw the diversion of an Air 2000 Boeing 757 from Orlando–Gatwick, reported to be Bournemouth's first transatlantic passenger flight for forty years. A new local holiday firm was Islanders, which introduced flights to Jersey by Aurigny Short 360s in summer 1994, with Gerona served by European One-Elevens two years later.

RECESSION

The recession of the early 1990s continued to affect the airport's business, with a number of staff laid off in October 1992. This was compounded by Jersey European closing its operations base in autumn 1991, followed by the pulling out of its winter services in 1992. This left Bournemouth with just holiday flights over the winter months. So it was back to the gloomy days of 1966 when all the scheduled airlines had moved out to Southampton. To add salt to the wound, Southampton advertised its new services in the local press on the page opposite that giving details of Bournemouth's job losses! In April 1993 plans were announced for the rebuilding of Southampton, including a modern terminal building. One unwise local comment was that this was 'unlikely to have any major impact on Bournemouth'. Jersey European found that its daily service to the Channel Islands was still uneconomic, so again cancelled its winter services during 1992/93. The reason was a 20 per cent drop in holidaymakers, plus a reduction in business travel. Services resumed in April 1993 for the summer (fare £61 single) but, come the following October, the airline withdrew completely to concentrate on its operations from Southampton. This broke the run of scheduled services to the Channel Islands from Bournemouth for a few years.

NO CASH FOR EXPANSION

The airport announced in November 1993 that under a new master plan the main runway extension was ready to proceed, along with terminal improvements. Controlled airline growth would cover local business and leisure needs, not those of London. Initial spending of £5 million was required, the aim being to increase passenger numbers from an existing low of 72,500 a year to 425,000 by 2000 – all very optimistic at a time when there were no scheduled services. However, the main problem was how to finance the extension and improvements; the runway alone was expected to cost £1.6 million. Both councils had their monies committed elsewhere, although Dorset initially thought it might be able come up with £1 million. In June 1994 both councils, as sole shareholders, decided to sell a majority of their shares in order to introduce public-sector funding, although this idea was opposed by the Airport Board.

EURO DIRECT COMES – AND GOES

Hope for scheduled services was restored in the spring of 1994. This followed the announcement in February of a wide range of routes operated by Euro Direct with a fleet of BAe Jetstream 31s and ATPs. Launched for business people early in April with a blaze of publicity, initial services were twice-daily to Amsterdam, Brussels, Dublin, Leeds with Paris CDG from the end of the month. Initially eighteen-seat Jetstream 31s were used, with business fares being Brussels £170 single and Dublin £160 single. ATPs and further destinations were introduced during the summer, including the re-establishment of the Manchester link in July, with Exeter and Humberside being added as further hubs. Some of the Jetstreams received names at civic ceremonies – *Spirit of Bournemouth*, *Poole* and *Christchurch* – the latter not being so appropriate when the aircraft was transferred to Euro Direct's Belgian associate company. All

Passengers boarding a Jetstream 31 of Euro Direct, which offered a wide range of destinations during 1994. This was a bold attempt to boost services from Bournemouth, but, as is often the case, finances did not work out as planned.

appeared to be going well, although there was some contraction of services over the winter months. Problems emerged at the end of November, when it was announced that passenger numbers were down on target – 35,000 in six months, with 250,000 p.a. required. The directors commented on a lack of support from Dorset businesspeople. Euro Direct's Humberside hub was closed at the end of November and the winter timetable was cut back further in mid-December. Then, suddenly, Euro Direct announced that it would cease flying at the end of February; its final service was to Paris on 26 February 1995. The end had been brought about by high operating costs and landing fees at major European airports, plus the withdrawal of the original financial backing. The only good point was the airline did not leave a trail of debts as many others had done. Once again it was down to the holiday flights to continue passenger services for the next few months.

VISITORS

An unexpected arrival early one morning in September 1988 was a privately owner Gazelle helicopter pursued by two RAF Pumas! The occupants had smuggled in drugs from Holland, dropping them off at Andover without realising they were being followed. On take-off, the Gazelle was chased by the Pumas and forced to land at Bournemouth. Those on board were arrested, and later convicted, with the helicopter being impounded.

August 1991 saw a fly-past of the last airworthy Vickers Varsity – a trials aircraft from RAE Farnborough. For its final flight it included Bournemouth in recognition of it being one of those built at the airport in 1952. July 1993 saw the very low fly-past midday of the last airworthy Sandringham flying boat. It was en route from Calshot to its new owner in Florida. February 1994 saw the low pass of a Virgin Airbus A340 on a murky afternoon whilst on a crew-training flight out of Gatwick. September 1994 saw pleasure flights offered by Lufthansa in their restored 1930s vintage Junkers Ju52/3 which was on a UK tour. October 1994 saw a number of cattle flights to Holland operated by an Air Algerie Boeing 737; the activities brought animal rights demonstrators to the airport with the threats of firebombs! The flights were moved away with the Boeing tragically crashing at Coventry six weeks later. The fiftieth anniversary of American Airlines first transatlantic landplane service was marked on 24 October 1995 by dignitaries from both the airline and the airport. A plaque, based on the author's design, was unveiled to mark the event and the airport's early involvement in post-war international air travel. Unfortunately, the hoped-for visit from the United States by a Skymaster did not materialise.

Receiving press publicity in January 1997 was an HS.125 executive jet which arrived from South Africa for overhaul. Following a tip-off, Customs and Excise officers were waiting in hiding with two of the jets' occupants making a run for it when they spotted them. The reason was that the aircraft was carrying £500,000 of cannabis, with the owner later appearing at Bournemouth Court where he was sentenced to jail.

Not all the visitors to the airport were airliners. RAF Hercules continued to call, as did those of Oman AF and UAE AF, to collect cargo for the Middle East. As well as normal military loads, the cargo was known to include Rolls-Royces, luxury Range Rovers, powerboats and zoo animals. One of the Sheiks in Dubai was a keen power-boat racer. Other RAF traffic brought Chinook helicopters from the early 1980s, distinguished by the thwack-thwack of their rotor blades. These would be crew training from their Odiham base or on a post-overhaul test flight from Fleetlands. It was possible to see any front line RAF or RN aircraft on a training sortie, ranging from Tornado to Sentry, Sea Harrier to Sea King. The variety was boosted by aircraft of Empire Test Pilots School at Boscombe Down, with the likes of Basset, HS 748 and One-Eleven.

FINAL VISCOUNT

Bournemouth was to see its last Viscount on 30 November 1997 when the airport was one of a number visited for farewell flights by enthusiasts. Bournemouth had been left off the initial list of airports until the organisers realised that Bournemouth was the home of the majority of Viscounts. The aircraft arrived from Southend and for £59 undertook an hour's local flight before returning, so marking not quite fifty years from when the famous airliner was first seen at Bournemouth. Another notable visitor was a preserved Constellation which arrived from the United States in June 1998 to visit a number of UK airports before flying to Berlin to commemorate the fiftieth anniversary of the Berlin Air Lift. Painted in USAF colours, it arrived on 8 June, but plans to operate flights were thwarted by regulations (including no British passenger C of A, plus hardly any fitted seats), so the enthusiastic crew had to settle for showing the public round their pride and joy. It was planned to depart to Middle Wallop which only had a grass runway, so the experienced pilot checked it out first. He reported back saying it was better than some of the hard runways he had previously landed the airliner on.

19

NATIONAL EXPRESS GROUP

NEW OWNERS...

In November 1994 Bournemouth and Dorset Councils offered the airport for sale. After years of indecision they finally agreed not to sell outright but to offer a 999-year lease. Despite statements that the airport's paper assets were worth £25 million, only two bids were received – one for £4 million, the second £7.1 million. This was from the National Express Group who had purchased East Midlands Airport for £27 million in spring 1994, and were also bidding for Cardiff. The timing of the withdrawal of Euro Direct services in February 1995 was not good news, but it did not stop the negotiations. The deal was concluded in April 1995 with National Express announcing that they would improve the facilities and attractiveness of the airport. This would start with the £2 million, 20 per cent extension of the main runway to 2,020 yards. This would hopefully attract back scheduled services, also appealing to holiday operators and freight operators with aircraft of Boeing 767 and DC-8F size. At the time there were 100,000 aircraft movements a year, 70 per cent of which were training flights. National Express advertised in spring 1996 that it was transforming the scale of operations of the former little, local airport by investing £10 million into the enterprise, including £2 million on the runway extension – the new Bournemouth International Airport.

... NEW RUNWAY

Sunday 21 April 1996 was the day the runway extension was brought into use. To mark the event, Bath Travel chartered Concorde from British Airways to operate a subsonic flight from Heathrow (which cost £199). It spent two hours on the ground before undertaking a £499 supersonic flight 'Round the Bay (of Biscay)' before returning to Heathrow. Harry Longhurst, the former airport director, was proud to be a special guest on this flight. There was an unprecedented demand for the flights with the first from Heathrow sold out within five hours and the return one in three weeks. There were huge traffic jams around the area on the day, with over 25,000 people turning up at the airport to see Concorde. The airport's publicity called the event 'Big Nose Day', with Doug Wilson remarking, 'This is the most important 400 metres of concrete in the south west'. The airport was also able to announce Ryanair's intention to commence low-fare

Concorde's proud crew on the occasion of its first visit to Bournemouth in April 1996. This proved to be the first of eighteen charters organised by Bath Travel until the airliner was grounded in 2003. Bournemouth's Aviation Museum applied unsuccessfully to put one on display.

operations into the airport, with one of their 737s making an appearance. The day also saw a Dove to mark the aircraft's use by Bath Travel back in 1947, pleasure flights in a Dakota and the unconnected arrival of a Tristar which was persuaded to make a low pass before landing.

TRANSATLANTIC CHARTERS

The runway extension was soon put to good use. Thomson's IT flights to Majorca were due to be operated by Boeing 757s, but high demand saw Boeing 767s frequently used from May 1996. Bath Travel organised a charter direct to Orlando on 30 May operated by a Leisure International 767, followed by a second in October. This did not go according to plan as the 767 went unserviceable and could not fly the passengers home. Hence the strange sight of a Douglas DC-10 of the Mexican airline Taesa at Bournemouth, having brought the passengers home. The flights marked the start of Bath Travel's transatlantic holiday operations. Following the success of the Concorde visit, Bath's arranged a second visit in August with a supersonic flight out over the Atlantic and then to Paris. £795 bought you Concorde to Paris, two nights in the Hilton Hotel and then home by Palmair 146 (or vice versa). Bath Travel's business included sea cruises, with the *QE2* being to the fore, and this resulted in further Concorde visits. The directors' aim was a New York flight, but because of its fully loaded weight this could still not be undertaken from Bournemouth's extended runway. So the passengers sailed to New York in August 1997 and spent three nights in the Waldorf Hotel at a cost of £2,595. Two groups then returned to Bournemouth in just over three hours on supersonic Concorde flights. (The problem was solved in August 1998 when Concorde was able to operate the outward leg from the military base at Boscombe Down – 'Salisbury International' – for the day.) Fly/cruise holidays to the Caribbean were also introduced, frequently operated by Britannia 767s, with an Air Cruise to Egypt in 1995 flown by 146 as part of the development of Palmair Day Trips. To keep the 146 fully utilised, one day a week was set aside for trips to European capitals. These quickly proved very popular with the Palmair clients, taking the management by surprise. In 1997 seven day trips were operated; by 2005 this had risen to thirty-two.

RYANAIR – START OF LOW-COST OPERATIONS

The early 1990s saw a number of low-fare airlines formed in Britain, although some only lasted a short time. The idea, still quite novel, was promoted vigorously by the Irish airline Ryanair. Their managing director had a different way of dealing with the airports that Ryanair intended to use. The airports were told that as they would make profits from the additional new passengers, there was no need for the airline to pay any charges. Ryanair commenced a Dublin–Bournemouth service with Boeing 737s in May 1995, at the time offering a return fare 'as low as £59' (this seems rather expensive ten years on). Originally, the flights flew in an almost direct line to Bournemouth, but after a few months this was changed for safety reasons. The flights now head for Bristol, along the A4, turning south over Newbury for the A34 and down to Southampton, before finally heading for Bournemouth. The airline introduced the first of its flying advertising hoarding in October with one of the 737s painted with Jaguar car logos. This was followed by others, including Hertz car rental, Kilkenny Beer, News of the World/Sun and Tipperary Crystal.

The introduction of low-fare flights by Ryanair was a novelty to Bournemouth passengers in 1995; it is now accepted as normal. Ryanair use some of their fleet for publicity purposes, and here are trying to bring about the demise of Italian airline Alitalia.

OTHER AIRLINE CHANGES

On a smaller scale, South Coast Airways set up operations in April 1996 with a luxury-equipped Dakota, offering the chance of nostalgic flights of bygone times. Its director, who had many years of Dakota flying under his belt, also frequently flew the B-17 *Sally B* at airshows as well as instructing with the Flying Club and (for excitement) flying new Cherokees from Florida across the Atlantic on delivery flights to Bournemouth.

June 1996 saw a special event at Heathrow to commemorate its fifty years as a major international airport. There was a fly-past of airliners from over the years, which included publicity for various Bournemouth connections. Channel Express provided a Herald, with their chief executive flying his Dragon Rapide, South Coast provided their Dakota and, although not now at Bournemouth, a Jersey Airlines Heron which had been a regular visitor in the 1950s.

Channel Express introduced its first Airbus A300F Eurofreighter in July 1997, but these were for use on the European express parcels services, rarely being seen at Bournemouth. However, their introduction was a big step up for Channel Express into the league of major freight carriers. Their Heralds were gradually replaced by F.27 Friendships which provided higher payloads and flew faster. The final Herald was retired to the Bournemouth Aviation Museum in April 1999, proving to have been the last Herald flying in the world. The Friendships continued the daily Channel Islands and Royal Mail services as well as a large number of ad-hoc charters to European destinations.

TERMINAL DELAYS

In March 1997 National Express announced plans for an impressive new terminal for 1.2 million passengers, hopefully to be ready by 2000. By then they hoped to be handling 500,000 passengers per annum, who could not be adequately handled in the existing terminal. The Airport Director said, 'Terminals form a vital first impression. I want this airport to be an international gateway in which local people can share a pride'. (Unfortunately, the improvements are still awaited ten years on). This optimistic news was followed by another new airline, Euroscot Express, which commenced daily Glasgow and Edinburgh services in September 1997. Operated by a One-Eleven, the flights were aimed at the leisure market with fares from £39 single, plus tax. Euroscot replaced their One-Eleven with an ATR.72 turbo-prop in August 1998, its director explaining that it would be more environmentally friendly and cost-efficient (anything would be compared with a One-Eleven!). Plans to operate to Amsterdam from March 1999 dragged on throughout the winter, but had not commenced by the time the airline went out of business in July 1999.

Dorset County Council regarded the airport as an important influence in terms of transport and as a major employer. It recognised the need to improve transport choices so as to reduce car usage by passengers (5 per cent) and employees (20 per cent). A ten-year plan was drawn up to improve the local roads, mainly to be funded by the airport.

Almost one third of the airport's area is designated a Site of Special Scientific Interest. This is mainly the heathland on the northern side. As well as wildlife, the airport takes care of trees and plants. Here, pruning is undertaken on one of the boundary hawthorn hedges.

As usual, finance proved the stumbling block, so preventing any real practical work. The winter of 1998 saw the commencement of regular ski holiday flights from Bournemouth – Crystal Holidays to Chambery by British Airways BAe 146 and Innsbruck by Tyrolean Airlines (later Lauda). Airport passenger numbers had risen during 1998 to 314,000 (Southampton 756,000 pre FlyBe), but this was not enough for National Express who had hoped to be getting nearer 500,000. Unexpected news in October 1998 was the swift departure of airport director, Doug Wilson, 'by mutual agreement' with National Express. He was replaced in August 1999 by Glyn Jones who remained in post for just over four years. There was also bad news regarding the terminal plans; they were called in by the Department of Environment in January 2000 as the airport fell within Green Belt Land. This was despite it having being in business for fifty-five years! National Express decided to move the location to the southern end of the soon to be closed north–south runway with the plans put on hold to await an upturn in passenger numbers.

CONCORDE HICCUP…

Concorde had been chartered by Bath Travel for a Rome trip in May 1999, but the night before, British Airways announced that they had no Concorde to spare and that a Boeing 737 would be sent as it had the same passenger capacity.

Peter Bath explains that this was the worst day of his life (and there must have been many problems within the holiday travel business).

I received a phone call from British Airways at Heathrow the evening before to say that three Concordes were out of action, but they had arranged a 737 replacement. There were just over 400 clients expecting a Concorde flight and no way of contacting them beforehand. So it was down to the airport at 5:30 on the Sunday morning to break the news to the distraught passengers, many who had travelled long distances. I also had to break the news to our tour manager in Rome asking him to handle the passengers due to fly home. The 737 turned up mid-day but only sixty of our clients decided to continue with their holiday to Rome. In the end British Airways paid compensation and laid on a replacement flight a month later.

... AND PALMAIR GROWTH

Palmair increased capacity when its 146 was replaced by a Boeing 737 in November 1999. Now under the Palmair European name, services were operated by a European aircraft on behalf of Palmair. The 737 gave greater range and capacity, obviating the need to refuel en route on some of the holiday flights. From the passengers' point of view regarding comfort, it was not fitted with a full compliment of seats, so giving them more leg room. A 'one-off' trip by a Monarch 757 to Egypt in April 2000 proved so popular that it had to be operated on three consecutive days – twice to Cairo and once to Luxor. Demand for the Palmair day trips was also increasing, this type of operation being unique to Bournemouth.

In March 2001 Palmair was voted the third best airline in the world by the *Holiday Which?* magazine. The presentation of this award was soon picked up by the national press who pointed out that the airline only had one aircraft, but that the attention to their passengers was exceptional.

Four Concorde visits had been planned for 2000, but the fatal crash of an Air France aircraft at Paris in July meant that the two scheduled for September were cancelled. This included one from Bournemouth–New York, which was to call at Shannon to refuel. All Concordes were grounded until September 2001 when limited transatlantic services were reintroduced by British Airways. Bath Travel hoped it would be able to charter the aircraft again during 2002, but this was not possible as British Airways did not return all their fleet to service. Concorde had operated twenty-one flights into the airport on twelve days over a five-year period, with each of the seven aircraft of British Airways fleet having been used. This was well in excess of Peter Bath's original dreams and expectations:

One of the Concorde pilots commented during a visit to Bournemouth that this was a shame as they and the crews liked operating such flights into local airports. They had the opportunity to meet enthusiastic passengers who had a real love of the aircraft (as did the

The largest aircraft to have visited Bournemouth is the Antonov An-124 freighter. This one of the Russian airline Volga Dnepr carried Nimrod fuselages to and from FR Aviation. Despite being Russian, the RAF frequently uses An-124 for carrying large loads.

crews). It certainly made a change from the Heathrow New York 'day job' where the flight crew were remote from the passengers and did not get much feed back. At Bournemouth they were treated like heroes.

Any hope for future flights from Bournemouth came to an end in October 2003 when the Concordes were taken out of service for good. Some residents of Bournemouth had their last brief glimpse of the airliner on the evening of 18 July when one flew low eastwards along the coast whilst on a test flight out of Heathrow.

FIRST JUMBO ARRIVAL... AND OTHER BIG JETS

A diversion from Gatwick in May 1999 included six British Airways Boeing 737s, which the local press reported as eight Jumbo Jets, although nobody had noticed any noise. Going back to the early 1970s, there had been outcry from the local residents when mention was made of 747 Jumbos possibly using the airport. This had never been the intention as the introduction of the runway extension was to cope with the likes of Boeing 767s. So the paper was able to regain some credibility when it published photographs of a Jumbo undertaking crew training in May 2000. It was, in fact, a luxury VIP version operated on behalf of a Middle Eastern sultan, returning again in December to make use of 'cheap' parking. Whenever visiting the UK, it would leave its 'passengers' at Stansted and then fly down to Bournemouth where the parking fees were cheaper, becoming semi-resident over the next few years.

Although it was the world's largest passenger aircraft at the time, Bournemouth's first 747 had been preceded by other large jet freighters. A giant USAF C-5 Galaxy made a fly-past during the 1984 Air Show. June 1987 saw a USAF C-141 Starlifter collecting US Marines fresh from training at Hamworthy Marines Camp. May 1996 saw the first visit of a massive Antonov An-124 freighter which called to collect flight simulators. Further visits were made in November when other An-124s arrived with Nimrod fuselages for FR Aviation. January 2000 saw the first visit of an Airbus Beluga freighter, when it called to collect fuselage sections of a surplus Airbus A300 from Channel Express for Airbus Industries. January 2005 saw a RAF C-17 Globemaster arrive unexpectedly to undertake a crew change before quickly departing. Although an older turbo-prop, February 2004 saw a night-time visit of an Antonov An-22 to collect engine spares from Channel Express. The freighter was almost as long as its stablemate An-124. So unless there is a highly unexpected visit by the new Airbus A380 airliner, the An-124 remains the largest aircraft to visit Bournemouth Airport.

20

AROUND THE AIRFIELD

FLYING TRAINING AND CLUB FLYING

Bournemouth saw limited private flying in the 1950s and had no based light aircraft. At the time, Christchurch catered for such needs but its impending closure brought changes. Seeing the need for continued club flying, the Bournemouth Flying Club was formed in September 1961. Housed in a wooden hut on the south-east side of the airport, it used the title of the pre-war club at Christchurch. The club was officially opened in December by Lord Montague, whose father had been a keen supporter of early flyers. The club's initial aircraft was an Auster, with a Dragon Rapide appearing in spring 1962. By the early 1970s Cessnas were in use, with flying rates now £8ph. Due to its success, the club was able to move to more substantial premises on the north-east side in summer 1973. The club suffered a number of problems in the late 1970s, resulting in its takeover by A&G Aviation in June 1980. A&G had been forced out of Ford airfield, and were looking for a replacement hangar to continue its maintenance business. That used by the club proved suitable for A&G and on arrival they decided to continue the flying training side as well. An inaugural fly-in in March 1981 was ruined by bad weather, with only four aircraft attending (although there were plenty of left-over burgers). On the club side, the fleet of Cessnas was built up. The maintenance and overhaul side, titled Anglo American Airmotive from 1987, expanded, becoming a Piper light aircraft agency in July 1993.

A&G Aviation was owned by the Norris family. Ken Norris, managing director, was also interested in aerodynamic design and engineering.

Ken had been an apprentice with Armstrong Whitworth Aircraft. In the 1950s Ken and his brother designed the Bluebird VII boat in which Donald Campbell first achieved the water speed record in 1955, but lost his life in 1962. The brothers had also designed his record breaking Bluebird car. In the 1980s Ken was taken on by Richard Noble as Team Manager for his Thrust II car which achieved the world land speed record in 1983. Richard was a member of the Flying Club and learnt of Ken's talents whilst there. In 1993 discussions were held in the Clubhouse which led to the Thrust SuperSonic Car which broke the sound barrier in 1997. Ken then turned his thoughts back to water and the design of a boat to retake the water speed record – Quicksilver. His last project was working on the design of a 1,000mph car.

Anglo American held a Piper fly-in in July 1994, including a navigation competition which was won by a Cessna! Two of the Club Cessnas made headlines locally in the autumn of 1995, following engine problems. In September one force landed on Barton Golf Club, but was able to be flown away by one of the engineers. However, the following month the pilot of another had to make an emergency landing on the beach at Highcliffe; this time the aircraft had to be dismantled before returning to the airport. The club was visited by a newly restored DH Gipsy Moth in September 1996, the biplane having been part of the Bournemouth Flying Club fleet at Christchurch back in the 1930s. Other visitors included the likes of RAF Hawks and Tornados where the pilots gave talks to club members. The Norris family sold the flying-club side of the business in spring 1998 when there was a downturn in light aviation. The new club owners decided that as there was less demand for private flying they would set up the Bournemouth Commercial Flight Training Centre. Commencing business in summer 2002, the centre provided CPL commercial training from premises at the western end of the airport. The maintenance side of Anglo American was acquired by the Meridian Aviation Group in February 2002 and the Piper Aircraft Agency passed into the hands of Senate Aviation. The Flying Club currently provides PPL private training on its fleet of Beech Duchesses and Piper Cherokees, with an hour's trial lesson available at £135 – a sign of rising fuel costs. The Clubhouse, situated in one of the 'temporary' wartime buildings, offers excellent views of the runway and airfield.

Professional Air Training is another company happily based in one of the still functioning wartime buildings on the south side – in their case a Mess Room. Since the early 1990s they have operated a fleet of Beech Duchesses and Sierras for CPL commercial training. The activities of the fleet make up a large amount of the current movements at the airport.

In the 1990s helicopter training was provided by Buzzi-B Helicopters from premises adjacent to the Aviation Museum. In June 1994 the business passed to Bournemouth Helicopters, with its fleet including a Bell Jet Ranger, Robinson R.22s and Schweizer 300s. Flying training and self-fly hire are available, a trial lesson costing £89 early in 2001. However, mounting fuel costs five years later has resulted in this rising to £100 for a twenty-minute flight. Operating in conjunction with Bournemouth Helicopters is the Solent School of Flying. The school offers PPL and trial lessons with its fleet of Piper Cherokees and diesel-engined Cessna 172s. Again, costs have risen – an hour's trial flight in 2001 cost £79, which has risen to £125 five years later. Fuel prices are affecting every section of the aviation world.

One private aircraft owner was Neville Duke. As mentioned earlier, Neville had been a visitor to the airport in the 1960s. On his 'retirement' to the Lymington area in the late 1970s, Neville based his Cessna at the airport in summer 1978, as flying was still in his blood. To mark the 30th anniversary of his world air-speed record, he was invited by Mike Carlton to fly the course again, this time in his Hunter Trainer. This took place on 7 September 1983, with Mike reaching a speed of about 700mph – just short of the original record. The flight was repeated ten years later, by which time the Hunter was operated by Jet Heritage. Neville was requested by FLS Aviation to test fly their Optica and Sprint light aircraft projects in 1993. This continued for a couple of years and, although well into his eighties, Neville continued flying his Cherokee into the 2000s, with wife Gwen being his vital navigator.

Among the Robinson R-22s recently operated by Bournemouth Helicopters, this one carried an appropriate registration. It had originally been based at the airport with another operator in 1993 before returning for a short spell in 2003.

WARBIRDS

The late 1970s saw an increase in the country of privately owned fighter and trainer aircraft, mainly of Second World War vintage. However, Bournemouth was involved with a Messerschmitt 109 as early as 1966 when a battered airframe arrived for long-term restoration. The owner was rather secretive and not many people knew which hut it was located in. The Messerschmitt saw the light of day once when it appeared at the 1967 BAC Families Day, then returned to its hut for further restoration. This proved to be protracted and any thoughts of returning it to the sky were abandoned. Realising the project was now more than he could handle, the owner sold the Messerschmitt in March 1998 to the Imperial War Museum where it can be seen on static display at Duxford.

Not all people went for Second World War aircraft. London businessman Mike Carlton bought a Hawker Hunter jet fighter which arrived at Bournemouth in summer 1981. The reason for choosing Bournemouth was that Eric Hayward – a former Hawker senior engineer who had rebuilt the Hunter for its previous owners – had just 'retired' to the local area. With aviation in his blood, he could not turn down the offer to maintain the aircraft in its new home. Mike's next objective was the setting up of a fleet of classic British jet fighters, which included an Armstrong Whitworth Meteor night fighter, DH Vampire and Percival Jet Provost. Tragically, Mike was killed whilst on holiday in August 1986, resulting in the fleet of fighters being put up for auction in October 1987.

Rising Phoenix-like in February 1989 was Jet Heritage, formed by a group of enthusiastic businessmen headed by Adrian Gjertsen. Most of the aircraft remained behind after the auction to form the core of the new operation. This enabled Jet Heritage to host a '50 Years of British Jet Flight' celebration in May 1991. The event was attended by a who's who of test pilots: John Cunningham, Neville Duke, John Farley, Peter Twiss, to name but a few. The local press reported that the event was, 'To commemorate the Gloster E28/39... the jet will make a fly-past'. In fact, the E28/39 had been in the Science Museum since 1945! As well as display flying, restoration work was also undertaken under the guidance of Eric. The first of a number of former Swiss Air Force Vampires arrived during 1991, followed by Hunters in June 1995. The work and enthusiasm of Jet Heritage came to the attention of King Hussein of Jordan who was himself an experienced pilot. In a visit to the hangars in December 1993, he commented on being, 'most impressed on my most memorable visit'. This resulted in the decision to form a Historic Flight of the Royal Jordanian Air Force, with Jet Heritage undertaking overhaul work on the aircraft. These were two Vampires and four Hunters, which after completion were flown to Amman in May 1997. There had always been plans for the hangars to be accessible to the public, and this occurred in May 1998 with the opening of the Jet Heritage Museum. There was a display by most of the resident jets, plus a visit of Concorde (officially on a Bath Travel charter).

Further activity saw Warbirds of Great Britain build a hangar during summer 1990. This was for its fleet of Second World War fighters, although they did not arrive until the following year. Run by Doug Arnold, the fighters appeared at a few Air Shows but spent most of their time inside the hangar. Once a month, Doug and his pilot would arrive to check on the aircraft, with the pilot undertaking engine runs on the fighters to keep them in trim. Their airtests were infrequent, but the sight of a Corsair or Mustang was sure to turn a few heads. Doug died in November 1992 and over the next few months the aircraft moved away.

Returning to the jet fighter scene, Source Classic Jets arrived in May 1993 with its fleet of Vampires and Venoms, mainly former Swiss Air Force aircraft. Four of the aircraft were invited to display at Boscombe Down in June 1993 to mark the fiftieth anniversary of the Empire Test Pilots School. After further overhauls the fighters began to emerge, from the end of 1995, in a variety of special colours. In September 1997 Source was able to put up an eight-ship formation over the Isle of Wight. The main problem was finding eight pilots still qualified to fly the elderly jets; Boscombe Down was able to supply them. An HS Buccaneer arrived in September 1993, but hopes of returning it to the air were dashed by ministry 'red tape'. Lack of demand for Air Show appearances saw less activity with the fighters, which were put up for sale in 2002.

Over the years the airport has seen a number of visits by the Battle of Britain Memorial Flight. Their historic aircraft might call to refuel for a local display or else be en route to the Channel Islands (always a popular destination). The roar of their Merlins would turn many ahead as they flew overhead, bringing tears to the eyes of wartime veterans. The aircraft originally parked on the main apron during the 1970/80s if they were night-stopping, but more recently these ladies of a certain age have sought refuge in FRA's hangars. Transit flights across the Channel do not always go to plan,

A busy scene on the Jet Heritage apron in June 1995, following the arrival of a number of former Swiss Air Force Hunters. After overhaul, they were delivered to jet warbird owners in this country and the USA.

as the weather often changes whilst the flight is en route. On the way to the Jersey in September 2004 they found that strong winds had increased across the Channel and were forced to night stop. The local papers report that they had been likely to have been blown over the Atlantic were probably slightly exaggerated. For the May 2005 VE Day celebrations, the flight displayed over Southampton, but strong winds prevented them landing at the airport. So they arrived at Bournemouth, night-stopping again before proceeding to Jersey's celebrations.

The flight's commanding officer from 2004 was Sqdn Ldr Clive Rowley:

> My family moved to the Bournemouth area when I was about eleven and I went to school locally, joining the Bournemouth School CCF as soon as I was old enough. Naturally some of the air minded cadets wanted to be fighter pilots, chasing around the skies in Hunters or Lightnings. I was granted a RAF Flying Scholarship, undertaking my training with Bournemouth Flying Club. My initial application to join the RAF was not accepted, their saying they weren't ready for me. So I passed eighteen months as a conductor on the Yellow Buses! Eventually I achieved my aim of flying fighters, but never in my teenage days had I imagined that I would end up flying Hurricanes and Spitfires, especially over my home town.

BOURNEMOUTH AVIATION MUSEUM

Jet Heritage was now being run by new directors. Unfortunately, financial problems meant that the company went into liquidation in August 1999. This almost meant an end to the museum side, but the many volunteers rallied round to bring into existence

The Battle of Britain Memorial Flight usually stops off two or three times a year. Whilst refuelling of their Hurricane is underway in May 2005, the crews are discussing the routing of the rest of their journey.

the Bournemouth Aviation Museum. It is an excellent example of a working museum, with many of the aircraft flying, not gathering dust. Around thirty aircraft are on view, ranging from a half-scale Bleriot to a One-Eleven.

Ken Bradley, the one-time manager of the museum, recalls the early days:

Getting the Museum up and running initially proved very difficult. As well as lack of finance we were Dorset's best kept museum secret as few people were aware that we existed. The museum is now in excellent health and visitors enjoy the hands on experience that we offer with access to many cockpits and aircraft. Our picnic area has the best views of aircraft operations at Bournemouth.

De Havilland Aviation, also based at Swansea, arrived in March 2000 to undertake engineering work on the flying aircraft. De Havilland not only had their own Vampires but also the last airworthy DH Sea Vixen. Initially, the Vixen flew in the red and yellow marking of its last operator, RAF target drone flight, and many people thought this was not correct for a former naval fighter. So they were not impressed when *Red Bull* stepped in during May 2003 to sponsor it at displays in full *Red Bull* colours. However, this ensured that the fighter was kept in the public eye for a few more years, attracting more attention than had it been in Royal Navy colours. A Hunter Trainer was maintained for a German owner who lived in Stuttgart, flying over to the museum every couple of months or so in order to enjoy flying his aircraft. An immaculate Dragon Rapide seldom takes to the air these days, but when it does it undertakes sedate trips around the Isle of Wight and the Purbecks. Then there is the post-war Hawker Fury fighter which turns out to be younger than its pilot owner, plus a Buccaneer which taxies and hopefully will fly again one day. A local businessman became such a firm fan of the Red Arrows that he bought the Gnat displayed in the museum. This saw it return to the skies for the first time in twenty-six years. The majority of airworthy aircraft are displayed inside the museum, with a number of retired airframes outside. These include a Dart Herald loaned by Channel Express and a One-Eleven loaned by European Aviation. A novel use for the One-Eleven is to hire it out for children's parties. Stripped of most of its seats, there is plenty of room for children to dance and play. In August 2004 it was used for an Indian wedding reception, which gave rise to incorrect rumours that it was going to be turned into an Indian restaurant later in the year.

Amongst the collection of the Bournemouth Aviation Museum are a number of airworthy veteran fighters. Prominent here is a Sea Fury with a Hunter and Mig 17 behind. Hanging from the roof – and often missed by visitors – is a Grasshopper primary glider.

The Aviation Museum is frequently the setting for other events, not always with aeronautical connections. It was a stopping off point for a countrywide tour by the Rolls-Royce owners club in 2004. Here the connection was the Rolls-Royce-powered aircraft on display.

The Red Arrow Gnats depart the airport after their 1979 Bournemouth Seafront Display. What is interesting in this view is the lack of buildings in the background in an area which is now occupied by the huge FRA complex.

BOURNEMOUTH AND THE RED ARROWS

Despite their formation in 1965, it was 1971 before Bournemouth saw its first visit from the RAF Aerobatic Team. The Red Arrows, with their seven Folland Gnats, displayed over the seafront at the town's regatta on Wednesday 11 August. Their visit became an annual event, with crowds flocking to the airport and seafront to see the aircraft. In February 1975 the display was 'off' due to Government Defence cuts, but luckily the decision was reversed in time for the summer display. The Gnats frequently called at the airport to refuel whilst undertaking other displays in the area, such as Cowes, Portsmouth and Weymouth. Due to their frequent visits, the team were made honorary members of the Bournemouth Flying Club. The first appearance of their new BAe Hawks was at the July 1980 Air Pageant.

The twenty-first year of Red Arrow displays was in 1986, with their scheduled display on Saturday 1 June being their 2000th. However, due to heavy rain the birthday party had to be held in the terminal (not the Town Hall), with the display held over to the Sunday.

The twenty-fifth anniversary of the Reds saw them visit the Bournemouth Flying Club in September 1989. Almost 900 guests attended the event. The Hawks parked neatly in front of the Clubhouse, but the visit is remembered for their support Hercules blowing away the marquee as it applied reverse thrust when trying to park!

The main local event for the Red Arrows was their display during Bournemouth Regatta week, their visits being regarded as normal. It is not commonly known that the displays have to be paid for, and by the early 1990s the Regatta Committee were unable to raise funding from around the town. This resulted in no display for 1994. So a group of local enthusiasts formed the Bournemouth Red Arrows Association to ensure that the display returned for 1995 and subsequent years.

Terry Trevett is one of the enthusiasts:

> When the Association was formed it was not realised what a struggle it was to raise funding, with lack of enthusiasm from local business's and the Tourist Authority. So on the day of our first display the Committee had insufficient funds to pay the RAF's bill. Luckily one of the guests was so impressed that he gave us a donation which meant we ended up £5.83 in profit! Since then the annual display has been tied in with a Corporate Lunch to raise funds for Charity. The Bournemouth Echo has recently described this as the best such event in Bournemouth's Calendar.

If possible, the team members try and visit the airport terminal to meet 'their public' and have a chat. Youngsters are thrilled to be able to meet the pilots, get their autograph and perhaps have a photograph taken. For example, during August 2001 the team were at the airport on eight days, covering south-coast displays from Clacton to Dawlish. Sqdn Ldr Spike Jepson was team leader in 2002:

Operating the BAe Hawk since 1980, the Red Arrows continue to thrill the crowds with their visits to Bournemouth. The 1997 Team Leader, Sqdn Ldr Simon Meade, and the team pose with an enthusiastic young supporter of the Reds.

We very much enjoy coming to Bournemouth as we always get a very warm welcome. We sit in some pretty grotty terminals around the country, but always rely on the tremendous spirit that Bournemouth is famous for to get looked after and be made welcome.

MUDEFORD QUAY

Away from the airport, at Mudeford Quay, the inshore lifeboat would frequently be involved in exercises with the Coast Guard S-61 rescue helicopter based at Portland. In order to raise funds to support the lifeboat, local supporters organised annual open days. As well as visits by the S-61, these began to see other aerial attractions. By the 2000s there were displays by the likes of an RAF Harrier, the Army *Blue Eagles* helicopter display team and the *Red Bull* Sea Vixen.

21

AVIATION PARK/FR AVIATION

Following the departure of British Aerospace in 1983, many of their hangars and buildings were taken over by other aviation companies. However, a number of firms were just seeking office or storage space, and so business units were also developed. Under the management of the airport, the north-western area has developed over recent years as an Aviation Business Park.

In addition to this, the north-eastern area has been developed by Flight Refuelling/ FR Aviation, who now are a major force in the local aviation industry.

LOVAUX/FLS

Lovaux Ltd arrived in summer 1984, taking over some of BAe's hangars, initially dealing in military maintenance and spares support. It obtained the FRADU Hunter overhaul contract in September 1985 (previously carried out at Abingdon). This continued until April 1988 when the contract was obtained by Airwork; the change was aided by the switching of trained personnel between the two companies (Airwork lost it again in 1993). Other aircraft seen on overhaul included Hawk and Phantom from Boscombe Down. In summer 1987 Lovaux moved its HQ from Bracknell to Bournemouth, becoming more involved in airliner maintenance, with a number of former British Airways One-Elevens in 1989, followed by Boeing 737s. A more unusual visitor in August 1990 was a vintage DH Gipsy Moth. The site expanded further during spring 1990, with former BAe hangars being taken on to cope with an increasing workload. Lovaux became part of the Danish FLS Group in 1989, with its title becoming FLS Aerospace Engineering in summer 1991. The company continued airliner overhauls in the early 1990s, as well as regaining the FRADU Hunter contract once again in 1993. However, this proved to be short-lived as the FRADU decided to withdraw their Hunters from service. The final one left FLS in December 1994, only for them all to be withdrawn the following February! Among the airliners seen were some Latvian Tupolev Tu-134s during 1993, and in spring 1994 the first 737 for Ryanair – at the time still not a household name. Work continued until spring 1995 when FLS moved out to new premises at Gatwick and Stansted.

In July 1990 the rights to build the Optica observation aircraft were acquired by FLS, followed in October 1991 by the SAH.1 basic trainer. A Light Aircraft Division was set up, and after redesigns, both types were relaunched in spring 1992 with a small number of additional aircraft being built. During 1991 there had been optimistic talk of possible sales of 450 Opticas to the United States, but this became an unconfirmed order for twelve in December 1991. The SAH.1 emerged as the FLS Sprint two-seat aerobatic basic trainer with the first new build flying in December 1993. This Standard Club Sprint was intended for club flying and private owners, with the more powerful Sprint 160 for more advanced training. The hoped-for orders did not materialise so both projects were put up for sale in the summer of 1994. Two prospective sales to the Far East fell through, so the aircraft were moved out of the hangar in November 1997.

EUROPEAN AVIATION

European Aviation had been formed in 1989 by Australian businessman Paul Stoddart, initially dealing in aircraft spares. Sixteen former British Airways One-Elevens were bought in May 1993; the aircraft had been parked at Bournemouth awaiting sale. Its subsidiary European Air Charter commenced operations with some of these aircraft in February 1994, planning further operations from Filton. Most of the One-Elevens moved to the new base, but operational problems saw the aircraft move back to Bournemouth in April 1995. They were housed in the former FLS hangars on the north side (the original BAC hangars where the airliners had been built in 1968), which provided European with more space than at Filton. Plans were announced in the summer of 1995 to hush kit the One-Eleven fleet at a cost of £30 million. Initial trials were carried out in Florida in summer 1998, with one of their aircraft being displayed at Farnborough Air Show. However, the project proved too costly and was given up during the summer of 2000.

European operated ad hoc charters, with their aircraft frequently being chartered by major airlines such as British Airways, Ryanair, Sabena and Jersey European. No services were operated from Bournemouth in their own right, the majority being 'wet leases' undertaken on behalf of other airlines and tour operators mainly from Gatwick, Birmingham and Manchester. European purchased Sabena's fleet of Boeing 737s in spring 1998, with the first arriving for service in the summer of 1999. It was also the intention to use a number of former Air France A300s, but these never entered service. A luxury equipped fifty-seat VIP One-Eleven was operated, being joined by a VIP-fitted 737 in 2001.

Paul Stoddard was a keen Formula One racing enthusiast, driver and collector. As such he operated one of the One-Elevens as a VIP aircraft for the Tyrrell Grand Prix Team, which he had considered purchasing in the late 1990s. A wind tunnel was installed at Bournemouth during the autumn of 1998, frequently being used by Tyrrell design engineers. Stoddart then became involved with the Arrows F1 team, but eventually was to team up with Minardi F1. This led to him buying the team at the beginning of 2001 and providing them with an executive One-Eleven. The team was sold to Red Bull in the summer of 2005, enabling Stoddart to concentrate on a new airline he had set up in Australia – OzJet.

AIM AVIATION

Having been in the aviation-related business for a number of years, AIM Aviation commenced aircraft work at the airport in December 1989. In the following spring they undertook respray work on ATPs and 146s for British Aerospace, followed by Army and Navy Lynx helicopters during 1991/92. In 2000 they obtained an anticipated £100 million contract from Saab to paint Saab 2000 airliners with the first arriving in May 1993. Unfortunately there were early development delays with the airliner, followed by poor sales. This resulted in Saab ending production after only sixty-five aircraft and the loss of work for AIM. Other work included a highly colourful private Hunter in January 1999, 'prototype' Canberra and DRA Tornado in spring 1999, and DRA Harrier in June 2000. By 2001 the respray work had tailed off, the firm now concentrating on its core business of designing and building airliner interiors.

CITATION CENTRE

IDS Fanjets took over one of Airwork's hangars at the western end of the airport in the summer of 1979, becoming a Cessna Authorised Service Centre for Citation executive jets. Over the years the range and size of the Citations has increased, as has the business. IDS became part of CSE Aviation of Oxford in June 1999, with a new hangar capable of holding nine Citations being brought into use the following summer as the 'CSE Citation Centre'. CSE became part of the BBA Aviation Group in March 2000, along with Dallas Airmotive who uses part of the hangar.

AIRTIME AVIATION

Airtime Aviation built up overhaul and maintenance facilities from small beginnings in 1993. Commencing in what had been the cattle lairage shed, it had expanded into a number of the former Second World War hangars by the early 2000s. One housed its Paint and Refurbishment Division which undertook respray work up to Citation and Islander-sized aircraft. This work has included a preserved Spitfire, Sea Vixen and Gnat, whereas Cessnas and Piper are the norm. Airtime has expanded to become the major light aircraft facility at the airport, with up to fifty aircraft around its hangars.

FLIGHT REFUELLING

After his Aerodrome's campaign of the 1930s, Sir Alan Cobham turned his attention to a new project: the ability to refuel airliners in the air to extend their range. To develop the system he formed the aptly named Flight Refuelling Ltd (FRL) in 1934. However, the early trials from Sussex terminated on the outbreak of the Second World War. These

The majority of wartime hangars situated on the northern side of the airport are still in use, although heavily refurbished over the years. Airtime Aviation currently use two of them for their expanding maintenance and overhaul business.

resumed after the war, with the company moving to Tarrant Rushton in 1948 where their hard work was rewarded in 1949. A Gloster Meteor fighter was successfully refuelled during trials in April. This was followed by an endurance flight in August where the fighter remained airborne for twelve hours, aided by ten refuellings over the Isle of Wight and Bournemouth area. There was talk in 1951 of the company moving to Bournemouth where they would have made use of former BOAC hangars, but they remained at Tarrant Rushton. FRL finally arrived at Bournemouth in June 1979, at which time they did not anticipate a long-term need for the site. Their office and hangar on the north-eastern side had a staff of just fifty in summer 1981. In fact, FRL were to expand over the following years to become a major operator and employer at the airport.

It was the Falklands War in 1982 that brought about FRL's expansion at Bournemouth. At great cost, the war had shown that the Royal Navy required more training in repelling attacks by aircraft and missiles. FRL already had experience of operating the Royal Navy's Canberra target tug fleet at Yeovilton. The company made proposals to the Navy to cover the training and updating of their target towing capabilities. A fleet of Dassault Falcon 20 executive jets was acquired in 1984, not for VIP duties, but their strong wings proved ideal for attaching underwing pylons. As well as the existing targets, these were for the various pods that contained electronic equipment or targets required for the new Electronic Warfare Training and Threat Simulation role. This increased activity led to the formation of FR Aviation Ltd in January 1985.

From autumn 1983 FRL maintained six F-100 Super Sabres which were operated in Europe as target tugs by the USAF, the work lasting about ten years. On one occasion in July 1989, one of the Super Sabres ran off the end of the runway and, although the pilot was unhurt, the aircraft was considered beyond repair. These 1950s vintage fighters were not what one would normally expect to see flying from Bournemouth.

FR AVIATION

FR Aviation (FRA) initially operated the Falcons from Yeovilton, pending provision of a new parking apron at Bournemouth in May 1986. The Falcon fleet expanded over the years, at one time reaching a maximum of twenty. Initially, the majority of training exercises were held with the Royal Navy in the English Channel, working up to what became known as 'The Thursday War'. This was the day of the week everything was geared up to, with the Falcons 'attacking' the warships by acting as enemy aircraft or missiles. Their underwing pods could be changed to suit different roles such as jamming the ship's gun alignment radar, undertaking target towing or laying chaff by way of deception for the naval guns. Initially, the Falcons operated in conjunction with RN Hunters, but more recently with Hawks (a far cry from the similar Airwork FRU operations thirty years previously). A base at Teesside was brought into use in 1995 where seven of the Falcons were based for similar operations with the RAF.

A contract was obtained to undertake servicing of RAF Canberras from February 1989. This kept on being extended with the final aircraft eventually departing in January 2005. The majority were of the PR.9 version where new digital cameras and sensors were fitted during the late 1990s. March 1997 saw a trials version arrive, which was familiar to some of the workers as it had originally been delivered to FRL at Tarrant Rushton in 1954.

As principal subcontractor to British Aerospace, FRA undertook conversion work on RAF VC.10s to convert them to dual transport/tanking roles. A large new hangar was erected on the north side of the airport with the Minister of State for Defence opening it in February 1991. The RAF's need for more tankers was soon shown with the outbreak of the first Gulf War. The initial contract had covered eight aircraft but this was soon followed by a contract for a further five, with the final aircraft handed back to the RAF in February 1997. The contracts totalled £60 million and by now the company workforce had increased to 500.

Following their VC.10 work, FRA became a major subcontractor to BAe again in July 1996 with the Nimrod 2000 project. An additional new hangar was constructed during summer 1998, with the first of four airframes having already been flown in by Russian Antonov 124's freighter during February 1997. At the time this was a world record for the largest single volume load to be carried by air (there was 6in door clearance!). Work on preparing the airframes was well underway when the contract was cancelled in November 1999 by BAe, who now proceeded with the Nimrod rebuilds 'in house'. (The planned date for entry into RAF service – originally set for 2001 – is still some way off.) The four fuselages were flown by An-124s to the BAe factory at Woodford, with rather less publicity than when they had arrived.

On a lighter theme, trials were undertaken on behalf of the CAA during October 1996 with a 'James-Bond' style VPM, two-seat autogyro. These trials were to prove how an autogyro really flew, as in theory – like a bumble bee – it should be incapable of flight! The trials were repeated by a team from Glasgow University in October 2000. To mark the fiftieth anniversary of the successful Meteor refuelling flight back in 1949, a fly-past of a VC.10 tanker and Meteor took place over FRL's Wimborne Headquarters and the airport in November 1999.

FR Aviation's fleet of Falcon 20s have recently been receiving major refurbishments to their airframes and equipment. Now flying with dark blue colour schemes, the fleet will remain in service for some years to come.

With a large hangar now available, FRA moved into civil business with overhaul work on airliners. These included One-Elevens for European in 1993, executive Boeing 727s in the late 1990s and Short 360 freighters for Federal Express in 1999. BAe 146s and further One-Elevens followed, and it was hoped that more work on these airliners would follow. Although this was not the case, the experience gained was not wasted as in December 2001 FRA became a partner in a new airliner maintenance business, BASCO. FRA also continued with overhauls on various civil and military One-Elevens in its own right.

From autumn 2000 the Falcon fleet began to receive dark blue paint schemes, so making them more visible in the air. Even the FRA Flying Club Cessna acquired the new dark blue colour. From spring 2003 the Falcons were upgraded and equipped with the latest style of glass cockpit. This ensures that they will continue to be a valuable asset for both FR Aviation and the MoD for many more years to come, the current contract running until 2014.

The Cobham Group is part of the AirTanker consortium which has been selected as the preferred bidder to supply the RAF with Airbus A330s as its future tanker/transport aircraft. The requirement is for just under twenty aircraft. The A330s will arrive from Airbus to have their air-refuelling equipment fitted by FRA; the contract also covers future maintenance and servicing of the aircraft.

BASCO

Bournemouth Aviation Services Co. (BASCO) was set up in December 2001, and is a joint venture between Singapore Technology Engineering and FR Aviation. BASCO took over the former FRA Nimrod hangar and commenced business in July 2002 with overhauls of a variety of airliner types. Although intended to concentrate on Airbus wide-bodied airliners, other early visitors included executive Boeing 727s and Douglas DC-8Fs of MK Cargo. From 2004 there was an increase in Airbuses, including a number of A300F freighters of express parcels carriers Channel Express, DHL and TNT. A300Fs seen from other countries included those from China, India, Kuwait and Turkey. Airbus A320s are also frequent visitors, many being owned by Singapore Aircraft Leasing (SALE) and leased to major world airlines such as Hapag Lloyd, Monarch and Thomas Cook.

22

MANCHESTER AIRPORTS GROUP

MANCHESTER AIRPORT

In September 2000 the National Express Group announced that they were moving out of the airport business to concentrate on their other transport operations. This resulted in both Bournemouth and East Midlands Airports being put up for auction. The Manchester Airports Group (MAG) was successful in its bid for both airports, with the £241 million deal completed on 28 March 2001. Bournemouth then became part of the Regional Airports Division of MAG (the others being Nottingham East Midlands and Humberside), with 200 people employed directly and another 3,000 around the airport site. At the time, MAG said it was initially concentrating on East Midlands, although it continued to pursue planning permission for Bournemouth's new terminal. 'Regional airports have a crucial role and we intend to make Bournemouth more successful. Bournemouth is well placed to capture the forecast growth in the south'. Unfortunately, this was a time of falling passenger numbers again, not helped by the events of 9/11. By autumn 2002 the 'International' part of the airport's title was quietly dropped, the reason being that 'International' was no longer included in the title of the other airports within the group.

Early 2001 saw a number of diversions from the London area due to bad weather. These included up to eight Ryanair 737s from Stansted on a couple of days. For its second route from Bournemouth, Ryanair introduced a service from Hahn (Frankfurt) in January 2002. Passenger numbers soon increased sufficiently to result in a competing British Airways service from Southampton being withdrawn. In January 2001 Alderney businessman Noel Hayes commenced operations with an Islander to fly fresh and chilled produce to Alderney hotels and supermarkets. Operating under the name of Le Cocq's, the service proved so successful that passenger flights were offered from the following January at a fare of £99 return, initially under the title of Le Cocq's Airlink.

Channel Express took over a hangar in the spring of 2001 in order to undertake in house overhaul and maintenance on its F.27 Friendships and Electras, although the Electras were not to remain in service much longer. One oddity to be seen during 2001 was an Antonov An-72 freighter wet leased from Estonia, operating horse charters and freight work for Channel Express. The Electras were well liked by their crews, but were now getting elderly and becoming expensive to maintain. So the aircraft were withdrawn during 2002, with just one remaining until the following spring. This departed Bournemouth in May 2003 for a new life as a water bomber in Canada. The Electras replacement arrived in the shape of Boeing 737QC (Quick Change) aircraft which entered service in June 2001. Following their successful introduction into the freight and passenger charter markets, the first of fourteen further 737s from Ansett Australia arrived at Bournemouth in May 2002. The airline now expanded its passenger charter work, although this was to be undertaken from other airports. A major change of direction for Channel Express occurred in October 2002 with the launch of Jet2.com. A low-cost scheduled passenger airline operated by Channel Express, it initially operated flights from Leeds, Bradford with some of the newly acquired 737s.

EUROPEAN JUMBOS

In December 2001 European Aviation acquired five 747s from British Airways at a knock-down price, flying them to Bournemouth prior to their entry into holiday services from Gatwick and Manchester. Again, the local residents imagined services being operated from Bournemouth, not helped when, for a time in May 2002, there were six Jumbos lined up on the secondary runway! However, by the summer they had mostly disappeared, with the odd one or two returning from time to time for cheap parking or minor servicing. European undertook some long-distance flights with the Jumbos in connection with Formula 1 races around the world. One flew all the race cars to Australia and another operated direct to Brazil from Bournemouth (the first time ever).

Always on the lookout for something new, Bath Travel chartered one of the Jumbos for a direct flight to New York in November 2002. Up to then it had not been thought that such an operation would be possible from Bournemouth, but the Jumbo with full passenger quota, minimal luggage and not full tanks of fuel, proved this wrong. However, the take-off was a bit hairy as there had been a cloudburst whilst the passengers were embarking. The pilot waited twenty minutes at the end of the runway for the water to drain away before moving, and then seemed to take forever to get the aircraft into the air. This was confirmed by those on the ground and in the aircraft where 95 per cent of the runway appeared to have been used before the aircraft leaped eastwards into the sky prior to making a slow turn to the north to head for America. Bath Travel later used one of the Jumbos for a charter to Moscow, with two further flights to New York at the end of 2003.

ONE-ELEVEN FAREWELL

The last scheduled One-Eleven service was the Turin ski flight from Bournemouth on 30 December 2001 by European, although one replaced a 737 in February. One-Eleven airliner passenger services finally came to an end in Europe on 31 March 2002, following the introduction of strict noise regulations. The occasion was marked at Bournemouth by a number of last flights operated by one of European's aircraft. There was the final Palmair One-Eleven (commemorating its use back in 1965) at £50, the final fare-paying passenger (for Ian Allen Travel) and the (very) final one for European staff. The 'Farewell' aircraft was later selected by Paul Stoddart for preservation at Bournemouth Aviation Museum.

Bournemouth continued to see a number of One-Elevens, mainly visiting FRA for overhauls, as the noise ban did not apply to executive or military aircraft. It was left to surviving aircraft from the Defence Research Agency (DRA) fleet at Boscombe Down to mark the 40th anniversary of the One-Eleven's first flight. Amongst their fleet was the oldest One-Eleven still flying, the fourth production series 200. Its final flight in June 2003 included a circuit at Bournemouth. For the actual 40th anniversary in August, another of the DRA fleet visited Bournemouth whilst on an 'extended' trials flight from Boscombe Down.

BUZZ 'OFF'

Manchester thought their faith in purchasing Bournemouth had paid off when, in October 2002, no-frills airline Buzz announced they were setting up a hub at Bournemouth with two based Boeing 737s. 'Bournemouth Airport's biggest ever deal' anticipated 750,000 Buzz passengers a year, with services to Amsterdam, Belfast, Malaga, Paris CDG and Prestwick, with fares commencing at £19. The first hint of trouble came at the beginning of December when Ryanair announced they would also operate a Prestwick service from the New Year at only £9.99 single! Tactfully, Buzz pulled their plans for this route. Then, at the end of January 2003, Ryanair purchased Buzz completely, saying that they would not proceed with Buzz's operations from Bournemouth which were due to start in eight weeks time! This left many unhappy prospective travellers, and it was a major blow to the airport. Most travellers had paid for accommodation and suchlike at their destinations, and this money was lost as Ryanair only refunded the fares. Amongst all this, Ryanair's own Prestwick service commenced at the beginning of February, becoming twice-daily in October, at which time a further new service to Girona began, but at the expense of that to Hahn. Passenger numbers on the Hahn route had been high, especially with Germans travelling to this country. Ryanair explained that Spain was its strongest growth market and, in the event, this proved to be the case.

Another flight which caused a bit of a buzz was a non-radio micro-light lost in the area in July 2002. It was eventually 'found' by the Coast Guard helicopter and escorted into the airport where the pilot was given directions.

UPTURN BEGINS

Palmair European was voted the 'World's best airline' by *Holiday Which* in March 2003, moving up from third in 2001. This brought plenty of national publicity with the press commenting on the one plane airline whose chairman saw off each flight. In April Palmair introduced a second 737, mainly to cope with their expanding European day-trip flights. In July 2004 their New York flight was operated by a British Airways Boeing 777, being the first 777 service from the airport (but not the first visit).

As well as its range of Mediterranean holidays, Bath Travel have greatly expanded their range of holidays by offering flights to the USA and West Indies. July 2004 saw this British Airways Boeing 777 chartered for a shopping trip to New York.

Southampton Airport was frequently in the news during summer 2003 in connection with the expansion of FlyBe flights to European destinations. These services attracted a large number of passengers, making it more difficult for potential operators from Bournemouth. One heartening point was the fact that, on occasions, a fully loaded BAe 146 could not take-off from Southampton's runway during hot weather. So it took off with little fuel, calling in at Bournemouth to top up. There were also occasions when FlyBe flights were delayed returning to Southampton, which was unable to remain open after 11 p.m. This resulted in the flights diverting to Bournemouth which was open to handle the mail flights.

In 2002 Newmarket Air Holidays offered a one-week holiday to Lake Garda which proved so successful that additional flights were added. The number of flights offered increased over the following years, with the summer of 2006 seeing weekly flights to Verona, plus other Mediterranean destinations. The flights are operated by a number of different airlines, so adding to the variety of airliners seen at Bournemouth. The Le Cocq Airlink services proved successful, the airline rebranding itself Rockhopper in September 2003 to reflect a change of focus in operations. It now intended to provide services between the (rocks) of the three main Channel Islands, doubling its previous years passenger numbers. In March 2004 Aurigny commenced a daily service from Guernsey and Jersey, operated by Short 360s, and, as a result, Rockhopper decided to cut back on these two routes, concentrating on Alderney. However, Aurigny ran into financial problems the following autumn, ending its services into Bournemouth in January 2005, whereupon Rockhopper were able to expand once more. Further Islanders and Trislanders were added to their fleet, with fares costing £89 return to Alderney and

£119 return to Guernsey and Jersey. From spring 2006 the airline rebranded itself as Blue Islands, expanding its routes and introducing Jetstream 32s. The large increase in passenger flights was countered by a drop in freight operations from Bournemouth, with 2004 seeing 75 per cent less flights than five years earlier. The main reason was the reduction in Channel Express services to and from the Channel Islands.

There were major problems for European in March 2004 when the airline almost went out of business. Worldwide charter operations with the 747s proved to be very different from that of short-haul 737s. An extension of a contract to operate holiday flights to Florida from Gatwick and Manchester was lined up, only to be cancelled at the last moment. This meant no work for the 747s with the resultant loss of many aircrew jobs. The 747s were stored at various airfields, but 737 operations continued with two still operated on behalf of Palmair. However, by July there was renewed activity with the 747s again undertaking various charters, although it was often the case of switching the engines around between the aircraft to keep them flying. The year 2005 saw two of the 747s fully employed again, frequently on charters to other major airlines. The 737s still had busy schedules operating holiday flights from Birmingham and Manchester, with one still operated as a VIP aircraft for the F1 Grand Prix racing teams. The launch of OzJet services in 2005 saw four of the 737s temporarily transferred to Melbourne.

A Government report into 'Airport Expansion for the South East' was published in December 2003, where Bournemouth was regarded as being in the South East. (The previous December the Government had regarded the airport as being in the South West!).

Seen outside their hangars in summer 2005, this European Aviation Boeing 737 is VIP-fitted for use between race venues by the Formula 1 Grand Prix racing teams. This explains the black and white chequers under the rear fuselage.

However, the report did confirm that additional terminal facilities could be introduced at Bournemouth to cope with 3½m passengers over a thirty-year period. This highlighted the desire for MAG to expand or rebuild the terminal facilities, but they wanted to see passenger numbers nearer the 1 million mark before undertaking any major expenditure. A new managing director, Keith Kerr (former British Airways), was appointed in December 2003, but he took extended leave the following September. MAG raised £325 million in March 2004 to fund a group expansion programme, which included further investment for Bournemouth. The airport had seen continued growth, also being a major aircraft maintenance base which MAG saw expanding in the future. In July the Government asked the airport, along with Gatwick and Southampton, to advise them of their growth plans so that these could be considered together in relation to future traffic requirements in the south-east. MAG estimated that there were 2 million people within an hour's drive of the airport – now how to get them to use the airport? The answer soon came.

THOMSONFLY

The date 22 March 2005 was to be a Red Letter day for the airport with the commencement of scheduled services by low-fares airline Thomsonfly, as an expansion of their services from Coventry and Doncaster, Sheffield. 'One of the most important days in the airport's sixty year history', declared the new Managing Director, Peter Duffy. The services were welcomed by MAG as a magnet for flying from Bournemouth. Passenger numbers were 265,000 in 2001 and 495,000 in 2004, and Peter anticipated that 2005 should see the magic 1 million. Initial destinations were Amsterdam, Faro, Malaga, Palma, Paris CDG, Pisa and Valencia, with fares starting at £17.99 single. For these operations, the airline based two Boeing 737s at Bournemouth, each undertaking a busy daily schedule. At the beginning of the year the most popular routes from Bournemouth were Ryanair's to Gerona and Prestwick, but by the summer Thomsonfly's Palma had caught up.

The author recalls the launch flight the previous October which carried the usual local Mayors and other dignitaries. We were advised to check in at 10.00 a.m. with our passports. The feeling was that we were off to one of the new destinations being served. But this was not to be. It was a typical British wet autumn morning and the only glimpses of land seen were of Weston-super-Mare and Cardiff! Still, there was a glass of Bucks Fizz.

Hard on Thomsonfly's heels came Jet2.com who operated a daily 737 flight from Belfast for six months with fares from £16. Other changes within Channel Express had seen the airline give up its newspaper and Royal Mail flights at the end of January 2005. The services were now operated by HS.748s of Emerald, ATR.72s of Air Contractors and a Boeing 737QC of Titan. This was to break twenty-six years of Channel Express services from Bournemouth. Their A300F Eurofighters were taken out of service in January 2006. with all operations now under the Jet2.com name.

The airline business has seen a massive rise in internet bookings in recent years, with a drop off in business for travel agents. Bath Travel found that their own bookings had

Real expansion started at Bournemouth with the introduction of Thomsonfly low-cost flights in spring 2005. Their earlier publicity flight took place on a typical winter's day, so encouraging passengers to book flights to the sun.

levelled out, but they still had their own local passenger following; many used them to make bookings for low-cost flights as they did not have access to the internet. Palmair again received excellent publicity at the beginning of 2005 by being voted second favourite airline in *Holiday Which*'s bi-annual survey. (First was Singapore, third was Jet2.com.) In addition to this, Peter Bath received an MBE in the New Year's Honours List. In spite of the large number of passengers flying with low-cost airlines, Palmair's holiday passenger numbers held up at 70,000 a year.

FURTHER LOW-COST EXPANSION

There was a further boost for Bournemouth with the introduction of two additional lost-cost airlines in December 2005. EasyJet commenced a daily service from Geneva with Airbus A319s with fares from £29.99 single, thereby providing access to the Swiss Alps for many skiers. Air Berlin introduced a thrice-weekly service from Paderborn with Boeing 737s at fares from £24.99 single. Of extra importance was that Air Berlin had been operating the service into Southampton, but found that they were unable to operate a fully loaded Boeing from Southampton's runway.

Further good news for the airport is that during the summer of 2006, all four of the UK's major travel operators will be offering holiday flights from Bournemouth: Airtours, First Choice, Thomas Cook (switched from Southampton) and Thomson, not forgetting the flights by the more local Palmair and Newmarket. Both Thomsonfly and Ryanair have added further destinations.

WORLD RECORD BOOK

When the airport's main runway was extended in 1995, it was to enable flights to transport holidaymakers greater distances. However, a flight of 26,389 miles was not envisaged! This was the case on 11 February 2006 when Steve Fossett in his Global Flyer made an emergency landing at Bournemouth. Having left Florida three and a half days beforehand, he had established a new solo flight World Record on passing Shannon (the second time). His planned destination was Manston, Kent, but a generator failure over the south coast meant an immediate return to earth was necessary. A safe landing was made by the Global Flyer, thus enabling Bournemouth to enter the Record Books as the landing point at the end of the seventy-six-hour, forty-five-minute flight. Richard Branson, in an accompanying executive jet, called to collect Steve Fossett and fly him on to greet the crowds waiting for him at Manston – without his Record Breaking aircraft.

THE FUTURE

With the increase in passenger numbers, plans were finally announced in December 2005 for redevelopment of the terminal area to cater for the increasing number of flights. This would give Bournemouth the capacity to handle 2 million passengers a year from 2009. As well as the new terminal, the apron area was greatly expanded in order to handle up to twelve airliners at the same time. The future looks bright.

The large number of low-cost flights being operated has enabled Bournemouth Airport to welcome its 1 millionth passenger in a year for the first time during 2006. At last passengers have realised they no longer have to suffer a frustrating road journey to London.

Appendix

For comparison in different decades, here follows details of passenger movements at Bournemouth Airport. Those shown for the spring 1946 are just before all services were switched to the new London Airport. Those for summer 1961 are shortly after the airlines moved to Bournemouth, when they thought Southampton was about to close. Compared to these figures, the present-day movements seem low. However, the 1961 movements produced 220,000 passengers compared to the present day's 1 million.

AIRLINE DEPARTURES – APRIL 1946

Monday	07:00	BOAC	York	Cairo & Calcutta
	13:00	BOAC	Dakota	Malta & Lydda
	14:00	BOAC	York	Malta & Cairo
	16:00	Pan American	DC-4	New York
	18:15	American	DC-4	Washington
Tuesday	12:00	BOAC	Lancastrian	Sydney
	12:45	BOAC	Dakota	Lisbon & Accra
	14:00	BOAC	Dakota	Malta & Cairo
	15:00	BOAC	York	Johannesburg
	16:00	Pan American	DC-4	New York
	18:15	American	DC-4	New York
Wednesday	14:00	BOAC	Dakota	Malta & Cairo
	16:00	Pan American	DC-4	New York
	18:15	American	DC-4	Boston/New York
Thursday	07:00	BOAC	York	Cairo & Calcutta
	12:00	BOAC	Lancastrian	Sydney
	12:45	BOAC	Dakota	Lisbon & Accra
	14:00	BOAC	Dakota	Malta & Cairo
	16:00	Pan American	DC-4	New York
	18:15	American	DC-4	Chicago

Friday	14:00	BOAC	York	Malta & Cairo
	15:00	BOAC	York	Johannesburg
	16:00	Pan American	DC-4	New York
	18:15	American	DC-4	NY & Washington
Saturday	12:45	BOAC	Dakota	Lisbon & Accra
	14:00	BOAC	Dakota	Malta & Cairo
	16:00	Pan American	DC-4	New York
	18:15	American	DC-4	New York
Sunday	12:00	BOAC	Lancastrian	Sydney
	14:00	BOAC	Dakota	Malta & Cairo
	16:00	Pan American	DC-4	New York
	18:15	American	DC-4	New York

AIRLINE DEPARTURES – SUMMER SATURDAY AUGUST 1961

08:10	Silver City	Superfreighter	Cherbourg
08:30	Silver City	Superfreighter	Cherbourg
09:00	Silver City	Superfreighter	Cherbourg
09:05	Jersey	Dakota	Jersey
09:40	Cambrian	Dakota	Le Bourget
10:00	Silver City	Superfreighter	Cherbourg
10:15	Jersey	Dakota	Guernsey
10:25	Jersey	Dakota	Coventry
10:30	Silver City	Superfreighter	Cherbourg
11:00	Silver City	Superfreighter	Cherbourg
11:20	Air Safaris	Hermes	Gatwick
11:25	Jersey	Dakota	Gloucester
11:30	Jersey	Heron	Guernsey
11:35	Air Safaris	Viking	Exeter
11:40	Jersey	Dakota	Guernsey
11:45	Silver City	Superfreighter	Cherbourg
12:30	Silver City	Superfreighter	Cherbourg
12:40	BEA	Viscount	Jersey
12:50	Silver City	Superfreighter	Cherbourg
12:55	Jersey	Dakota	Jersey
13:10	Air Safaris	Viking	Dublin & Belfast
13:15	Jersey	Heron	Jersey
13:50	Jersey	Heron	Guernsey
14:00	Jersey	Dakota	Guernsey

14:00	Silver City	Superfreighter	Cherbourg
14:30	Silver City	Superfreighter	Cherbourg
14:35	Jersey	Herald	Jersey
14:40	Jersey	Heron	Jersey
15:05	BEA	Viscount	Jersey
15:05	Silver City	Superfreighter	Cherbourg
15:25	Air Safaris	Viking	Birmham/Newcastle
15:35	Cambrian	Dakota	Bristol
15:50	Silver City	Superfreighter	Cherbourg
16:05	Jersey	Herald	Jersey
16:25	Silver City	Superfreighter	Cherbourg
16:35	Jersey	Dakota	Guernsey
17:00	Silver City	Superfreighter	Cherbourg
17:25	North-South	Heron	Leeds Bradford
17:45	Jersey	Dakota	Jersey
18:10	Silver City	Superfreighter	Cherbourg
18:20	BEA	Viscount	Jersey
18:30	Jersey	Herald	Jersey
18:35	Silver City	Superfreighter	Cherbourg
19:00	Silver City	Superfreighter	Cherbourg
19:25	Jersey	Dakota	Guernsey
22:30	Air Safaris	Viking	Ostend/Amsterdam

AIRLINE DEPARTURES – JANUARY 2006

06:45	Thomson	737	Paris Orly
06:55	Thomson	737	Alicante
08:05	Air-Berlin	737	Paderborn
09:00	Palmair European	737	Mediterranean
10:00	Rockhopper	Trislander	Alderney
11:05	Ryanair	737	Dublin
11:30	EasyJet	A319	Geneve
11:30	Rockhopper	Trislander	Jersey
11:40	Thomson	737	Faro
15:35	Ryanair	737	Prestwick
16:00	Rockhopper	Trislander	Alderney
16:45	Ryanair	737	Girona
16:45	Thomson	737	Malaga
19:00	Thomson	737	Amsterdam

Index